SANE Book of the Year 2010.

Highly Commended Certificate in the Human Rights Commission's Non-Fiction Award 2010.

Shortlisted, *The Age* Book of the Year 2010.

Calm, clear, honest and it oh so gently lifts your soul until you unexpectedly find yourself gliding in the clouds before gently coming back to earth. And weaving in the rhapsody works a wonder and evinces deep hope.

—Jack Heath,
Former CEO SANE

Flying with Paper Wings is anything but a misery memoir. Glittering with black humour and without self-pity, it shifts other people's perceptions of mental distress beyond kindness, compassion, sympathy and fear into some deeper perception ...
Read this exceptional book. It takes you beyond your own narrow terror towards something that might be called insight.

—Helen Elliott,
The Age

The biggest satisfaction I gained from reading this book was the realisation that this is an exceptional record of someone who is still gravely ill, and yet is able to surface over and over again, with mind and humour still intact. It has a depth which gives it strength. It has a warmth and honesty that is refreshing.

—Anne Deveson

[illegible] 2020

Highly Commended [illegible] the
Human Rights Commission [illegible] Award 2019

[illegible] Stories [illegible] Books of the Year 2019

[illegible] and [illegible] unexpectedly [illegible] of [illegible] And [illegible] the chapters [illegible] understand [illegible]

—Jack Heath,
[illegible]

[illegible] Marker [illegible] but [illegible] with black humour [illegible] [illegible] people [illegible] beyond [illegible] [illegible] [illegible] your own [illegible]

—[illegible] Elliott,
[illegible]

[illegible] reading this book [illegible] on that [illegible] one who [illegible] and [illegible]

Photo credit: Sabin Fernbacher

Sandy Jeffs OAM grew up and went to school in Ballarat. She has lived with schizophrenia and all its moods for more than 40 years. Sandy has published many articles, eight volumes of poetry and two other books concerned with the disparate topics of madness, domestic violence, the trials and tribulations of playing midweek ladies' tennis and the mad world in which we live, including during the times of the pandemic – and some of these have inspired other artists to compose music, libretti and dance. Sandy has also become a community educator who speaks to school kids, university students, community groups and clinicians about what it is like to live with a mental illness. Her home, with friends human and animal, is in Christmas Hills on the outskirts of Melbourne, 'where it's Christmas every day'.

Also by Sandy Jeffs

Poems from the Madhouse (1993, 2000, 2002)
Loose Kangaroos (co-author, 1998, 1999)
Blood Relations (2000)
Confessions of a Midweek Lady: Tall Tennis Tales (2001, 2009)
The Wings of Angels: A Memoir of Madness (2004)
The Mad Poet's Tea Party (2015)
Chiaroscuro (2015)
Out of the Madhouse: From Asylums to Caring Community? (co-author with Margaret Leggatt, 2020)
The Birds of Eltham (co-author with photographer Tony Robinson, 2020, 2021)
The Poetics of a Plague, A Haiku Diary: The 2020–2021 COVID-19 Pandemic (2021)

FLYING WITH PAPER WINGS

Reflections on Living with Madness

SANDY JEFFS

We respectfully acknowledge the wisdom of Aboriginal and Torres Strait islander peoples and their custodianship of the lands and waterways. The Countries on which Spinifex offices are situated are Djuru, Bunurong and Wurundjeri, Wadawurrung, Gundungarra and Noongar.

First published by The Vulgar Press, 2009
Reprinted by Sandy Jeffs, 2016
This edition published by Spinifex Press, 2024

Spinifex Press Pty Ltd
PO Box 200, Little River, VIC 3211, Australia
PO Box 105, Mission Beach, QLD 4852, Australia

women@spinifexpress.com.au
www.spinifexpress.com.au

Cover design by Deb Snibson
Typeset in Sabon
Printed in the USA

A catalogue record for this book is available from the National Library of Australia

ISBN: 9781925950946 (paperback)
ISBN: 9781925950953 (ebook)

For my angels —
Robbie, Dido, Lynne and Felicity

In the peaceful quiet you create for me
And the way you keep the world at bay for me
The way you keep the world at bay.

Dixie Chicks

And Something's odd—within—
That person that I was—
And this One—do not feel the same—
Could it be Madness—this?

Emily Dickinson

CONTENTS

SANDY JEFFS,
TANGATA WHAIORA – 'PERSON SEEKING WELLNESS'

The first time I met Sandy, she thrust into my hands her business card, which read: *Sandy Jeffs . . . poet . . . lunatic . . . insanity consultant.*

I was at a mental health conference, making a documentary for the ABC called *Angels & Demons,* seeking to talk to those who had experienced mental illness first hand, to find out what it looks like from the inside.

Pretty much everyone I met said "oh, you've got to talk to Sandy". So here I was, being invited into the private hell of a woman whose business card was an eloquent statement of intent: *madness is not going to stop me.*

We talked for over an hour, as Sandy described to me the two tormenting voices in her head she had dubbed Tweedledum and Tweedledee. The pain they had inflicted on her over the years – and the strength required not to be overwhelmed by them – was stark. Here is how Sandy ended that interview:

When I wake up in the morning I lie in bed thinking 'Get out of bed. Have brekkie? Top myself? Have brekkie? Top myself? I'll have brekkie today'. Then one day it mightn't happen. One day I mightn't have brekkie, I don't know. You know it's scary stuff.

Just how scary, I didn't fully realise till I read this book.

From an abusive and spiteful childhood, filled with threat and degradation, Sandy's inner life began to unravel while she was still at school. By university, voices inside her head were shouting at her: *Your rotting body is poisoning the world, Hide yourself! Cringe and cower, slut.* In the more than 30 years since, during which they seldom abated, those voices have tried everything in their power to destroy Sandy.

Diagnosed with schizophrenia, Sandy went through episodes of deep psychosis. Convinced she was evil and a danger to the world; sometimes with the sensation that maggots were in her brain, squirming and chewing; several times she found herself inside the Dickensian wards of Victoria's mental institutions.

If there is a deeper circle of hell than to be mad amongst the mad, then Dante never wrote of it. For us, Sandy lays this world bare. And, despite her own torments, she manages to find within this world the still-glowing embers of humanity. For Sandy, an old woman emerging from the bedlam to gently brush her hair and whisper soothingly was a moment that showed "*not everyone was a monster*".

Despite the horrors of her journey, there is no self-pity in this book. Rather, there is a sense of wonder that a woman who entered her forties with no *future, identity or self-esteem*, finds herself, a decade later, a published author, sought-after speaker and a human being with hope.

Her gratitude to the angels in her life, Robbie and Dido, is profound. Their advice, when Sandy was being swept away on the winds of self-delusion, to *keep your feet on the ground and your hand on the vacuum cleaner,* is typical of the practical and loving way they have approached Sandy's illness, and there is much here that other carers can take from their example.

Sandy knows better than anyone that there is nothing romantic about madness and she doesn't gild the lily here. Not a week passes where she doesn't question her sanity – she found herself back in hospital while finishing this book – but as she writes:

We may never understand what makes us mad but we can seek to understand what makes us well.

Ultimately, it is Sandy's insight into fighting the monster of psychosis, which makes this book valuable to the many people – too many – in our society that have had to fight similar demons.

Whether Sandy's voices will ever be stilled is hard to say. She says of them: *It's like a war of words between us. I hope it will be me who has the last word.*

With this book, that will outlive both her and them, I believe she has.

Andrew Denton

PREFACE TO THE 2024 EDITION

Spinifex Press has decided to reissue this book, which was first published 15 years ago in 2009. In the intervening years, my original publisher issued several print runs and, along with me, distributed many thousands of copies to readers of many kinds – those who had lived similar experiences, and those who treated or cared for them, including many mental health professionals.

To this edition of the original text, I have added an Afterword, which brings readers up to date with how I am going now, in 2024. In that, I reflect upon my telling of these most difficult years of my life, and the life I have gratefully made since.

Over the years I have seen a lot of upheaval in the mental health world. With the 2020 Royal Commission and the beginning of a reconfiguration of mental health services, there is much to think about. Always on the fringe of mental health politics, I have stood as witness and as an observer of ongoing events and have tried to offer my observations about the mental health system and all things mad, with thoughtfulness and honesty. As always, my ideas are continually evolving. These days the more radical advocates see me as a conservative because I still talk about mental illness. I draw on over 47 years of living with schizophrenia and feel I have something to offer the advocacy world. Wisdom or folly?

The role of trauma in people's mental distress is now given more credence. My story is one of many where childhood trauma laid the foundation for my descent into madness. This book is worth revisiting to understand that relationship.

I thank Jackie Yowell for ongoing editorial advice and Margaret Leggatt, Jack Heath and Julie Dempsey for casting their wise eyes over the new chapter. Thank you to Susan Hawthorne and Pauline Hopkins for their sensitive editing. And thank you to Susan and Renate Klein at Spinifex Press for giving this memoir a new dress, a new life and the chance to reach a new audience.

PREFACE TO THE 2009 EDITION

> Pleasant looking, brown-haired girl of medium height and build with rimless glasses and worn old jersey, jeans and boots. Fully co-operative with examination interview. Speech precise and rather pedantic with occasional malapropisms. Slight stutter (had severe speech impediment as a child), mood detached, rather blunted and at times inappropriate. Sandra appeared to be very concerned with her mystical experiences relating to her wish to die beneath a particular eucalypt tree. She was perplexed about the events leading up to her admission and was unable to give any very clear account of the preceding two or three months. No formal thought disorder, no current hallucinations. Orientation and memory within normal limits. Intelligence estimated at above average. Insight lacking.

The clinical notes above are about me, and they are from a madhouse – Parkville Psychiatric Unit, 13 December 1976. I never thought in my worst nightmare that I would end up in a place like that. I sought these records 23 years later, in 1999, when my curiosity about my past intensified. I wanted to understand my madness and what had led me to the madhouse.

How does one explain the experience of falling into madness; one's mind fracturing? Somewhere in there festers my fraught relationships with my parents, the early experience of sexual assault, a confused attraction to Catholicism, and contradictory feelings of self-loathing and self-aggrandisement. I can understand all this only through painful, retrospective investigation: digging into the past, dredging through my fickle memory, straining to be honest against the need for self-justification, and to rationalise my irrational self.

This is the story of how I became a Poet and a Madwoman, of uncovering the seminal life experiences that led me to their door. My childhood was awful. I have wondered many times whether its crushing weight was what tipped my fragile mind over the edge. Or was my madness simply a biochemical imbalance that would have developed anyway? The question of nature and nurture in the onset of mental illness has long been debated, with a cacophony of opinions. It is a question that has occupied my thoughts since I was diagnosed with schizophrenia 33 years ago.

I have had five volumes of my own work published. Poetry has allowed me to talk about painful and disturbing things in a safe and creative way. This gift of creativity has been a lifeline because it has allowed me to look at myself, and the complexities of being a human being, both intuitively and critically. But more importantly it has enabled me to recreate myself, construct an identity, and so survive the disintegration of madness. My poems were often able to communicate my feelings and thoughts when I was unable to articulate them any other way, so I have included a few of them. They speak as honestly as I can.

Yet I have felt the need to understand my experiences more deeply and have turned to prose in the hope that, through the process of uncovering and reconstructing my life in sequence and through reflection, I can make sense of it. In writing this book I feel as though I have been having a conversation with myself as well as with you, the reader. While it has been deeply unsettling, the process of writing has ultimately been therapeutic and helpful. But I want it to be more than that; I want it to help other people who may have pondered similar questions about mental illness – for themselves or those for whom they care. This is not just a memoir about being lost in the jungles of madness and coming back to tell the tale; it is my attempt to help people understand the subjective complexities of insanity – the idea of which all too often frightens and repels people. By telling my story I am exploring the relationship of my life-experience of mental illness but I recognise that I can speak only for myself.

We are the sum total of our experiences – or rather, of how we remember them. Our memories are all we have of the experiences we accumulate over a lifetime. Memory, imagination, reality are hard to distinguish. Certain memories are clear while others are elusive: I see some things in minute detail; other incidents have a haze over them, but what is left is a powerful impression. We are our memories, unable to live in the present or look to the future without recollecting what brought us to where we are. But how reliable are our recollections and how much are they impressions of what we think happened? Are we having a memory of a memory?

Memory is a recasting of our life experiences, coloured and forged by emotions that temper the reality. Memory has to reconcile recollections with the emotions they bring forth. Because I was so troubled by my childhood, my impressions of that time are also often dark – despite memories of both ordinary and good times. My sister remembers our home life as being far less traumatic than I do. I question my memories of childhood and life events continuously, often not trusting the mind that has also taken me to unimaginable places; the mind that has betrayed me on too many occasions.

My sense of self was always fragile, but with the onset of schizophrenia my centre could not hold. Can the interior of a mad mind ever be revealed? Can rational words ever adequately express the experience of profound irrationality? I have tried to explore my madness as candidly as I am able. All I can do is offer these glimpses into the dark, bizarre world of schizophrenia, the struggle to keep my self together, and the slow reconstruction of an identity that I can live with.

Sandy Jeffs
Melbourne, April, 2009

Part One

Childhood, Girlhood, Youth 1953–1971

Copy cat from Ballarat
Sitting on a witch's hat.
Anon

BROKEN CRADLE

Long before the voices of paranoia broke over me, I was condemned to suffer the shrill, vicious voices of my parents ruthlessly savaging each other. I was born in the provincial city of Ballarat, which was built upon the riches of the gold rushes of the 1850s. The gateway to the abundant farmlands of Western Victoria, it is renowned for its bitterly cold and changeable weather. The grim uncertainty of that weather reflected the capricious and turbulent life of my family. I grapple with recollections of growing up and seeking warmth beyond my troubled home. It is the memory of those winters, both physical and emotional, that stay with me.

My parents, Max and Mavis, married in 1946. Like most newly-weds they must have felt passion and commitment to each other, but by the time I was eight they had descended into anger and bitterness. Alcohol destroyed their lives, and their children's. According to my Auntie June it reared its head early in their marriage by disrupting their honeymoon. Their wedding reception was held at the home of my maternal grandmother. Grandma Bryant was reputedly a fierce woman who forbade alcohol in the house. However, my mother's brothers defied her by supplying the guests with alcohol which they had stashed outside in the washhouse. They and my mother were all heavy drinkers from an early age. After my parent's reception, when they finally climbed into the mourning coach borrowed from Uncle Ted's funeral parlour, they were so drunk they forgot my mother's bags. My uncle had to make a mercy dash to Melbourne early next morning in a vegetable truck to deliver the bags so that my parents could catch the boat to Tasmania. It would be a funny story if this were an isolated occasion instead of the beginning of an emerging pattern.

They must have been a fine couple. Auntie June said my mother was very beautiful and my father was handsome and so much in love with her. But when my mother married she had expectations that were never to be met. Her father owned a big vegetable market in Ballarat and was moderately wealthy. It was always a source of disappointment for her that her marriage to my father had let her down socially. She wasn't able to live in the manner in which she had lived with her own family – from all accounts they had rather spoiled her. My father worked in a factory where he made and tested gas meters. He gave her an allowance, which she always said wasn't enough. They argued bitterly over money.

My sister, Marilyn, was born in 1948. My brother, Keith, followed soon after in 1949. I came along in 1953. I think I was an accident. I used to assume that each of our arrivals was happily embraced, but now I wonder about my parents' early relationship and whether it was doomed from the beginning.

I sensed that something wasn't right between my parents but there were some reassurances that we could do normal and enjoyable things like other families. For example, they would take us to the drive-in cinema. We sat in the FJ Holden while the windows fogged up and the film's soundtrack buzzed on the small portable speaker hung from the car window. We would be wrapped in a brown woollen rug that kept the cold from our small bodies. My father would go to the kiosk and buy chips and drinks for us at interval because there were always two movies to see. Or we occasionally went to the cinema, where a highlight was seeing

South Pacific. I sang the songs from it for months afterwards (and can still sing them). Another memorable film was *Breakfast at Tiffany's*. I cried with my mother when Audrey Hepburn threw the marmalade cat into the alleyway in the pouring rain, only to retrieve it in a moment of redemption. (I only recently learned that the character Audrey Hepburn played in the film was a high-class prostitute. Childhood is so innocent.)

There were visits to see aunts and uncles and to play with cousins. We spent a lot of time with Uncle Wal and Auntie June, and played with Cousin Judy and Cousin Walt. We would go mushrooming with them in the crispness of autumn, finding paddocks on the outskirts of the town chock-a-block with mushrooms among the cow dung. Like a lot of kids we sat in the car outside pubs waiting for our parents; my father used to bring out lemonades and sarsaparillas saying *We won't be long*.

As kids we wandered far and wide around the town: on foot, on bicycles and on the old green and yellow trams. On the weekends, or over the holidays, if we weren't playing sport, we amused ourselves by riding our bicycles around Lake Wendouree in the centre of the city, up and down the streets or visiting friends. We roamed all over the place with no fear. My friend Rosie and I spent a lot of time together. One of our favourite haunts was the drain that ran beneath the streets of the town which we explored with excitement and trepidation. In summer, we spent our days at the city baths from morning until sunset. The freedom we had then would be unheard of today, perhaps because there was no sense of 'stranger danger'. Our parents would have no idea of where we were and what we were doing. Nor did they ask. All they wanted was for us to be home in time for tea. They had an extraordinary trust in our safety and we did too. I don't know if this laid-back attitude was the product of living in a provincial city or whether times have changed and we are a much more cautious and fearful community.

I'm not sure when we got our first television, but on its arrival a new world opened, with sitcoms, comedy shows, westerns, dramas and afternoon soaps. Before television, we had always eaten our evening meal at the kitchen table, a ritual that we performed as a family. At first my parents, like normal parents of the time, resisted our pleas to eat in front of the television, but eventually the television won out. After a few years of doggedly eating in the kitchen, we moved to the lounge-room armchairs, with the trays of food precariously balanced on our laps. While we ate, we dutifully watched the Australian Dream turning into the American Fantasy. Before us was a parade of fresh-faced American actors. I especially remember the *Dick Van Dyke Show*, a sitcom with a wholesome young couple whose lives were an ongoing sequence of easily resolved problems. I wished that my life could be as funny and easy as theirs.

On wintry Sunday nights we sat around the open fire and watched *Disneyland*, eager to know which land it was coming from that night. Was it to be Tomorrow Land, Frontier Land, Fantasy Land or Adventure Land? The fantasy of Disneyland brought me a surreal calm after a stormy night in which my parents had fought and argued. It was the one night of the week when I felt we were almost a 'real' family. After school, I would rush home to watch *Superman* and involve myself in his mission to save the world from evil. I'd have done anything to have the strength of Superman, to fly like him and *bend steel in my bare hands,* be *faster than a speeding bullet, more powerful than a locomotive* and *able to leap tall buildings in a single bound*. If I had his powers, maybe I could change the world to make it a happy place. But the show that made the strongest impression on me was *The Adventures of Ozzy and Harriet*. I longed for Ozzy and Harriet Nelson to be my parents and I longed for our family to be happy, caring, temperate and relaxed, just as they were: for our house to be a home, and not the madhouse I imagined it to be.

* * *

The first time I saw my father beating my mother, I was about eight. It was a Friday night. My mother had been at Uncle Charlie's pub. I'd watched my father pacing around the house, waiting for her. There was an awful, sinister feeling about that night.

The sound of the car hitting the gate stirs him. In she staggers. My father pounces. *Where have you been? I've been out*, she slurs. And says nothing more. He slaps her and pushes her around, smacks her face, the dull thud is his fist into her stomach. They wrestle and she screams *Little Hitler! Little dictator! You coward!* He is screaming back at her, *whore, slut, bitch, all you think of doing is boozin' and rootin'*. He corners her in the passageway, standing over her slumped body, hurling abuse at her. Her dress is torn, her makeup smudged and her limbs limp. He grabs her and wraps his chunky hands around her throat.

Why is my father calling my mother a *whore*? What does that mean? By the way he is saying it, I know it must be something shameful. He raves, lashes out and shoves her into the wall. My brother, who would have been twelve, stands between them and yells *Men don't hit women*! I am bewildered. Then the three of us stand between them and try to fend him off. *Where have you been?* he yells at her again. *I've been out!* she screams back. I implore her *Just tell him*, naive, thinking this would stop the fight; that *she* had the power to stop it. My father grabs at her again. She screams, *Call the police!* He wrenches the phone from the socket, throwing it against the wall. She slurs to all of us *I'm going up to the lake*. We plead *Don't go, please don't go*. He sneers at her: *You're mad. You need to see a fuckin' psychiatrist. You need ya head read, ya mad bitch*. Then he says *he* is leaving and makes his way outside to the car, and again we plead *Please don't go*. Neither of them leave. Windows have been smashed, doors slammed, crockery hurled against the wall and furniture thrown around. We all finally go to bed, to fitful sleep. I contemplate the unthinkable: if my parents split up, who would I live with?

Next morning we behaved as though nothing had happened, putting on a brave face for our neighbours who must have heard the screams. But there was evidence: my mother's bruises and black eyes, and the shambles of the house that had to be cleaned up, the telephone man called to reconnect the phone, the glass man to fix the windows. And my father bringing a cup of coffee to my mother in bed, in a room which reeked of stale beer.

This was a night that was to be repeated over and over in an unrelenting pattern. The violence in our family life went on until my father's death almost 30 years later. In particular, I came to dread Friday nights. The Australian writer Noel Tovey, in his story of survival *Little Black Bastard*, says he hated Fridays too. His mother would do the rounds of the pubs in North Melbourne and come home drunk. All day at school my stomach would be in a knot; I never wanted to go home. As I watched television, I felt sick with worry and anticipation. Sharing Tovey's dread is a strange comfort. I suspect a lot of people dreaded Friday just like us – the day after payday and before the weekend.

Every Friday night
you lie in wait
eyeing your prey
craving a carcass.

Every Friday night
we await the mauling
praying intercession
that never comes.

Every Friday night
your savage moods

shroud us in dread
steal from us our joy.

Every Friday night
in she walks
senses numbed
to endure your devouring of flesh.

Every Friday night
we visit the shades below
as you cut our hearts into pieces
tossing the bleeding bits to your cur
that guards the gate–
every inexorable Friday night.

It wasn't until much later in my life that I realised how terrifying it must have been for my mother to walk into the house on those Friday nights, knowing he was waiting for her. Did she numb herself with alcohol to endure the beatings? I can't imagine what was going through her mind, but she must have expected them. Something had turned my father into a wife beater and it was related to his question, *Where have you been?*

The beginning of the violence seemed to correspond with our shift in 1960 from the corner shop we had in Mair Street to the grey, solid brick house in Creswick Road. I was happy at the shop, which was a little mixed business my parents owned. My mother ran it while my father worked at the gas meter factory. I used to wonder if this house was haunted by angry ghosts who turned my parents into monsters.

Over time, the fights didn't happen just on Friday nights or the weekend. If it were a week night, and I had to go to school the following morning, I would walk to the tram-stop with images playing over and over in my mind, the yelling still clanging in my ears. After a beating, my mother would hide herself from the curious world until her battered face healed. Once she even ended up in hospital with broken ribs. Yet my father visited her regularly, giving her a peck on the cheek when he arrived and supplying her with beer. None of this made sense to me.

Festive occasions like Christmas were often the worst. My mother would go out and invariably get drunk. When she'd arrive home, a fight would start. One Christmas Eve my mother stabbed my father in the hand with a carving knife. He told our visitors who came the next day for Christmas dinner that he had slipped while cutting the bread. That awful night my mother had thrown our presents at us as she staggered to the door saying she was going to the lake to kill herself. She was soon back, not having gone far, and took some tablets, but they had no effect. I saw the empty bottle lying on the floor in the morning.

I never looked forward to celebrations – Christmas, New Year, birthdays. Alcohol would be consumed and an ugly fight would start. I willed them to be happy celebrations, but any joy was brief, unsustainable, always quickly crushed by heavy disappointment. Perhaps this is what shaped my pessimistic outlook, as I learned to expect the worst. My glass is always empty.

THE RAGE OF MAX

I don't believe I knew either of my parents. I have no bundle of family photos, no faded sepia reminders of them as young lovers having fun with their friends. I don't have a store of memorabilia from which to piece together their lives, or those of my siblings and me. My parents were not good communicators; they never revealed their feelings to us – except those of rage. All I have to go on are my memories of their relationship. As I try to paint a picture of people so central to my life, I wonder if my memories, my sources, are reliable. I don't know. I have always felt this inadequacy and lack, wondering if it has more to do with me and my own shortcomings rather than them being enigmas. Or it may simply be that my relationship with them blurs and skews my understanding.

My father had a profound inability to express his emotions and this made it difficult to know him. He was born Keith Maxwell Jeffs in 1920, the elder of two boys. My father wasn't a tall man but he seemed large to me because he had legs like a weightlifter's, with huge calf muscles and bulging thighs. His face was long, and he had a long nose and a pointy chin. His hair was jet black and straight, and only slightly greying in his old age. Similarly, my hair has retained its natural brown even though I am now in my fifties. My father's hands were chunky, the hands of a manual worker, not the hands you would expect of a musician, yet they could navigate the intricate keys on his saxophone and clarinet.

I recall my father telling me: *It's not what you know, it's who you know*. I think he was right. He also used to say: *If you can't be the player, look the player*. He was emphatic that we all must be gracious and sportsmanlike in the way we approached our sport, and look clean and neat in our uniforms. But as to life? His temper was far from his edicts about sportsmanship. He was a man of extremes. He was violent. Yet he could be moved to tears when he heard music. He had a huge collection of old 78 rpm records. His love was swing: the music of Glenn Miller, Benny Goodman, Bob Crosby, Tommy Dorsey and others like them. He loved playing their music on his saxophone and clarinet.

My Auntie June said my father was deeply in love with my mother when they married and was a devoted husband. He did a lot of caring for us children too. He would wash my long hair for me when I was a child, rinsing it, I recall, with the cold hose in the backyard, making fun of the whole operation. Sometimes he arranged my lathered hair into a cocky's crest on top of my head and we would laugh uproariously as I screeched like a cockatoo. He bathed me too sometimes when I was very young. In the early years of marriage he was away at night a lot because of his music. He played in dance bands in Ballarat many nights of the week and got home very late. My mother was left at home with us and became lonely. She sought company elsewhere and my father found out. This contributed to the souring of their relationship. She had been unfaithful to him and he was insanely jealous. He knew the answer to his question *Where have you been?* Beating her wasn't going to stop her seeking other men; indeed, it drove her to them. His violence turned me against him. My brother's words still echo in my mind: *Men don't hit women*.

My father was a man who had no self-control and very poor social skills. He had little self-knowledge or understanding about how to deal with conflict. There was no negotiation with my mother, no quest to determine the truth or understand her point of view. He was self-righteous, never wavering in his right to punish my mother. He was ruthless in tracking her and her transgressions. He would get a map of Ballarat, take a reading of the petrol gauge and odometer in the car before my mother went out and after she had returned, and calculate how far she could have driven and the possible places she could have been. This was an obsessive mind at work, a man in the grip of a furious jealousy. I hated his rages. Every morning, when he prepared his breakfast, he threw the pots and pans around the cupboards in a vile temper, deliberately creating loud, angry noise. What made him so furious, I'd wonder? Many times in my teenage years, when I was the only one at home with my parents, I had to stand between them while they fought. His rage would continue unmoved by the havoc he was creating.

My father would rail at the world, and more pointedly, at my mother. He clashed with my sister who herself has a fiery temper. He had definite opinions about things and was unshakeable in his conservative political views. In my later temporary certainty as a university student I believed his views were not well informed. His stubbornness infuriated me. When someone told him they had seen me in front of the Ballarat town hall in a Moratorium demonstration against Australia's involvement in the Vietnam War, he was furious. Yet all I had done was hold up a placard saying *Educate, don't escalate*. This was in 1970 and I was a young and intense 17-year-old, exploring the world and its meanings through politics and social action. Australia was engaging in a debate about its future, and left-wing politics was on the rise amongst the youth of the day. I was eager to participate and change the world. I even had my own *Little Red Book,* Chairman Mao's manifesto, which I read but did not really understand. My father couldn't engage with my views. He came from the world of conservative, Anglo-

Saxon, Protestant, white Australia. His politics had been formed during the Menzies Cold War years. He still believed that Menzies had protected society from all the dreadful, threatening, unnamed forces, as well as from the unions, the Labor Party and 'the Commies'. My father thought my actions rebellious and dangerous. He forbade me ever to demonstrate in public again. I was resolute and determined to pursue my beliefs.

It's a puzzle to me trying to reconcile my father's bellicosity and his love of music. He was a very good musician whose saxophone and clarinet playing were well regarded in dance bands in Ballarat. Music had played a big part in his early boyhood years, too, when he played the euphonium in the Pleasant Street School Brass Band and later in the Ballarat City Brass Band. I loved it when he shut himself in the kitchen and practised his saxophone. I listened from the front room and heard the mellow tones floating through the house, up the passage to my eager ears. Through his passion for music, I began to love all kinds of music. Music transported me to another world where reality fell away and the senses held sway.

We had Grandma Bryant's piano at home and I would play little ditties by ear and spend hours tinkering with tunes. I wanted to learn, but my passion for sport was time-consuming and my parents weren't pushy about me taking lessons. Strangely, for a man so passionate about music, my father did not teach me one note. I did finally learn an instrument, the viola, when I was 23 and just out of the madhouse. I had time on my hands then, and a friend who encouraged me to take up an instrument. I play violin too. I play neither instrument well. Sometimes, in the nether world of early morning, when I am half asleep and half awake, I have a dream that I am learning the piano. In the next life, I might realise this dream and play the piano beautifully, accompanying my father on his saxophone, our music melding together in a sonorous duet.

My father had his muso mates, some of whom came home and partied on with him, but they weren't a feature of his social life. He had friends at the Golf Club, but didn't spend much time with them away from the golf course. He belonged to the Masonic Lodge but didn't seem to have any friends from there. (We would ask him to show us the secret handshake the Masons were supposed to have but he would never disclose it and I suspected it was a myth. I would sneak into his wardrobe and get out his little case of trinkets, not really knowing what the blue apron with all the silver tassels and baubles was for. It looked a little ridiculous.) I have the sense that he had no close friendships with anyone – I don't recall a particular mate with whom he did things. He was someone who didn't know how to do friendship, but didn't seem perturbed at this. He was self-contained. He was an arrogant man who wasn't a good listener, being too certain of his own thoughts and opinions. My father never spoke of his parents but I think his own father might have been violent too. His mother, in contrast, was a loving woman my sister remembers fondly.

Childhood is a precious time and parents have the responsibility to protect their children from the perils of the world. I never felt protected. My father's violence was pervasive. But I also have vivid memories of my father's insensitivity to my feelings. My first memory is as a ten-year-old watching my father drown a stray cat. He lured it into a noose and then dunked it into a big bucket of water. It struggled as its legs and body twisted and flailed before it fell limp. I was traumatised by what I saw. My father didn't shield me from this. Too cruel a reality can batter a child's psyche. The other lingering memory I have is of being in the car when my father ran over a dog. I heard the dull thud and immediately looked back through the window and saw the dog tumbling into the gutter. I wanted to scream *Stop!* but the word caught in my throat. My father didn't stop. He didn't say a word. I sat immobilised in the car, tears welling, as I wondered whether the dog was alive and injured, or whether it was dead. It was someone's pet; someone's loss and sadness. I never forgave my father for this cruelty and to this day I still wonder: why didn't he stop?

Friends have asked me if I think my father would have been a wife-beater even if my mother had not been unfaithful. I can only speculate. He never hit me once for any of my transgressions, but then I was careful not to create much of a fuss. My sister did incur his wrath and he did physically throw her out of the house on several occasions. He also belted her so severely with the strap one night, for using too much hot water, that she went to school the next day with the welts and bruises still on her legs. When he found himself in a rage with my mother he could express his fury in only one way. The fact that he was always suspicious of her meant that he belted her many times when she hadn't actually done anything wrong. He reacted to any little thing she did: the way she held a cigarette in her mouth or spilt coffee from her cup were enough to incite him into a rage.

The bashings became more unprovoked as time went on. My feeling is that he would always find some reason to beat her: the violence was in him and expressed itself so easily. Perhaps if he had been able to work his way through problems by talking rather than bashing, things would have been different, and I wonder if he would have benefited from 'anger management' courses offered to violent people today. But while wife-beating is often associated with drunken men, my father also bashed my mother while he was stone-cold sober. Being top dog was important for him and he knew no other way of dominating and imposing his will, of ensuring her compliance.

He always had a maniacal look on his face when he was beating her. Sometimes, when he beat her ruthlessly, he then forced her to have sex. I heard them in their bedroom; I heard her pain.

Out Patient Appointment 4/4/78
Also used to hear them have sexual intercourse where Fa would force himself upon Mother & she learnt sex = aggression.

I thought this must be what sex is about: violence and pain, demands and submission, power and powerlessness.

As for myself, I'm too afraid to show anger. Instead, I ruminate and seethe about things, until the gall becomes an internal claw. I don't want to create scenes like my father did, but on the other hand I know I am living with a stultifying introspection that cannot resolve conflict in a healthy or mature way. I try to be as calm and as even tempered as possible and not be the source of anyone's distress. I am afraid of causing conflict and the irreparable damage it may leave in its wake. When I cannot deal with conflict, I bury my head in the sand and wait until it blows over. I want a peaceful world at all costs. Is this any better than raging? It has to be.

S

ALL THAT GLITTERED

My mother was the youngest daughter in a large family, with five brothers and one sister. She was born Mavis Dorothy Bryant in 1923, three years after my father. I don't know what her relationship with her parents was like; she never mentioned them much to me. Her eldest brother was 17 years older than her, and from all accounts, all her brothers doted on her. They nick-named her Fluff because she had such a healthy head of brown curly hair. But she was envious of her siblings because they were all better off than she was. When one brother bought an expensive house in a prestigious location near the lake she was scathing, her envy fuelled by her own failure to climb the social ladder. She often criticised her siblings for no real reason, and this was always magnified when she was drunk. I rarely heard a kind word for any of them, except for her brother Wal, whom I think she did love in her clumsy way. Often she was thrown out of Uncle Charlie's pub because, in her drunkenness, she would become bitter and acrimonious. One night Uncle Ted and Auntie Thel threw her out of their house because she caused so much trouble. She fell in the garden amongst the roses, and lost her marquisette watch.

Despite my mother's social misdemeanours, she was a surprisingly devoted housekeeper. She scrubbed and waxed the kitchen lino floor by hand twice a week: down on her knees with the

Wunder Wax and rags, shining the floor until it gleamed with her reflection. She eventually bought a Hoover polisher, which had brushes to spread the liquid wax and lambskin buffers to shine the lino. This appliance was a beast with a mind of its own: it jolted and jerked over the floor, with you hanging onto it lest it career into the furniture. When I tried to use it I felt turned inside out, my small arms barely holding the monster at bay. The ironing was one of the rituals I remember well. In the morning my mother dampened the clothes. She used water in a sauce bottle stopped with a cork that had small holes in it. She then wrapped the damp clothes in a sheet. In the afternoon she ironed them with the Sunbeam steam iron, using a blanket and sheet on the end of the kitchen table as the ironing board. As well as ironing the clothes, she pressed the sheets, towels, pillow slips, underpants – all with meticulous care. To my mother, how well she ironed the clothes, and how crisp they looked, was a testament to how good a housewife she was.

I never felt my mother gave the same care to her mothering as she did to her house, or that we mattered as much. It was as though the only way in which my mother could feel some control in her life was through providing a clean house, and that in this she was making a home.

People said my mother was beautiful, and certainly men found her attractive. She had played netball in her youth and became a keen golfer in later life. When I was in year ten I saw a picture of her in *The Ballarat Courier*. In the photo she is in full swing with a golf club, her athletic body trim and agile. She ran swiftly, well into her thirties: I have a silver tray inscribed with the words: *Ladies Gift won by Mrs Jeffs, Canberra Hotel 1960*. She had won the open athletics championship at Ballarat High School, and it was a thrill for me when I won the same championship.

She had a slender body, with shapely legs. When she walked into a room she became the centre of attention. She dressed with elegance. She took great care with her make-up. Her brown hair went grey early, and she used to put a pink or blue rinse in it each Saturday morning. She spent hours manicuring her hands and beautifying her face before going to the Golf Club for a night out.

Her long bony fingers, which grew gnarled over the years, knitted hundreds of exquisite woollen jumpers. My own hands and fingers are long and bony just like hers. A cluster of diamonds glittered on her ring finger. She had several rings: engagement, eternity and wedding rings, her mother's wedding ring, and other rings she had bought when she and my father went to Hong Kong. She was consoled by her rings because they represented the social standing that she craved, and she was always chuffed when people made flattering remarks about them. The more she glittered, the happier she was. On her death, I chose to have her wedding ring and my grandmother's wedding ring. My sister opted for the diamonds. They were valued and found not to be worth very much, certainly not as valuable as my mother had imagined. All that glittered wasn't diamonds.

My mother was a mix of bravado and insecurity. At parties, she would be at the centre of the crowd with her loud and hearty laugh. But her demeanour was a performance masking her troubled life, her insecurity, and the unfulfilled and abusive relationship with my father. Did she drink to make it more bearable to be with him, or to forget she was with him? Or was she with him only because of her insecurities? Whatever the reason, drinking only made her life worse, and when she got drunk she would bemoan the fact that other people were better off and luckier than she was, her humour giving way to snide and provocative remarks. Her gregarious nature would become grating to others as she started to lurch and demand attention. Sometimes, when I could hear her laughter becoming hard and forced, I felt she was trying to conjure happiness into her life.

She would sing *Please release me, let me go* and *So release me and let me love again,* as though that song were written for her. She would also sing the Beatles' ditty *Bang, bang, Maxwell's silver hammer came down upon her head.* Was she alluding to her bashings? Her friends laughed with her, but I sensed the significance of the words. But eventually her beery jollity would become wearing and they would stop laughing. She was a sad drunk and the drunker she got the more pathetic she became. One day she accused her brother of disloyalty because he had banned her from his pub after she had caused a drunken scuffle.

I was aware of her drinking from an early age. She seemed to be at Uncle Charlie's pub a lot, particularly Fridays, from where she would always come home drunk. Then when she started playing midweek golf, she would come home tipsy. On Saturdays, if she wasn't at Uncle Charlie's she was at the Golf Club. She would come home very drunk on these nights. That she didn't have more accidents is a miracle, for she would have been way over the alcohol limit allowed today. In the mid 1960s they bought a second-hand two-tone brown EH Holden which she drove. We called it 'the concertina', because it had so many dents in it. Our gate was permanently bent and twisted.

One night she drove into the back of a stationary car. If she hadn't leapt out of the car and abused the other driver, he wouldn't have called the police, and she would have been saved the ignominy of being taken to the police station and charged with drunken driving. That night, the police rang home. I knew something was wrong when my father, in a seething rage, left the house on his bicycle. A few hours later, I saw him walking up the street with my mother staggering in front of him. He was abusing her loudly enough for all the street to hear. He had made her walk home through the cold, damp streets shouting at her all the way. When she staggered into the house, he raged at her, belted her, and went to bed.

For all her drinking, I never saw her with a hangover. However, every morning, whether she had been drinking the night before or not, she had a Bex headache powder, before having her usual cup of weak, black, instant coffee. It was a ritual. She would dextrously open the specially folded paper and tap the white powder into a little mound in the middle, fold the paper in half to guide it onto her tongue and then wash it down with a glass of water. The combination of the Bex and all the alcohol she consumed over the years cannot have been good for her stomach, but she didn't seem to suffer any problems.

My mother's drinking worsened over the years, intensifying when my parents sold their house and took up the licence of a hotel after my father lost his job at the gas meter factory in 1972. The pub provided unlimited alcohol for my mother, who thought she would be in control if she drank small beers. However, she drank them continuously, from the time the pub opened to when it closed. She held court in the bar and consumed vast amounts of grog. She was dressed to the nines and coiffured beautifully. But her dependence on alcohol was growing and much of the time she was in a stupor. By the time my parents left the pub and moved to Melbourne, six years later, my mother was pickled on beer and had descended into an alcoholism that was destroying her. By the end of her life she was drinking all day, every day. I would ring her once a week, before noon on Sundays, because I knew that time was my window to speak to her while she was sober. It's as if she thought that starting at noon, and not some random time, meant she was in control and didn't really have an alcohol problem. Once I said to her that I hated her drinking and she looked so witheringly at me that I shied away. Her face was white with anger. She never accepted she had a problem. She drank right up to her death.

My distress about my mother grew to the point where I was fantasising about killing her. I was sure death would be kinder to her than the miserable life she had with my father. I also couldn't stand watching her deteriorate. Even though I loathed and despised my father for what he did to my mother, I never had a fantasy about killing him. Isn't that interesting? Can it be that we expect so much more from mothers than from fathers?

My mother must have been miserable in her marriage, and perhaps the drinking and infidelity were her way of making her life liveable. I never really thought about how she felt, about her needs or how unloved she must have felt. I was too involved with what I was experiencing – in the way a child does, not really aware of my siblings' feelings either. Although my mother was antagonistic towards her family, she was accepting of her friends' foibles. Perhaps she was aware of her own flaws. She often said: *You can only treat people the way they treat you*. One of her friends told me what a loyal friend my mother was because she didn't let gossip destroy their friendship. But when my mother got drunk her better qualities became lost in the fog of liquor. As she declined into alcoholism she lost the will to keep a clean and beautiful house, and lived in squalor. Her friends and family deserted her until finally no-one was left. Even as an adolescent I knew I didn't want to be like her.

In later life I came to realise that I had been guilty of victim-blaming. I now understand that we can be powerfully influenced by social attitudes that suggest women bring abuse upon themselves, and I had internalised these to blame my mother for my father's violence. I thought she should have the power to stop it and I blamed her for her powerlessness. Later I was to feel a similar powerlessness in my own circumstances. Although I blocked her from my life, I had a desperate need for her. I didn't have the same kind of longing to know or understand my father.

Could I have done things differently? I wish I could let my mother know how sorry I am for my ignorance and neglect. What would have brought me close to her? The fact that society still blames women victims suggests it wasn't just a product of the time, that perhaps it has more to do with the way women are still at the mercy of a male-dominated culture that has power over their lives in ways even men themselves don't realise. I think it must be the same way white people don't understand the power they have in a white-dominated culture that subordinates black people. I feel my mother was ultimately in a no-win situation and was doomed by forces of which I was unknowingly a part.

* * *

Out Patient Appointment 4/4/78
She only wants to be cuddled by someone - always looking for a mother.

I spent much of my life looking for a mother – someone to give me the love I felt I wasn't getting, to heal my sadness and make my life less painful. Even though we didn't talk about it, I was aware that my siblings were doing the same: seeking alternative families. I knew my brother had a close set of mates with whom he spent a lot of time. They were his family. My sister, in trying to find the love she craved, entered a series of disastrous relationships. I always longed for the mothering touch, for someone to hug me in a maternal way, for a great matriarch to furl her wings about me in a warm, womb-like space; for a mother who could tell me everything was going to be all right. It is ironic the wings that closed around me were to be the wings of madness, with strident voices forbidding me to be touched at all – a cruel twist.

My anxiety and desperation about my relationship with my own mother made me turn to my friends' mothers. Mrs Anderson, my friend Rosie's mother, was one such substitute. It was her I asked where babies came from, not my mother. But she too had an abusive husband who had what was called 'war neurosis'. He was an alcoholic who beat her and neglected their six children. Yet Mrs Anderson was a pillar of the community who played piano for the girls' calisthenics and made cakes for church stalls. I loved the sing-alongs we had in the front room with Rosie and her sister Glenda, and her mother at the piano. We sang songs from musicals, popular songs and old-time favourites. For a moment we forgot ourselves and were transported to a happy place where we sang along with Judy Garland, Doris Day and all the other stars. Years later, in the madhouse, singing along with a bunch of other loonies, I felt the power of music to transport me from my immediate sorrow, and my thoughts drifted back to those days in Mrs Anderson's front room.

My other 'mother' was my favourite Auntie, June. She was always there. She watched me grow up and, as an angst-ridden teenager, I would lob in at her house and lie on the lounge-room floor in front of the open fire, letting myself drift into dark thoughts. Auntie June later told me that she felt there was an impenetrable wall around me. She said she wanted to fold me in her arms, just like the matriarch I longed for. She wanted to tell me everything was going to be all right, but she couldn't because of my reticence.

My mother-search has been a compelling need, sometimes so intense that I have pushed friends into this unwanted and unhealthy role. In my later years, the need has subsided with the easing of my angst and a better understanding of who I am and what I need to sustain my life. But I still have moments when I become the needy child again, and this regression suggests a deep need I am still unable to assuage.

SILENCE IS GOLDEN

For years no-one knew what was going on inside our family, or if they did, it was never acknowledged. Neither we, nor our extended family or neighbours ever spoke about it. In such a silence you turn in on yourself. You feel guilt and blame. I was a child, without any understanding of what I was witnessing, or the social forces that might explain it. I didn't have the language to articulate what I was feeling, or a safe place in which to talk about it. Silence for me was denial, and denial a defence. But internally I suffered, blaming myself for not being able to stop the terror and feeling utterly alone with it. This fuelled anger in me, but I didn't know how to express it, fearing the destructive power in the rages of my father. Consequently, as an adult, any anger in me is ill-formed and suppressed. I still find it difficult to distinguish between conflict and healthy disagreement. But I will not be a victim; I have had to learn how to deal with conflict in my own way.

My psychiatrist's note from the early days of my psychotherapy shows my world view seems shaped by pessimism. Bearing witness took its toll.

Out Patient appointment 4/4/78
Has been in psychotherapy for 1 year, 2 weekly appointments. Sandra has a very pessimistic,

> depressing view of life, mainly originating from very negative experiences as a child. Fa & Mo alcoholics, frequent fights & blood baths, Mo stayed away in hotels until 12MN & Fa would be cursing her, calling her vulgar names etc.

My siblings and I didn't talk to each other about our family life. We had shared the drama of trying to restrain my father from beating my mother. We had heard her screams and witnessed his abuse. Even worse, we had shared the awful experience of trying to stop him from strangling her. We lived with that constant horror, yet we never asked each other how each of us were handling it. I didn't know anything of their suffering, nor did they know about mine. We lived our separate lives, suspended in an eerie silence. My sister left home at 17, when I was 12. She was gone before we could develop a proper relationship. My brother, who is four years older than me, had more freedom and was always out with his mates. So I didn't have the chance to know him well either. Their absence left me alone with my parents and I bore the brunt of their disintegrating relationship. I had no support and no-one with whom I could talk or compare my experiences.

This silence between my siblings and me was a personal agony. When I was twelve I saw my mother kissing a strange man in the car park where I was once again waiting in the car. I didn't tell my brother and sister. I carried that memory for years. I felt betrayed, puzzled and angry with my mother. All the time we had been defending her against my father's accusations, and putting ourselves between them to protect her, because we believed her. Then I saw her with this other man. When she got into the car to leave she said to me *Don't tell Daddy – these things happen.* I didn't know what to think and sat silent in the back of the car stifling my tears. I felt so insecure and vulnerable, insignificant – how could she do this to me? Is this what a mother does to a child she loves – to expose me so easily to her betrayal, and expect me to carry such a heavy secret?

It was only at my mother's funeral that I found out my brother had seen my mother with other men in the car parked in the street around the corner from our house. Around this time I also saw my father kissing another woman in our back yard. I was shocked, but quickly squared up the ledger. He was no better than my mother, for all his anger towards her. I feared that my family was falling apart; I thought it would explode and we would be left as orphans with no-one to protect us from life's onslaught. As a child, you have a deep moral sense, and mine was outraged by my parents' duplicity and unfaithfulness. I was a child in a world that cared nothing about me. Everything was out of control and I felt guilty for not being able to bring it back to some order. I'm reminded of Macbeth on the night he kills Duncan, when nature and all the cosmic forces are out of kilter and terrible things happen. This Shakespearean turmoil was my home, with all its unnatural brutality and drama, and my siblings and I were at the centre of it.

THAT OLD-TIME RELIGION

Like most Protestant kids in the 1950s and 60s, my siblings and I were sent to Sunday school. We went to a congregational Sunday school, not because of our religion, but because it was close to where we lived. My mother was adamant, though, that we were Church of England because that is where we were baptised. What I learnt at Sunday school was in direct contrast to home. I could never reconcile the differences between the two worlds: the alcoholic fights with the temperate, God-fearing teachings of the Sunday school. The peace and humility of Jesus were not what my parents practised.

Going to Sunday school also meant I had to dress up in girls clothes. I hated wearing the little pink frocks, in which I felt not like a princess but a freak. I hated the black patent leather shoes my mother forced me to wear. I wanted to wear more practical shoes, like my school shoes, and pants instead of a dress. I was a tomboy from an early age and was more interested in climbing trees and playing sport. I wanted the freedom I saw my brother had. Before setting off for Sunday school we were each given threepence to put in the collection plate, but sometimes I spent this on raspberry lollies at the shop on the way. I was fearful God was watching and judging everything I did and would thunder at me from the sky, dash the lollies to the ground and punish me for my sin. So I became more cunning and spent only twopence on lollies and put one penny in the collection plate, thinking God wouldn't mind this.

At that time, the church had a policy of asking members of the congregation if they would be willing to have an Aboriginal child from the local orphanage home for Sunday lunch. We never did. I wondered who these children were and why they were in an orphanage? What had they done to be put there? Were these children bad? Where were their parents? Today we know that these children were 'the Stolen Generation', taken from their families as part of the government's assimilation policy. Who were we to lead by example when our own lives were in disarray? But the reason why my parents would not have had these kids home was, however, more than likely simple apathy. My guilt about the assimilationist policies is ironically appeased by the fact that we didn't engage with the church's wishes.

At Sunday school I learnt about the all-loving Father, and the Son who died for our sins. I was taught about the miracles Jesus performed and the power of prayer. I had a deeply religious inclination as a child and I wanted to believe all I was told. On Good Fridays I was solemn and respectful, especially around three o'clock, which I thought was the time Jesus died on the cross. I watched the silent movie *King of Kings* on television and felt all the solemnity of the final moments of Jesus' life. In fact, I was always more moved by the death of Jesus than His birth. After Sunday school we would go into the church for the Sunday service and I always wondered why my parents weren't in the congregation and didn't share my religious feelings. Yet, like most of their generation, they felt duty bound to send us to Sunday school even though they didn't care about religion themselves.

When my father belted my drunk mother, I retreated into my bedroom and recited the prayers I had learnt at Sunday school. Amidst the yelling I begged God: *Please, stop Daddy from hit-*

ting Mummy, and *Please God, stop Mummy from drinking*, and promised to be a good girl. I prayed fervently, hopefully, with deep conviction and sincerity. I was desperate, feeling that I was being punished for some sin I had committed unknowingly. I had been told of the fiery realms of hell and damnation and feared we must all be destined to go there.

'Now I lay me down to sleep.'
Sleep was broken
by the noises that
came from their room.
Something was going to happen.
Indeed, sleep did not come
with the tension in the air
the hate, the bitterness
the night about to explode
. . .
'I pray the Lord my soul to keep.'

I wanted God to stop the awful things we had to witness, to bring peace to our lives. It seemed a simple thing to ask and I didn't think it unreasonable given that the Lord was all-powerful, loving and merciful. When He didn't help me, I felt abandoned and betrayed. I couldn't believe that God would let children live such miserable lives and I began to doubt that He existed. The faith I lost then was never regained, even during a later intoxication with Catholicism in my late teens and early twenties. When madness descended upon me years later, religious imagery was to be the centre of my deluded, persecutory world.

This was a period in Australia's history of sectarian bigotry between Protestants and Catholics. My father would tell us that Catholics, derisively called *Micks*, had guns in the crypts of their churches and were going to take over the world. He often told us the story of how, when he was little, he was nearly made a Catholic. Some dastardly neighbours had secretly taken him to a

Catholic church and almost had him baptised, but some miracle saved him. The fact that my mother had had to confront and interrogate Patricia, a Catholic kid from St Joseph's Primary School, about stealing a lolly from our corner shop only went to prove that Micks were indeed dishonest. And not only were the Micks a problem, but the Commies were going to get us as well. There was nowhere to turn without being in some peril: Ballarat was under siege from forces huge and irresistible.

In spite of my father's warnings, or perhaps because of them, I became fascinated by Catholicism. I knew that Catholics went to mass and ate fish on Fridays and demanded that everyone who married a Catholic had to convert: all of this intrigued me. At the public swimming pool I would see Catholics with their trinkets around their necks and wonder about these displays of religious devotion. I was beguiled when I found forgotten scapulars and medals in the changing rooms, knowing these had something to do with the ritual life of Catholics. I wondered what the images and words on the medals meant and wished that I, too, had something mystical to hang around my neck. The closest I came to a medal was a green plastic Tiki I got from a peanut butter jar, which I put on a piece of string and placed around my neck. I liked it dangling when I bent over, and felt blessed by its charm.

My fascination with religious icons is consummated in my continuing collecting of religious icons and trinkets from all over the world. I have been given many pieces for my eclectic shrine. Friends are still trawling the world's religious trinket shops for pieces of Catholic kitsch and icons of devotion. What this fascination means I don't know. Why am I, an atheist, drawn to such blatant displays of belief? There is something poetic about Catholicism: the art, the prayers, the Virgin Mary, Stations of the Cross, the rosary, incense. Catholic priests in ceremony are, to me, like peacocks, their vestments like shimmering feathers, mesmerising their audience with a beautiful and seductive performance. Perhaps this aesthetic fantasia touched in me a poetic sensibility then unformed.

I had to walk past St Patrick's Cathedral on my way to and from primary school. A constant stream of people was always coming and going from its huge dark-brown doors. I would sneak up to these forbidding doors, above which hung a picture of the Pope. I would tremble in fear of meeting a nun or priest who might ask me what I was doing there. These people dressed in strange clothing were frightening. We made fun of them to allay our fears, calling the nuns 'black crows'. These were doors to a world my father would denounce as an incarnation of Hell. But Hell, to my delight, was a work of art. I would peek behind the doors into the dark, cavernous interior, where people lit candles, splashed themselves with holy water, and kneeled in front of statues, wrapping rosary beads around their hands. Religious pictures, statues, candles burning in every nook and cranny, the strange smell of incense wafting into my nostrils, the flowers – it all made me gape, entranced. I hadn't seen such a display of opulence before, certainly not in the congregational church. There was something comforting about the way the Catholics blessed themselves, as though it meant God were really present in their lives and taking an interest in them. In my childish ignorance, the Catholics were God's Chosen People, before I found out about the Jews and the Promised Land.

My father's worst fears about Catholicism were realised when one of my mother's brothers, Derek married Myrtle, a devout Catholic. My mother's family never quite coped with Auntie Myrtle: there would always be snide remarks and pointed comments about her intransigence on religion. Her children were, as matter of course, all educated at Catholic schools, and when her son, also called Derek, decided he wanted to enter a seminary and become a priest . . . well, that was the end! There were family rumblings and much dismay at Cousin Derek's decision. This could only be a Catholic plot to take over the world. If Auntie Myrtle were alive today she would also have been proud of her sister's son: he is the conservative Australian Cardinal George Pell.

Cousin Derek was ordained in 1974 at St Patrick's Cathedral, Ballarat, when I was 21 and in my second year at university. The ordination was on the same day as an abortion rally in Melbourne. I wanted to go to both events but chose to go to Cousin Derek's ordination. My compromise was to stage my own abortion rally in Ballarat before I went to the ordination. I stood alone in Sturt Street, with a huge placard saying *Abortion a right, contraception a responsibility*. It was a Saturday morning, and I stood across the road from Myer, the big department store where everyone who was anyone in Ballarat met. I saw old school friends who looked at me as though I were mad. A woman came up to me and called me a murderer. I was shocked she could see me as such; I thought I was only trying to enlighten people about something essential for a better society. My protest was part of my emerging feminism. Here was I, flirting with a conservative, reactionary religion and engaged in a desperate search for meaning, but at the same time developing a social conscience informed by radical, left-wing feminist politics. How could I embrace both worlds?

I was drawn to Cousin Derek's spiritual journey. I wished I could be so sure of God, or of a spiritual way. Derek looked splendid in his ornate vestments, a vision of Catholic religiosity. The church was beautiful with displays of flowers lovingly placed all through it by some hardworking women. The perfume of incense permeated the candle-lit cathedral. Cousin Derek was radiant as he vowed to take his religion out into town and country as a parish priest. At the conclusion of his first homily, he was applauded. Now he was all set to re-enter the world in his new incarnation, in the role he had been destined for; he was now shepherd to his flock in a world where wolves were baying. Cousin Derek blessed the congregation and then blessed everyone separately. He blessed me. As he was blessing my mother, I made a silent prayer that this would save her from herself and my father's brutality. Maybe the hand of God would lead my mother beside still waters and restore her soul. Again I was invoking God to intervene, wanting the spiritual life-force to bless us all. Surely the supernatural powers now invested in 'Father' Derek would work their magic to bring the miracle of love and peace?

When Uncle Derek died, Auntie Myrtle gave him a Catholic funeral. Cousin Derek officiated at the ceremony. I wasn't able to go but I know from family gossip that burying a Protestant as a Catholic was considered sacrilegious. How dare they bury Uncle Derek as a Catholic! Someone claimed that Auntie Myrtle was heard to say: *We couldn't get him while he was alive, but we got him in his death*. This only confirmed for my family the predatory nature of the Catholic Church and gave credibility to my father's story of his childhood near-miss with the Catholics.

My lack of faith today has much more to do with scepticism. Various Christian denominations ask you to believe in stories of the creation, the fall, the holy trinity, the resurrection, heaven, purgatory and hell, transubstantiation, pre-destination and the elect, a virgin birth, an immaculate conception, a son of God, miracles, the power of the sacraments, papal infallibility, speaking in tongues – the list is endless. Such beliefs are no less fantastic than some of the visions and ideas I've had when I was mad! The Christian religion is only one spiritual understanding of the world, no more nor less legitimate than Hinduism or Buddhism or the Aboriginal cosmologies. That there are many creation stories and many ways of seeing the world only reinforces to me that Christianity cannot have a monopoly on truth. I understand now, however, that there is comfort in the familiarity of the ritual and symbols of the religion one has grown up with, and for many this is why they still perform their religious duties. Comfort in this world is sometimes hard to find and I envy anyone who finds it, even if it is in religion.

SHAME

I was in year eight when my mother's conviction for drunken driving was reported in *The Ballarat Courier* for all my school friends to see. I dreaded going to school that morning where some of my 'friends' delighted in asking me if it was my mother who was in the paper. I wanted to crawl under a rock when I saw their smirks and heard their asides. My mother was a public drunk: she had let me down and made me a victim. Kids can be merciless when they scent an opportunity to shame someone. This shame was crippling and made me question my friendships. Some friends were loyal and I appreciated them more. I needed to be reassured, not ridiculed, because of my mother.

What is shame? Shame is a personal admonition, something you feel in relation to your own values and insecurities. If you have a good self-image and confidence then shame is easier to deal with, but I was insecure and vulnerable to people's cruelty. One time I was in the FJ waiting for my mother. I would have been about ten and I was lolling on the back seat with my legs slung over the front seat. A sleazy man walked past and said: *Close ya legs luv, I'll get back to you when you're older*. I didn't understand why he had said that to me, yet blushed with shame. Worried that he would come back, I sat rigidly on the seat until my mother came out to take me home. I didn't tell her about the sleazy man.

In 1967 shame touched me in a more brutal way. In my desperation to escape the family and succeed at something that was going to give me a sense of self, I was open to suggestion and very impressionable. I often took my cues from others who seemed more worldly and accomplished. Sharon was one such person. I went to school with Sharon; she was a year older than me but seemed ten years older. She was intelligent and interesting and seemed 'with it' and in touch with all the latest pop culture and fashion. I admired her worldliness and outrageous left-wing politics. Her parents were union people and very big in the labour movement in Ballarat, while I was a child still living under Menzies' star. Not that my parents knew much about the political landscape, unlike Sharon's family who seemed so well informed.

Sharon was refreshing. My discussions with her, as we rode our bikes to school together, were partly responsible for the leftist political views I was to develop around the age of 15 or 16. I remember in year ten giving a talk to my current affairs class about why Australia should get out of the Vietnam War, and in the following year, 1970, taking part in the political demonstrations that were against the war. My mother wasn't very happy about my association with Sharon, who she thought was a bit rough.

One day Sharon and I caught a bus to a tiny township 20 kilometres from Ballarat, where we were going to spend the weekend with Sharon's sister. She had a boarder at her house, called Bruce, who was 24 and seemed pretty groovy to us young girls. Bruce offered to drive us to a dance in Maryborough, 60 kilometres from Ballarat, in his light-blue Mini Minor. All the way there we drank beer and by the time we arrived we were drunk.

This was the time of the swinging 60s when military clothes were fashionable. Bruce looked so handsome in his blue-and-red military jacket with gold epaulettes and braid. I had on a brown corduroy jacket, also with epaulettes, which Sharon had lent me, and blue-and-white checked bell-bottomed slacks. I felt so grown up, but I was only 13.

After Bruce and I had danced for a while he suggested that we go for a drive. I trusted him. We drove into the bush and drank some more beer. We kissed and he fondled me. He wanted to have sex. I resisted. In the back of my mind I knew this wasn't right. *Do you think we should?* I slurred. He reassured me, but beneath his reassurance I sensed a threatening and nasty man. I gave in because I was too scared to refuse. It was an isolated place and I feared he would hurt me. I felt I had no choice. The sex was awful, awkward, painful and humiliating. We returned to the dance. He stood outside with the boys who habitually stand outside dances with their beers, and boasted about his conquest. They laughed at me and made snide comments. I felt betrayed. I felt dirty, sullied, a tramp, a whore, everything that goes with the shame of having surrendered myself to a man who used and abused me. I wanted to disappear into a hole to escape their taunts and derision, their scathing laughter and leers. They asked me for sex. I was anyone's now.

I faked my way through the rest of the night. I didn't show how gutted I felt. In my child's mind I blocked my thoughts and started a process of denial to survive the shame. I drank more beer. When we finally left the dance I left my childhood there, at that unforgiving place, with Bruce and those leering boys.

I came home to the place where my misery was already profound and although I could not imagine that things could get worse I learned that Whiskey, my beloved cat, had been hit by a car. He lay on a cushion, barely alive. I felt a crushing guilt. If I had been home this would not have happened. It was all my fault. When I got up in the morning Whiskey was gone. My father had taken him somewhere and buried him. My throat ached as I began to wail. Whiskey's death was punishment for my sin. And I hated myself, as I still do, for the death of my innocence.

I grieved for Whiskey. I grieved for what had happened to me. I felt the world was a fiercely unjust place where nothing was given to me without my being betrayed or hurt. And there was no-one I could share my grief with or unburden my shame and guilt.

I became someone who was unsure of how to be with boys. My self-esteem had been taken from me. I had no self-respect and little regard for how I behaved. I placed myself in dangerous situations, allowing boys to fondle me. I started drinking alcohol and often got blind drunk because I felt worthless. For many years I carried the shame of what happened with Bruce. It wasn't until a friend of mine went through her own struggle with sexual abuse that my own experience finally overwhelmed me with its awful reality. I had for years suppressed my emotions as I tried to find a way of coping with my hurt. I had always blamed myself for what had happened. Now I could see that an adult man had taken advantage of a naive, drunk 13-year girl, and that even though he didn't violently assault me, his boastful betrayal of me was a cruel emotional violence; it was emotional rape. Yet even now I remain ambivalent about my role in the awful events of that night. I have to work hard at forgiving myself. I'm not alone in this self-blaming mind-set. Many women who have been abused have blamed themselves. We still live in a society that often blames women for being seduced, raped or bashed by abusive men.

People talk about resilience. I'm not sure what that is. I survived this trauma without any help from an adult or peer. I was left to my own devices and in the end they got me through. Denial was my first strategy and it eased the initial phase of the shame. I dissociated from the event, went into a mental vacuum where nothing seemed to touch me. I was stone. Anna Akhmatova, in the poem 'The Sentence', says, *So much to do today:/kill memory, kill pain/turn heart into stone,/and yet prepare to live again*. I did just that, but in my unsophisticated child's way. I lived most of my teenage years with shame in the back of my mind, trying to deflect my attention from it. I put my energy into establishing friendships. Anne Deveson talks about this in her book *Resilience*, saying the ability to make friends is an attribute conducive to surviving trauma. I could easily have withdrawn from people, but friends were always my saviours. Without the mental capacity to be bloody-minded and *kill the pain*, I may have foundered.

Not many of my friends know about my experience of sexual assault. I have been unable to talk about it. So, why am I writing this? Why the public confession? Why expose this secret to the world? I don't know the answer but there is something in the anonymity of the reader, the fact that I don't see you face-to-face. There is also a faith in the reader as a companion on a journey: the reader sitting impartially with my words, with my struggle to make the words meaningful. The will to explore my experience in words is a way of understanding, and confronting, something that has been a painful memory; a way of owning and perhaps moving on from the pain. Perhaps my words will help someone else, or at least tell them they are not alone, and that many of us share similar secrets. Or perhaps I want to make a public confession, hoping for absolution, something I have never been able to give myself.

AT THE LOONY BIN WITH DAD

Sometimes there are events in your life that have a resonance much later. In year ten, I found myself witnessing a human drama with characters both humorous and tragic. Once a month my father would traipse up to the local mental hospital to play his saxophone with his trio at social functions for the inmates. One day he said to me: *Come up with me to the loony bin and have a laugh at the loonies.* I would have been about 15 and had never knowingly seen a mad person before. I was intrigued. Lakeside was a cluster of redbrick buildings, surrounded by parklands and gardens. Those dark buildings were forbidding. What would I see behind the thick brick walls?

I stood on the stage of the dingy hall and looked down at the loonies dancing to the old-time music of the 40s, while Pat vamped on the piano, Ivan caressed his drums and my father blew his saxophone with a mellow tone. The loonies were a show to behold. They shuffled and tottered with unsteady gaits. They were a mumbling bumbling lot, waltzing with each other in tenuous embraces, taking tentative steps. (I only understood years later that it was their medication that made them like this.) There were wonderful characters amongst this bizarre gathering. I think deep down my father had a kind of compassion for these mad people and was intrigued by some of the stories he heard. There was the woman, dressed as a green frog, who waved to me all night. My father told me of the loony who was a great artist before her mind shattered. There was the former headmaster who had succumbed to gibbering madness, and the genius who went mad after his skull was slashed by a chainsaw. My father was always saying with awe in his voice: *Genius and madness are related, you know*. Another loony actually played my father's saxophone and played it with flair. There were many stories in that tragic hall, of people lost to madness and now living in this dilapidated and desolate place. And yes, I laughed at this procession of madcaps snaking its way around the hall, denying their humanity and betraying my own.

Madhouses have been places of curiosity for centuries and this event reminds me of the cruel days when well-off people used to visit them to watch the loonies who were seen as sources of ridicule and entertainment. William Hogarth, in a scene from the series of 1735 engravings called *A Rake's Progress*, poignantly captures this awful attitude. The artist shows a chaotic assembly of stereotypical incurable lunatics – a lovesick melancholic, a mad scientist, a mad tailor, a mad musician, a crazy Papist, a religious maniac, a mad king and a mad astronomer – at the old Bedlam Hospital in London. Two high-class ladies of fashion are gazing unfeelingly and unsympathetically at the lunatics, one concealing her amusement behind her fan while the other whispers in her ear. Surrounded by raving madness it was easy for these women to take comfort in the knowledge that it was someone else who was mad. My father and I were hardly better, laughing at the unfortunate people with the crazed eyes and troubled faces who stood before us. But I do recall that although at first scathing of the loonies, on reflection I too had felt a pang of compassion, perhaps tempered by my father's constant accusations that my mother was mad. Could she end up a loony in Lakeside? How could I have known that eight years later *I* would be walking the grounds of a madhouse as a madwoman?

RESPITE

All through my childhood and teenage years I played sport. I played A-grade softball all year round. I also played squash, basketball, volleyball, hockey and netball at various times, depending on the season. I loved to run, to throw, catch or hit a ball. I took refuge in sport. Having success helped too: my performances in softball led some to think I might even play for Victoria or perhaps Australia. It was a dream I entertained briefly, but in the end I didn't have the temperament to withstand the pressures of top-level sport, or the ambition to get me there.

On the sporting field I felt a rare confidence in my own abilities, while off it I felt awkward and clumsy. The kudos from my peers helped me begin to see myself positively. The camaraderie of team sport was exhilarating. It was inspiring and comforting to feel connected to others, working with them to achieve a goal.

Without sport, I would have been crushed. The frustration and anger that welled up out of my troubled home life were laid to rest when I played a vigorous game. It was marvellous therapy, channelling my wounded emotions in constructive and socially acceptable ways. I wavered on the brink of trouble – alcohol, drugs, street fighting – and the self-destructive impulses could have taken over, but sport kept me on the rails by focusing on something positive.

My parents were supportive of my sporting interests and never minded taking me to wherever I was playing. I'm sure they were proud of my sporting achievements. I didn't appreciate then their efforts to encourage me or their generosity with the time and money my sport needed. All of that was overshadowed by their awful behaviour. My mother was a source of embarrassment as she watched me playing softball – always drinking and often getting drunk at a game. After any game, I had the knot of worry in my gut about returning home, where I would have to hold them apart. Sport was only a respite from the dramas at home.

AWAKENING

My last two years of high school were a crossroad. I might have descended into a self-pitying decline of alcohol and drugs, into a half-lived life with no intellectual stimulation or creativity, and no future. I hated the idea of being shackled to my violent parents. Instead, I found a new world, one in which the intellect and creativity were celebrated, a world that began to gather me into its words and ideas, showing me a part of life I hadn't known.

To my parent's credit, they encouraged us to continue on with our schooling. There was no pressure to leave early and find a job. To assist us, my father bought each of us a reading lamp for our beds and a huge *Webster's Dictionary*. He also bought us a set of Arthur Mee's *Children's Encyclopaedia*. He believed in education and its transformative powers and wanted us to do well at school. My brother and I fulfilled this ambition, though it took me a long, convoluted journey to harvest the fruits of my education. I started year 11 at Ballarat High School in 1970. It was a moment of synchronicity, with me starting to take more seriously the fact that I was now in my senior years of high school, and the arrival at the school of a set of young, intelligent and dedicated teachers. They were to change my life. Until year 11 I had been a bad student and a badly behaved one. My academic results were mediocre and no-one thought I had any potential to further my studies. I had no self-belief and never thought for one moment that I could go to university. My future was an uncertain void into which I couldn't see. Anything could have been lurking there. And was.

I had a stammer. I don't know when it started, but I was acutely aware of it in my early years of high school. It was a disabling impediment and made me dread communication in class. I was too embarrassed to speak, feeling the eyes of my classmates on me whenever I tried to say something. I was very self-conscious at this time of teenage angst about identity. Acceptance by your peers was paramount and anything that got in the way of that was a disaster. My confidence wasn't helped by my brother and father who secretly recorded me speaking and stammering one night, while I was washing the dishes. They played it back to me and laughed. I was devastated. The stammer peaked in year ten, when home was a battlefield, my school work was suffering and my confidence was low. As I gained a little more self-confidence in year 11 with the support of my history teacher, Miss Vines, my stammer began to subside and I was relieved to be able to utter a sentence without struggling to get the words out. But the stammer did not disappear completely.

As I settled into being a senior student, I found myself modifying my behaviour. I took on responsibilities by being voted a house vice-captain. It might seem unusual that I was given such a vote of confidence by my peers, when the picture I have painted of myself is one of a deeply dysfunctional teenager. Perhaps I wasn't as hopeless as I thought, and others were aware of capabilities beyond my self-perceptions. Part of this vote of confidence was a response to my achievements in sport. But the real stimulus for change came when Miss Vines walked into the classroom as my new Modern History teacher. She had started teaching at the school the year before, and I had heard she was a good teacher. I thought she was charismatic. She was a folk singer and at the school eisteddfod had performed a couple of folk songs, accompanying herself on the guitar. I was entranced: she had a wonderful voice, and with long black hair she looked just like Joan Baez. I looked forward to a year I knew would be interesting and challenging.

Miss Vines introduced herself and asked if anyone knew what nationalism was. I gingerly put my hand up and talked about China: that it was nationalistic because it was proud of its political system. I was interpreting what I had seen on the news on the television. I think Miss Vines was impressed. I had never impressed a teacher before with an answer to an abstract question like that. I was off to a good start. She later told me she thought I had academic potential and that what I said in class was worthwhile. History was to be full of questions about the human condition and conflict. I already had an intuitive understanding of conflict.

My parents were fighting relentlessly and I was always anxious about what might happen. My teachers were unaware of my situation. In English, with Mr Clift, another of the young teachers, we explored social issues, and the essay questions he gave us were thought-provoking. *Does society create the man or does the man create society?* I had never thought about that before. It was a question that challenged my whole teenage way of thinking. To the proposition *It is indeed a rare and beautiful thing*, I wrote a meditation on death. Was this my pessimism beginning to show itself? We studied poetry and Shakespeare, and read J.D. Salinger's *The Catcher in the Rye* and James Joyce's *A Portrait of the Artist as a Young Man*. I learned about anti-heroes and rebellion, and wanted to be a rebel too.

My mind was expanding in unexpected directions. I was intrigued by the imponderable questions we all ask: *Who am I? Why am I here? What happens after death?* I wrote pieces of meditative and exploratory prose in which I ruminated on these questions. These were my first forays into writing and trying consciously to understand who I was in a world that gave no easy answers. My essays were achieving good marks. It was a revelation to me that my thoughts and words could impress my teachers. With such encouragement I developed an interest in current affairs, ideas and poetry, as well as a new desire to express myself in my own questioning way.

The music of the times still resonates with me. The folk singers Simon and Garfunkel echo through these years. I was captivated by the poetry of their soul-searching lyrics, which made me think deeply about the world. I remember the spine-tingling sensation I had when I first heard their rendition of '7 O'Clock News/Silent Night', on their album *Parsley, Sage, Rosemary and Thyme*. The newsreader's litany of world misery dubbed over the Christmas carol gave a chilling sense of the world's disarray and its contradictions. Whenever I looked at myself in a mirror their words came to me: *The mirror on the wall/casts an image dark and small/yet I'm not sure at all it's my reflection . . . I wander in the night without direction.* I was consumed by the process of trying to understand myself, but felt deeply disconnected. Teenage angst made it impossible to see the *pattern of my life/and the puzzle that [was] me.* The poetry of Simon and Garfunkel gave me solace. When I didn't have the words to express my real emotions, I would turn to their lyrics because they seemed to know what I was feeling and said it so beautifully. They were the first poets to reach me.

I cannot forget the impact the Beatles had on me too. Like many young girls of the 60s, I was a devotee while still in primary school, when I fell in love with their music and personalities. I always preferred the Beatles to the Rolling Stones. At the time opinion was polarised: radical and adventurous teenagers favoured the Stones, while those in the more conservative mainstream were Beatles' fans. I saw the Stones as ratbags and creatively inferior. The Beatles' Australian tour of 1964 was covered extensively by the media and I was glued to the television and newspapers, eagerly tracking their movements and every word they uttered. I cut out pictures of them and plastered them all over my bedroom walls. My mother would show my room to her friends, who were amazed at my love affair with the Beatles. When *Sgt Pepper's Lonely Hearts Club Band* came out in 1967, my sister gave the album to me for Christmas. I played it over and over non-stop for months. I had heard nothing like it before. As The Beatles became more outrageous, particularly John Lennon, I was even more taken with them. Their creativity was limitless and yet they were voicing my generation's thoughts: we did want peace, we did want to make love not war, we did want to change the world and make it a better place. They were our spokesmen, but my father hated them with a passion. Their music offended him; he hated the loud twang of electric guitars. His ultimate dismissal was to say they weren't 'real' musicians.

Bob Dylan was another voice of our generation. Miss Vines brought his records into class and gave us copies of his lyrics to study as part of our course. His poetry and acidic observations of the world caught my attention and made me think the ideas of my family were stale and bankrupt. *Your sons and your daughters/are beyond your command/your old road is/rapidly agin'/please get out of the new one/if you can't lend a hand/for the times they are a-changin'*. I was well aware by this time that my home life was not what it should have been. I wanted the times to be *a-changin'*. When Dylan sang: *How does it feel/to be on your own/with no direction home/like a complete unknown/like a rolling stone?* I thought he was singing to me, as though he understood my doubts and fears. He was a soul-mate who gave my inner life a new meaning in songs for all to share. I'm sure many people have felt the same connection with their favourite singers and songwriters, though perhaps not as obsessively as I might have. Finding solace in the words of others who have the gift of sharing their lives in songs and poetry can be lifesaving.

Miss Vines also introduced me to The Weavers who sang old folk songs, union and working songs, and songs of the Wobblies

(The Industrial Workers of the World). I always felt a joy from listening to their arrangements of folk music from all over the world. They believed in the goodness of humanity which was implicit in their music. I still listen to it.

Even though I was undergoing a radical change, I wasn't a hard worker or consistently studious student. I survived on my ability to produce an essay when it was needed, even if it was without the rigorous and careful work required. In year 11, the distractions of home did not allow much mental space. I had to push myself to complete school work. I used to see it as laziness and was critical of myself. Even now I am quick to label myself lazy – although I know that when I have a task I must perform, I usually do it. Was it my mental state or a heightened sensibility that made it harder for me to concentrate in the sustained way other students could? I do know my mind was difficult to rein in and discipline. My motivation was affected also, as I had so little expectation that I could achieve. Yet Miss Vines told me that if there had been a prize for History I would have won it.

The year I turned 17 I started to attract boyfriends. Prior encounters with boys had been quite horrible, and I had always felt clumsy and unattractive. Now boys started to look at me, and I at them. I was surprised when they asked me out for serious dates. My earlier experience of Bruce had scarred me but it didn't stop me from wanting to be like my friends and be seen as an attractive young woman. I repressed my self-loathing and fear, enjoying a respect I had not felt before. I even hoped for a relationship where I would be valued and not abused, where I might feel good about myself.

Despite all this, towards the end of that year I started to go off the rails. Sport, which had kept me safe, wasn't enough to distract me. I was overwhelmed by cascading images of violence and by black moods. I had thoughts of suicide. In retrospect, I wonder if I was suffering from an untreated depression during the latter stages of that year. I began drinking large amounts of vodka and vermouth. A girl I knew who worked in a cafe gave me some white pills which might have been speed. I didn't ask. Whenever I went out to a dance or a party with my friends, I would numb myself to the world by getting drunk. These days I'd be called a teenage binge-drinker. I wanted my mind to stop whirling at its frenetic pace. I had powerful urges, fuelled by my anger at life and my parents, to thrust my fist through windows and into walls, but resisted because I didn't know how I would explain it to the teachers I admired.

During the winter softball season, I would catch the train to Melbourne each Sunday morning. The train departed at around nine o'clock. and it was usually bitterly cold. I would sit by myself in the old red rattling train carriage, my feet resting on the metal cylinder filled with warm oil, and look out the window deep in thought. I was falling into a self-indulgent mind-set where I was the centre of the universe, saturated with my own thoughts and ideas, as teenagers often do. But this reflection was dangerous because I was becoming too immersed in myself, becoming consumed by my own darkness. I was convinced no-one else thought the way I did. Sometimes, after my game, with an hour or two before the train left, I would go and sit in a candle-lit chapel and pray. Or I went to the People's Palace, run by the Salvation Army, and had a cheap meal of roast pork and apple pie and watched the needy people who came in. I was drawn to these people. I would see a person and make up a story to myself about their life, why they were at the People's Palace, where they would go when they left. I felt an empathy with these homeless souls.

By October I was so overwhelmed by mental distress that I took an overdose of pills that the girl from the cafe had given me. On a cold, drizzly Friday night I wandered Ballarat's streets in a stupor, and found myself sitting for hours in St Patrick's Cathedral, where my mind whirled randomly from thought to thought. I staggered onto a tram and ended up at the lake. My mouth was so dry I gulped down some lake water. It tasted foul. Miss Black's flat was close by and I stumbled to her door and knocked. I remembered she and some other teachers were having a small get-together – Miss Vines and Miss Douglas were there. When Miss Black answered the door I mumbled: *I'm lost and can't find heaven.* (This is so melodramatic that I've never forgotten it.) Miss Douglas bundled me into her car and took me to the emergency department of the Ballarat Base Hospital, where I spent the night under observation. It wasn't a serious suicide attempt; rather, it was, as they say, a cry for help. I recognise it now as seeking attention from the teachers: I wanted them to save me. I was in such raw emotional pain that I was driven to misguided and extreme behaviour.

In the hospital I lay awake all night. It was an unnerving place. I heard patients being brought into casualty who had been in car accidents. People were screaming in pain, weeping, talking to injured loved ones, moaning in anguish. Nurses and doctors bustled about tending to patients. Because I had taken an overdose, the police were called and went to the Golf Club to notify my mother, who came to the hospital. She didn't ask how I was; instead she said *Why have you done this to me?* She never talked to me about this incident. Nor did my father. She rang my sister in Melbourne and said *Marilyn, you need to talk to Sandra.* So I was sent to Melbourne to stay with my sister the following weekend. Strangely, I can't remember if we talked about these things or not. I was reluctant to talk to anyone, running away from everything and everyone, including myself. I remained melancholic and burdened by troubles I couldn't express.

Miss Douglas was particularly kind to me, and as a troubled teenager I was often at her flat seeking help and counsel. She was young, funny and bright, and endured my fluctuating moods with patience. I trusted her, yet was unable to reveal the extent to which home was disturbing me. Yet I am sure she was aware that something wasn't right, so spent time with me, talking and steering me towards books and learning. After I turned up at school one day, evidently a bit high on drugs, she took me in her two-tone blue Holden FX to Clunes, a township near Ballarat, where we explored the small Catholic church and other old buildings. She tried to help me overcome the effects of my unsettled life which were leading me into trouble.

The school was concerned about my behaviour and sent me to an Education Department psychologist for an assessment. In 1970 there was no school counsellor to deal with normal teenage insecurities. An appointment with a psychologist was a big deal. Was I mad enough to have to see a psychologist? Why wasn't it my parents? The verdict was that I was insecure. Nothing was done to help me.

As the third term vacation approached, I decided I would leave school and find a job. What was I thinking? I went along to the Sunshine biscuit factory and asked for a job. Just like that. The woman who was the overseer of the factory took me on and suddenly I was on a conveyer belt picking up 'raspberry smile' biscuits and placing them in a white plastic box. It was soul-destroying work: boring, repetitive and meaningless. I lasted three days. I sheepishly went to the overseer and said I was going back to school. I knew I didn't want to end up having to do that kind of work for the rest of my life. School was a much more attractive proposition, and I hoped that an education would make me immune from having to do such labour.

I look back and feel lucky for the kindness and interest of my teachers. Even in sport, Mr Fletcher, a footballer, was encouraging and caring. We played golf together and swam at the local indoor pool. He sometimes gave me a lift to Melbourne when I was playing softball. It was he who drove me to the offices of the psychologist. He was an all-round role model of excellence

– trustworthy, caring, holding high standards. Perhaps I was so impressed because not only was he a recognised sportsman, he was the first male I really felt I could trust.

The model of my family had been a negative and destructive force. I was always looking elsewhere for something or someone to show me that there were other ways of dealing with the world. Mrs Anderson and my Auntie June were maternal models I found more acceptable than my own mother. People who had qualities I admired, like Miss Vines, Miss Douglas and Mr Fletcher, made larger-than-life impressions on me because they represented everything for me that my family wasn't. They were intelligent, educated, trustworthy and good role models. I was also exceptionally impressionable because of my deep insecurity and spiritual malnourishment. Over the years I have been able to identify people I thought might be able to help me and draw them into my world, making it a better place. My seeking of, and finding, these good role models was not just an effective survival mechanism; it was a sane response to the madness of my family.

Year 11 was a watershed in my life. My teachers' response to my dark moods restored a sense of trust in adults which I had lost. My leanings to left-wing politics, diametrically opposed to those of my parents, were firming. Perhaps initially I was adopting a stance simply to oppose them, but by the end of the year I was convinced of the value system I adopted then and carried on into my adult life. I had great sympathy for the working-class struggle, strong views on Australia's involvement in the Vietnam War and no time for conservatives of the day. I was primed for my next hurdle, my attempt to pass my Higher School Certificate. And as I moved into this next phase of my life I carried in the back of my mind the words of a friend of my sister who drew me aside and said: *One day you will do something important.* What could she mean?

NEW DIMENSIONS

I began year 12 and my Higher School Certificate with trepidation. It was well known that a lot of students failed HSC. The pass rate at my school the previous year, 1970, had been only 53 per cent. Failure was likely, but I was hopeful of a miracle. At the beginning of the year, we were asked to think seriously of our intentions, and to start making plans for our futures. What did we want to do after school? Professional employment still seemed limited for females: there was nursing, the public service, or primary or secondary teaching. Other professions like medicine or engineering were dominated by male applicants and only open to those with top marks. University was an aspiration quite foreign, and I never thought I could achieve the marks needed to win a place. For years I had thought I would like to be a physical education teacher, but that notion fell by the wayside when I started to develop an interest in academic and creative pursuits. I didn't think there was room for sport in my new life but I still didn't know what I might do.

Yet here again, in spite of a year still troubled by dark moods, I was to discover new strengths in myself through encounters with others. Early on in the year I became friendly with Simon and James who were academically smart and intensely creative. They helped reveal a world of poetry and words, ideas and creativity I had only glimpsed the year before. Now I experienced them intimately with two people of my own age who had a real understanding of their importance. Poetry was unknown in my home, art was just a picture on a wall and there was no discussion about creativity. Yes, there was music in the house, but I hadn't appreciated it as part of a creative impulse to make sense of who we were in the world; it was a nice sound made to entertain. Now I was trying to find words to describe what it felt like to hear Beethoven or tease out the meaning of Dylan's songs. Finding words became my pre-eminent task.

Simon came from an unusual and interesting family, with five artistic and eccentric siblings. He was the youngest. Simon had a wonderful mind capable of embracing many different ideas. I was in awe of him and fell for him and his captivating family. I had been involved with another boy for the first part of that year but became aware that I was drawn romantically to Simon and by June we were involved in a relationship. I was his first girlfriend and had to teach him about relationships, but we had a good time that year and he taught me a lot too. He was someone who had no sense of time and was blithely in a world of his own, often lost in his own cryptic thought, which I found endearing.

I enjoyed Simon's family immensely and wonder if I was more in love with his family than him. His mother Kate was a great matriarch, her husband having died when Simon was in year seven. She was a devout Anglican who went to church every Sunday morning. I sometimes stayed at their house overnight on weekends. I would go with Kate early in the morning and she would drop me off at the Catholic church, not far from hers. I was taking my religious feelings seriously at this time and had been going to mass throughout that year, a secret I kept from my parents. Miss Vines was a Catholic, and because I admired her, I wanted to be like her. I often saw her as she walked the few blocks from her house on her way to mass and wanted to join her. If she took her faith seriously and performed her religious duties devoutly, this legitimated my interest in her religion.

I confess that I had fallen under the poetic sway of Catholicism. The prayers were beautiful; the incense, pageantry, costumes and theatricality were seductive. I thought I wanted to convert. The Catholic Church offered a poetic, idealised model of community, friendship and companionship I was desperately in need of. I loved the ritual of offering a friendly hand to the person next to you in the congregation and saying: *Peace be with you*. In that brief moment of the offering of hands, I felt peace. Nothing like this had happened at the congregational church of my childhood, where dour and simple services were uninspiring, not poetic at all. But I could not share my enthusiasm with my family or friends – not even Simon understood my spiritual quest. When I finally told my parents, they seemed to feel that I was embracing the Devil's religion.

Each Sunday evening we would all gather at Simon's house in Buningyong, a small town south-east of Ballarat, for a communal meal. There would be Simon and me, and his siblings with their partners. It was a rowdy affair with affable and challenging discussion, lively banter and lots of fun. After the meal, we would then take off in cars and go trainspotting. We went at all hours, rugging ourselves in coats and scarves, going to all locations to witness the passing of a huge, dark diesel pulling freight and carriages to some distant destination. It was exhilarating. I really wanted to live with Simon and his family, instead of my own. I had had a glimpse of family life that wasn't marred by violence and drunkenness. I was biding my time, waiting for the opportunity when I could leave the family I so deeply despised.

James was the most creative person I had ever met. He was an artist and poet. Art and poetry was something only gifted people, famous people, did, so knowing someone who actually wrote poetry and painted was a thrill. I thought his poetry was profound and compelling. He had a command of language that astonished me. He used words I hadn't heard before and was able to conceptualise things that made them take on new and deeper meanings. Even his hands seemed poetic – sinewy and alive, with raised veins that gave an elegance and strength that suited his character. His hands were the kind an artist would immortalise in drawings and paintings.

James also had a sadness. His older sister was killed by a drunken driver when he was in year 11, and he would have been still grieving for her when I met him in year 12. I had no idea about grief associated with the death of a close sibling and never knew how much he was hurting. He didn't talk about it much. His mother was unstable. James told us how when he came home from school one day his mother was walking around the house talking to herself. From his descriptions of her behaviour, I now recognise she may have had a psychotic illness not unlike the kind I was to develop. His mother relied a lot on him as he was now the only child, and male, in the family. They lived on a small farm and she ran it by herself, her husband having died when James was about 12. He clearly had had to grow up quickly, yet had an infectious boyish enthusiasm for whatever he was doing. I did wonder how he managed to remain stable himself, with all this happening to him, although I did have some hair-raising car rides with him during which he drove like a maniac. I think his car was his release valve for all his pent-up emotions. But into our English literature classes he brought his creative flair, where his literary criticism was so incisive that we all learned much from it.

Hanging out with such gifted people was a learning experience I was privileged to have, but it was also daunting. The limitations of my family and upbringing made me feel as though I would never be like James or Simon; never be creative and interesting like they were. I always felt James had an exciting future and could have done whatever he'd wanted, such were his intellectual and creative gifts. He has gone on to become a chief conservator of painting at an important art museum. Simon's future was less certain. He was much more unsettled than James, possibly because he was weighed down by the expectations of his mother who wanted him to achieve academically. Consequently he took longer to find his feet in the world away from his family. I lost contact with him in my early twenties, but have heard that he eventually found his way to Adelaide where he completed a medical degree, something his mother had always wanted him to do.

In 1970 my brother was drafted into the army and the following year he was sent overseas to Vietnam. He had been studying metallurgy but was desperate to be conscripted. At the time I was perplexed that he was taking part in a war I disagreed with, but we never talked about it. In retrospect, I see that it was his way of getting away from my parents. When he left, he kindly gave me his Yamaha 250cc motorbike to ride. After I got my learner's licence in May, I spent a lot of time riding the bike. In a defiant gesture, I would park it in front of the principal's office at school. I was quickly asked to park it elsewhere. I took long trips out into the country, enjoying the exhilaration of the wind on my face. On the road I felt free, that nothing would stop me or get in my way. Everything was ahead of me. I hadn't read Jack Kerouac's *On the Road*, but when I did, many years later, I recognised the impulse in his epic freewheeling journey. There is something seductive about being reckless and taking no responsibility, just living for the moment, owning the road with a machine that is fast and dangerous.

Simon and I would ride the motorbike to James's farm. In the miserable, biting cold winter we wrapped ourselves in scarves, gloves, leather jackets and army great-coats, knowing that a warm house and good conversation were at the end of the journey. In front of the fire in the cosy lounge room, we talked well into the night about anything and everything, while Dylan played in the background. I loved those nights we spent at James's farm, musing about all that seemed important to an 18-year-old in the early 1970s. I look back on those days with great affection, knowing they were the beginning of something that has grown with me over the years. I built my love of poetry around these moments, fired with a fervour to make it part of my life. Words intrigued me and I wanted to explore their potential to help me express things I had never talked about before. I wrote in the same idiom as the authors I was reading at the time, not having a voice of my own, taking my cues from Shakespeare and T.S. Eliot, from John Donne and Gerard Manley Hopkins. Looking back I can see the prose I was writing for my English exercises was in a morbid and affected style.

Despite my new-found friends and interests, my view of life and my own prospects remained bleak. In July of that year I had gone to Melbourne to undertake a vocational guidance test because I had no idea as to which job I was suited. The psychologist more or less said I might as well leave school and find work wherever I could, because I didn't have a lot of aptitude for professional jobs. What I had put down for my choice of occupation was 'Poet'. This is without ever having demonstrated any ability at poetry – not like James, who was probably a poet all his life. The psychologist said I was not being helpful by choosing something so unrealistic. What had I known about myself then? The fact that I have become a poet is another miracle in my life. I was the product of a most unpoetic home but I was inspired by my teachers, and by James and Simon who gave me a poetic sense. There was much lying dormant in my soul that wanted to speak in poetry, but it stayed hidden until I found my voice.

The first indication that I might have the ability to pursue tertiary studies came after my mid-year exams. My report card was a revelation. My teachers commented on my independent thinking and the fact that if I applied myself I could do very well. Later that year I was recommended by my teachers for a place at the Australian National University in Canberra. When the letter came telling me my good news, I went straight to Miss Vines full of wonder and surprise. She said I was one of the first they had recommended. She had told me I had innate intelligence, but I had never believed her. There was no evidence to me of this. My parents had always focused on my brother's academic achievements; he had won scholarships and had done very well at school while I was seen as the sports champion. When my mother came home from a parent-teacher night she couldn't hide her surprise when she told me: *Mr Clift says you are very smart and have the ability to go on to university!* However, I needed a Commonwealth Scholarship in order to be able to take up the ANU offer of a university place, and I felt this was only a remote possibility.

Earlier in the year we had been instructed to apply for university places, Commonwealth Scholarships and Victorian Education Department studentships. I applied for everything, including a studentship, knowing it involved being bonded to the Education Department for three years after completing my degree and Diploma of Education, and having to go and teach wherever they sent you. I harboured a thought that I would like to be a teacher like Miss Vines, and help a student in the way she helped me – perhaps even be a positive role model, like she had been to me. Being bonded for three years might be a problem, but I'd cope with it. This was the way to leave home legitimately and easily. A rare wave of optimism came over me. There were however some serious hurdles to negotiate, ones that I hadn't foreseen and for which I was unprepared.

S

IMPLOSION

I had been bearing the brunt of my parents' violent relationship all year, with my sister now living in Melbourne and my brother in Vietnam. We had forged our own lives in each other's absence, but I missed their support when my parents fought. One September night I came home and walked into the kitchen to find it like a murder scene. Cupboards were splashed with blood, crockery smashed everywhere and furniture overturned. I thought my father had killed my mother and expected to find her body on the floor. My heart was pounding hard enough to burst my chest.

I left immediately and walked the streets. I was scared. I was angry and defiant. I wished I had somewhere to go where I could be safe. I was too afraid to go home. I had heard from Simon's mother, who ironically was a marriage guidance counsellor, that Lifeline was starting a service in Ballarat. I thought I could unload on them what I had just seen – what my fears were, where I could go to get help. Anything would have helped. I was frantic with worry for my mother, for myself, about everything that was in my life at that time. I rang Directory Assistance to get the Lifeline number and the woman apologised saying: *Sorry dear, Lifeline isn't connected yet*. I didn't ring Simon. I didn't ring Auntie June, I didn't ring anyone. I just kept walking the cold streets on that cold September night, in that cold, cold town.

It was morning before I could face returning home. I saw that he hadn't killed her. He had beaten her mercilessly. Bruises were splashed black and blue over her face. Her body was slumped in a chair. Her eyes were black and teary. And yet, that morning, I packed my bag, and with Simon and his mother, left to go to Mildura for a week's holiday. I didn't care that I was leaving her, not knowing if I would come back and find her alive. I fled like the criminal, stealing away with heartless disregard. I was taking myself and my sanity with me. I could think of nothing else to save me.

Mildura was warm, but a false respite from home because I could not stop wondering what my father was doing to my mother. He did such disgusting things to her in front of my siblings and me, what on earth did he do to her when we weren't there? It was too awful to contemplate. The day I came home my mother told me my father had beaten her every day. After she had told me this, she said she was leaving. I never understood why she didn't leave before, given how awful their marriage was. But then, at this time there were no supporting mothers' benefits, and without financial resources, leaving a marriage wasn't a simple option. She had no real education or qualifications. There were also social pressures to stay. What would their friends at the Golf Club have thought? Where could she have gone? To be honest, I had been hoping for what, in my earlier years, had been unthinkable: for my parents to split up. And now my mother was leaving. But would I want to stay at home with my father? I dreamt of living with Miss Vines.

My mother told me my father had not only beaten her, but had made her sit in the corner of the lounge room away from the fire, where it would have been cold. She was his prisoner, alone in the house with his rage. He punished her according to his law. She was bruised and battered. It had been systematic, cruel and sustained, like torture. When she told me she was leaving,

I didn't care or ask her where she was going. I wasn't upset or sorry. I was too numb to show concern for her. I wanted her away from him and out of my life. I wanted them both out of my life. I wonder now if she was hurt by my coldness and indifference. Perhaps she was too numb. I got my motorbike and rode into the country, trying to forget what had happened. When I returned, she had gone. It was the only time she left him.

My father tried to explain himself, telling me why he had beaten her, why he hated her. She had been unfaithful, not for the first time. He thought if he told me this I would change my mind about him, would assuage my ill feelings about him. Perhaps that I would put all that I had seen and heard behind me, forgive him and be his loving daughter. Instead, I retreated even more deeply into myself and my own thoughts.

I continued to live at home while my mother was gone, but I didn't spend much time there. I lived independently from my father. Miss Vines and some other teachers supported me through these times but I couldn't talk much to them about how I was feeling, about what I had seen. I sometimes had tea with Miss Black, who allowed me to spend time at her flat where I could study in peace. I stayed at James's farm on occasions and I spent a lot of time at Simon's place. I really liked his mother and wished she could use her marriage guidance skills to magically transform my parents' relationship.

My sister later told me my father would ring her and ask about my mother, saying: *Where's that bitch?* She didn't tell him for some time that my mother was with her. Eventually she gave in and told him, and my father set out to get her home. He courted her like a new lover. Why? I couldn't work it out. He hated her, yet there he was wooing her with charm and nights out on the town in Melbourne and then back to motels to have sex. She was gone for three months. How on earth could she go back to him?

My father's brutality and my mother's leaving upset me more than I would admit. I was mortified to hear from a friend of the family that my father had thrown a glass of beer over my mother's face at the Golf Club in a public display of his anger. He was suspended from the club for three months for inappropriate behaviour. I was to be repeatedly embarrassed by their vitriolic public altercations. Her return three weeks before my exams was to be just as disruptive, because nothing had changed. On her first night home, he belted her. The drunkenness and beatings continued as if she had never left. It became clear to me that I would have to make my way in the world without them.

Mein Kampf

One day I will
relinquish the memories
forget the violence
obliterate the angry words
block out the flashbacks
kill the sadness that lingers
cut out the tumour
erase what I witnessed.
one day I will
bury you forever
Mein Führer, forever.

S

MOMENT OF TRUTH

I had been on an extraordinary learning curve that year, involving much besides school work. I made some important life decisions at about this time. Like my brother, I decided I would not have children because I didn't trust that I would be a good parent. Neither of us would risk putting kids through what we went through. I also decided not to drink alcohol. I had flirted with it, had seen myself becoming like my mother and did not want to be destroyed by it like she was. Wine, champagne, spirits and beer have since tasted vile to me. Had I lived a century ago, I'm sure I would have been a member of the Temperance Union, standing on a street corner railing about the evils of the 'demon drink', proclaiming *lips that touch alcohol shall never touch mine!* I jokingly say to my friends that if I were supreme ruler of the world I would burn every vineyard, tear down every distillery and brewery, empty every drop of alcohol down the gutter. But deep down I really mean it.

I crammed, an act of desperation in the two weeks before the exams, hoping to save myself from the fate I could no longer bear – being trapped with my parents and their shrill voices. A studentship would be my salvation but far from concentrating on my studies I had this urge to sleep all the time.

I sat the exams in a state of bewilderment. I tried to recall a year's work and pour it onto the foolscap-size exam booklets.

I was examined in five subjects: English Expression, English Literature, Australian History, Reformation History and Biblical Studies. We sat upstairs in the old, drafty town hall where mayoral gala balls were once held. It was now a place of trial, in which a student's performance determined whether their dreams could be pursued or would be turned into nightmares. I sat in my allotted chair over a period of eight days, writing my heart out, recalling my learning and making up what I didn't know. I laid my pen to rest on my last exam, and hoped with all my heart that a miracle would occur.

The wait for the letter from the examination board was interminable. When it eventually came, one hot January morning, I held it in my sweaty hands and made my first bargain with God. I promised everlasting obedience to him for a pass with reasonable marks. I opened the letter trembling. Failure was one thing, but not doing quite well enough to get a studentship would have crushed me. Amazingly, I passed four of my subjects with good enough marks that might even win me a studentship. Interestingly, I failed Biblical Studies. I hadn't done well enough to win a Commonwealth Scholarship to take up the ANU place.

I had to wait for the studentship offers to be announced in the paper a week later. The wait was another agony. What would I end up doing? Where would I be in a couple of months? Judgement Day arrived and I nervously picked up the paper. My mother was with me as I searched for the results. I bargained a second time with God to make my name appear in the list of successful applicants. Thankfully, my name was there for all to see, amongst hundreds of others. I had a studentship! My mother shared my joy though I don't think she realised that I saw it as my escape route from her and my father. The relief was inexpressible. I can't recall if I remembered to thank God. My life was going to be different from that of my parents. I was off to La Trobe University in Melbourne, where a new life beckoned.

Part Two

Student Days
1972–1975

Knowledge comes, but wisdom lingers.
Alfred Tennyson

UNIVERSITY OF LIFE

One would have thought that finding myself with the chance to leave home and take up my studentship, being in the privileged position to pursue tertiary studies and being financially independent, the world was at my feet. There were crucial people who helped me through school, gave me a sense of my abilities and gave me encouragement when needed. Without Miss Vines (who I still count amongst my friends) and the other teachers, without the miracle of passing my exams, without the various people who changed the course of my life, I would not have found myself with such a wonderful opportunity. I was, in a strange way, blessed. It seems I was to find angels all through my life, who would pick me up while I battled with my demons and carry me with them to a safer place.

On a mild Sunday in late February 1972 my parents deposited me at Glenn College, a student residence at La Trobe University. La Trobe was an isolated campus and with no access to good public transport, you could feel trapped there if you didn't generate friends and couldn't leave at your own behest. The College was a cluster of fawny-brown brick buildings in a scattered bush landscape. Some of the gum trees were magnificent, with their candle-white bark. Their canopies of greeny-blue leaves shaded the courtyard. My room was small, its walls naked brick. It had a bed, a wardrobe, a table with a lamp, dark-blue carpet on the floor and a water heater on the wall under the window. Its Spartan interior was not homely or comforting and I had nothing to make it a place of welcome – an electric jug to make cups of coffee or tea for visitors, for example, as I saw most other students had brought. Yet I thought I could learn to like this new place.

This was a time when being a student was as much a lifestyle choice as a springboard to a career. Our scholarships and studentships paid our fees and gave us a reasonable living allowance, making it possible to live as a full-time student. We were poor, but accepted that as part of our rite-of-passage into the professional world for which we believed we were being anointed. Part-time work to supplement our finances was not essential, and rents were usually low. We spent our time on campus in the cafeteria arguing about politics and philosophical notions of reality and truth. We took part in demonstrations because we longed to make changes to a society we saw as materialistic and conservative. La Trobe in those days was a university with many experimental and radical courses: in 1972 a student could do a whole course in Revolutionary Studies there.

I was an anxious 18-year-old, not sure of what to expect but excited by the thought of a new life. In one sense, I was worldly for my eyes had been opened to parts of life that many of my contemporaries would not have seen. In another sense I was naive and inexperienced, an innocent in a world about which I knew nothing. The trip to Melbourne had been filled with emotion. I was entering a new phase of my life. I would be free from the physical presence of my parents, but haunted by their shadows. All I had was a bag of clothes and a guitar. I thought I could play this, until I heard another student at College play his guitar beautifully. I was a very small fish in a huge pond and 1972 was to be a year of great change in Australian politics and in me.

My studentship paid me $27 per week and my college fees of $18 per week included breakfast and the evening meal, cleaners twice a week and wonderful facilities designed to make living in college a good experience. By today's economic standards, the princely sum of $9 a week to live on, after the fees were taken out, sounds impossible. But in 1972 it was quite a liveable sum of money especially when you weren't buying meals. A hot chocolate cost 25 cents, a Penguin book $1.20 and a ticket to the movies $1.00 concession. In any case my needs and wants were simple, and I was very frugal. I never asked my parents for financial help because I didn't want to owe them anything, or be held accountable to them. I saw this as my opportunity to break away from them forever and there was no going back. However, later that year, after I had saved some money to put towards buying a motorbike, my father lent me $200 to help me make the purchase. I was reluctant to take the money but I was pragmatic enough to see how it would benefit me. I appreciated his kindness then, as I do now, when I look back. There is good in everyone, and we have to acknowledge and cherish it even if it contradicts the pattern we have come to know.

My first few weeks in college were painfully lonely: I didn't know anyone, and felt awkward in company. Simon was at another university and James had gone to art school in another city, and I missed them. Making friends wasn't easy and I was constrained by a rising sense of inferiority. I sensed competitiveness in everything but shied away when asked about my HSC marks, as many students did. People seemed to be testing each other out, finding their strengths and weaknesses, assessing who was smart, who was a fake. I'm sure many people presented counterfeit personae to get through this challenging time: trying to act adult, yet lacking the life experiences to be truly comfortable in an adult role. The students from Melbourne schools were more savvy than those like me from 'the country'. Even the size of Melbourne was daunting and I marvelled at those who could find their way around the maze of streets and suburbs.

I wasn't coping with my new life. I become nocturnal, walking the corridors of the college at night, sleeping during the day. I stayed up for days at a time and did little work. The baggage of home weighed upon me, my mind haunted by flashbacks of the kitchen splashed with blood and littered with smashed crockery. I smelled stale beer and heard my parents' curses. But there was no-one I could tell, no-one who could help me cope with these recurring images. I felt myself descending into a deep and dangerous hole, and as the year pushed on, I began to feel the pressures of study. I was not a good student: I was struggling.

One night I felt so overwhelmed and distressed that I burst into the room of one of the few students with whom I had been able to establish a friendship. Her name was Heather and I blurted out to her what I had been holding onto for months. I ranted about what I had seen in our kitchen and how I ached with awful memories. It was three o'clock in the morning and Heather had been peacefully sleeping. She didn't know what to say to me. I left her to her sleep and returned to my room. I sat there for hours and in my melancholy I built a wall around myself and my awful memories.

I didn't think to seek counselling for my emotional problems and no-one suggested it to me. I had to deal with them alone. To do otherwise would have signalled weakness. I remembered my father ridiculing my mother. His words – *you need to see a fuckin' psychiatrist* – echoed in my mind. To admit I needed counselling would be tantamount to saying I was mad, like her. Deep down I had a sense that something was wrong, but I didn't know what. My relationship with Simon petered out and I lost contact with James. My little world was changing almost beyond my comprehension, while in the wider world, left-wing politics and feminism were sweeping university campuses. Throughout the year of 1972 we watched the rise of Labor's leader, Gough Whitlam. He proposed radical reforms if elected to government, such as free tertiary education and withdrawing Australian troops from the conflict in Vietnam, fast becoming an unwinnable war for the USA. In December a Labor government was elected, with Whitlam at the helm. Their win ended 23 years of Liberal-Country Party rule in Australia. Meanwhile at the Munich Olympics Mark Spitz dazzled the world with his record of seven gold medals in the pool, only to have his triumph overshadowed by Arab terrorists killing eleven Israeli athletes. The world, like me, was entering a new and less innocent phase.

The prominent intellectuals of the day were left-wing and they exerted a strong influence on student politics. I took part in demonstrations, marching in the streets of Melbourne, arm-in-arm with my comrades, decrying the Vietnam War, wanting Australia to bring home its troops, chanting *Ho, Ho, Ho Chi Minh, dare to struggle, dare to win.* I railed against authority, participated in sit-ins in the administration building of the university, protested the imprisonment of a radical student for subversive political activities. Memories of the student protests of 1968 in Paris still influenced the culture of the university. Miss Vines had told us in year 11 Modern History that *students are the watchdogs of the world.* I took her words seriously. I had embraced Gough Whitlam's *It's Time* election campaign and had tried in vain to convince my parents to vote Labor, arguing that the Liberal government was fascist, hell-bent on turning the world into a class-ridden society where the rich lived off the labour of the poor. I was inflamed by the fervour of the time, but looking back I realise I had limited understanding of the issues. I was flying with paper wings.

I also felt unease when I went to demonstrations. They were mainly peaceful but I sensed they could turn into a mob stampede. There was a tension in the crowd that was precarious – I have felt the same unnerving tension in a football crowd. Some protests did become violent when radical protesters broke from the ranks to engage police, who could be rough with students. I was a cautious person when it came to political ideology. Even with my emerging feminism, I remained on the periphery rather than in the vanguard of this important movement.

I had thought I could recreate myself and be whatever and whoever I wanted to be in my new life away from home. I had won the chance to remake my persona, to forge an identity of my own making. My parents' incendiary relationship had reduced my sense of self to a pile of ashes and I wanted to resurrect myself. I decided to tell people I *was* a Catholic and actually behaved as though I were one. I loved going to mass at the beautiful and imposing St Patrick's Cathedral in East Melbourne. I even took the Eucharist from the Archbishop of Melbourne. While the world was careering towards political change, I immersed myself in religion, even though I could see that Catholicism was reactionary in its opposition to abortion and contraception, rulings which were challenged by feminism.

I embraced Catholicism with the solemnity of a true convert because it gave meaning to the wreck of my life. I know now that in the big real world, each day was a struggle, and Catholicism made it a little more manageable. But I lived in fear of meeting people from the Ballarat past I was fleeing for anyone who knew I wasn't Catholic would blow my cover. I convinced myself I was really a Catholic as a survival strategy. Even now, many years later, some people still think I am a Catholic, and I haven't the courage to tell them I'm not. My thought patterns were full of contradictions. I felt torn by extremes: the love that I ought to have felt, instead of disgust, for my parents; my ambivalence towards my mother. Although in some ways I felt I had decisively left home, I still yearned for the ideal family very different from my own. I wanted to feel comfortable in my own skin yet hated myself. I wanted to trust yet feared betrayal. I needed spiritual strength in the face of scepticism. How could anyone remain stable when torn by such contradictory forces?

The fact that I didn't actually believe in God did not deter me from attending church and enjoying its pomp and ceremony. It wasn't God who drew me to the Catholic Church, it was the ritual. The ceremony of the mass has a life of its own, like a piece of well-acted and well-scripted theatre. God had disappeared from my life years before, when my childhood prayers for help went unanswered.

Early in the year I made friends with two fellow students who were Sisters of Mercy: Sister Joan and Sister Paula. Their religious life fascinated me. They were in their third year of study and were popular, but I am sure other students saw them as I did – as strangers from another world. There were other nuns, brothers and Jesuit priests, studying at La Trobe. All were young, fresh, unworldly. I attended lunchtime mass with them, taking upon myself the commitment and sincerity with which they practised their religion. To my prosaic Protestant sensibilities they seemed exotic. They offered me an understanding of religion in general and of Catholicism in particular. More importantly, they were kind, dedicated and studious women. Their friendship helped to get me through the year.

Sister Joan and Sister Paula weren't like the nuns I had seen at home: black crows in long black habits, heavy black veils with white coifs, large rosary beads dangling from belts around their waists. My friends were 1970s nuns. They were liberated yet they still lived within the constraints of the religious life. They were beginning to benefit from the edicts of the Second Vatican Council of 1962–65, inspired by Pope John XXIII, which were then filtering into the church's doctrine and freeing many religious from the fetters of cloistered lives. Sister Joan and Sister Paula wore a scaled-down habit, with knee-length dresses. Their veils covered only part of their heads. Modest crucifixes hung around their necks. When they visited me in my college room, they would take off their veils and reveal their healthy heads of hair. This seemed such a subversive act!

When they weren't participating in their studies at the university, however, they still lived hidden from the world. I would visit them at their convent, an old red-brick building in the style of many Catholic buildings built in the early part of the 20th century. Statues were placed appropriately in its pleasant gardens, to provide a meditative place for prayer. The heavy front door had the most beautiful leadlight glass, but I felt apprehension when I knocked, not knowing how I would be greeted. The other nuns scared me because they were often not friendly and I wondered if they were a little peeved by all the visitors Sister Joan and Sister Paula received. I knew that my chat with my two exotic friends would have to take place in a staid parlour, overseen by religious statues and crucifixes.

In July Sister Joan and Sister Paula took me to a poetry reading in a room in the English department. It was my first such experience and I sat in wonder at the lofty aura of the occasion. I felt ungainly and uncomfortable, yet curious. The poetry reading was by the august Australian poet Vincent Buckley. I found his verse entrancing and thought he must be a genius. He read *Golden Builders*, and moments of that poem linger in my consciousness. Its evocation of Carlton's streets still resonate in my poetic remembrance. *The hammers of iron glow down Faraday./ Lygon and Drummond shift under their resonance./ . . .O Cardigan, Queensberry, Elgin: names of their lordships./Cardigan, Elgin, Lygon: shall I find here my Lord's grave?* Buckley's voice was rhapsodic. I was struck with the potency of poetry and the power of the poet to transform the starkness of the room. In my enthusiasm, I went back to my room and wrote a poem. It wasn't my first attempt at writing poetry, but I was motivated to see what I could create.

Books were knocking on the door of my mind: I was touched by the power of words and I was thirsty for knowledge. I recalled James and Simon, and my mother's friend Peg. Peg had none of my mother's passion for housework; she read the whole day. What was it she read? Was it romances, detective stories, historical novels? It didn't matter to me because I thought she must be intelligent and interesting because she was a reader. Books were a mystery to me because I was unfamiliar with them. I hadn't spent long nights under the bed covers with a torch, reading some fabled story or exciting adventure, as I have heard friends tell of doing. I hadn't read Enid Blyton, or C.S. Lewis, Rosemary Sutcliff or Mary Grant Bruce, or any of the children's classics. The only books we had in the house were my father's *Reader's Digest* Condensed Books to which he subscribed for a few years. We did have newspapers and the weekly magazine *Australasian Post*, a tawdry piece of journalism that came with scantily clad models on the front cover. Much later I found, in the back of a hardly used cupboard, a four-volume set of *The Book of the Thousand and One Nights* published in 1949. I don't know where it came from. With Peg, however, I sensed that books were a ticket to somewhere beyond the housework and drudgery of my mother's life. Even though I wasn't a reader as a child, I was inspired by Peg's love of books. Eventually I would find books, or they found me.

S

BRAVE NEW DIFFICULT WORLD

All year I skipped lectures and tutorials and did little of the required reading for my courses. I was never a natural reader, and although I loved books, I found the discipline of reading difficult. The year flipped by and I flopped through it, managing miraculously to pass two subjects out of three, with mediocre marks. I failed Philosophy. It was rare to fail first-year Philosophy, but I managed it, bringing me a bit of unwanted notoriety. I had scraped into university and now I scraped through first year. How would I get through the next few years of university, let alone qualify to teach? The thought of teaching terrified me. I felt stupid. If I were to teach, what could I teach when I knew nothing myself?

I began to suffer mental occurrences that I can only describe as mental blackouts or absences. I used to call them my *turns*. I would bang my head against the wall and fall into a mental torpor, oblivious to the things around me. I'm not really sure what I did in these states or how long I was absent, but I would come back to the world exhausted and bewildered. It happened many times and did not stop until I developed full-blown mental illness. Were these turns early symptoms of madness or were they more like emotional tantrums? Why did I not seek medical advice? Like so many things in my life, these turns were too frightening to talk about.

Feminism attracted me, but my thoughts about it were not fully formed. I knew there were gender antagonisms and I felt a personal ambivalence towards males as well as a sense of abandonment by Simon. Nonetheless, I started a relationship with a former school friend, Christopher, who was very loving toward me. I had growing misgivings about my sexuality, however. I did not feel sexually comfortable with men, and had felt awkward and unsatisfied with them since my late teens. Everything changed at the end of my first year of university. I fell in love with the woman in the room next door to me in college. Her name was Robbie and she was doing a science degree. I entertained the notion that one could love two people at the same time. The groundwork for this idea was laid by D.H. Lawrence in his book *Women in Love*, which I had read in my last year of high school. It was a radical but intriguing idea that captured my imagination; anything was possible in this life. The following year Robbie and I decided to leave college and rent a house with Christopher. I thought I must be bisexual. This was a confused time, which perhaps other women have gone through on their way to becoming lesbians. I found poignancy in my first kiss with a woman, with the soft brushing of cheeks, unencumbered by the stubble of a man's face. Our relationship grew over third term, and during the Christmas break I made several trips on my motorbike to Robbie's home in Sale.

The following year I also began a relationship with Jane, a woman I met while working over the Christmas break at Allambie, the child reception centre. It was a place to which children from broken families were sent, children who had been sexually abused and were wards of the state. I empathised with these children too much for my own good. I was drawn to Jane. She had integrity and I liked and respected her, but the relationship was unsustainable and after six months it ended. I had tried to juggle these simultaneous relationships with Robbie, Christopher and

Jane, thinking that if I were honest with everyone, it would be manageable. It wasn't. The logistics and emotional toll of such a complicated situation were hard for everyone. In retrospect, I fear I was thinking more about what I wanted than what was good for them. Christopher left after a year or so when he went to work in Sydney. It was an easy way to extricate himself from an unsatisfying and waning relationship.

Now I had to come to terms with being a lesbian. It was one thing to be attracted to, or infatuated with, women, but quite another to consummate those feelings. This made for some acutely felt insecurities. Was my shift to lesbianism a response to my incident with Bruce and my father's sexual aggression towards my mother? I can't be sure, even now. It is true that bad experiences with some men made me wary of them. And, for too long, I had seen sex between my parents as representing emotional and physical power and domination by my father over my mother. But I had always been a sporty tomboy. I had never liked dolls or cooking or girly activities. I had long resisted traditional female roles. I had been infatuated with a lesbian friend of my sister. She had been attractive, rebellious and full of fun and I had liked the fact that she was different. I wanted to be like her.

It was a difficult time for me. Society in the early 70s was still uncomfortable with homosexuality and I didn't easily acknowledge it myself. I felt I was breaking taboos and was unsure how to handle this. But for a while the university shielded me from wider society, and the growing influence of feminism meant that lesbianism was less frowned upon in that environment. Recognition of my homosexuality did nothing to strengthen my fragile sense of identity – who wants to be known as a lesbian in a society that extols the virtues of heterosexual marriage and the institution of the family? But it was not a negative experience. On the contrary, it was liberating. I enjoyed the company of women and the feeling of sisterhood that lesbians offered each other. Finding love, companionship and security among women reinforced my physical attraction to them.

Robbie and I continued to live together. We shared our lives and pursued our studies. Robbie was more studious than me, however. I was constantly fighting myself and my lax attitude to work: my mind was preoccupied with everything except my studies. We were surrounded by women on the cusp of the feminist revolution. They were involved in Consciousness Raising (CR) groups in which they explored their inner lives and the new ideas sweeping society. They went out into the community and talked about their sexuality, telling groups of unsuspecting suburban women about feminism and lesbianism. They lived in what we called the 'lesbian ghetto' in North Fitzroy, an inner Melbourne suburb, with a concentration of lesbians and a flourishing lesbian culture. They wanted to spread the word about this important political movement. They told women and the wider community that *the personal is political* and *sisterhood is powerful*.

Robbie and I were now renting a house in a leafy hamlet called Warrandyte on the city fringe, far away from the bustle and politics of the lesbian ghetto. Our connection with the feminist movement came through our friends, Sue and Sue, who were planted firmly in the middle of the revolution. We believed passionately in the movement and went to *Reclaim the Night* marches. But we lived quietly amongst the gum trees with our cats and dog and the burble of the Yarra River.

We were finding our way in the world when Dido, Queen of Carthage, came into our lives. It was 1974. Dido was a PhD student whom Robbie met in the science department. They shared an interest in botany and both liked camping and bushwalking. Over several months they developed a deep love. Somehow, in an unusual and wonderful way, it became a shared relationship, and the three of us bonded in a circle. We became enclosed in our own world. We explored each other and the possibilities of our unique situation. We devoted more energy to our lives together than to the outer world. It was streaming ahead at a revolutionary pace, but we lived with an intensity that was in its own way remarkable.

I bumbled through the last few years of my degree. Because I had a studentship, I had undertaken to do Education subjects concurrently with my Arts degree. This meant I was to do teaching rounds. In the second year course these were for observation only but by the time I got to the third-year course, in 1975, I was supposed to teach classes. I went to my assigned school completely unprepared, not knowing what topic I would have to teach. I trembled when I entered the school. The thought of teaching made me sick with worry. I knew in my bones I couldn't do it. When my assigned teacher-supervisor suggested I teach his year 11 class something about the French Revolution, I froze. I knew nothing about the French Revolution, even though I had done Modern European History in my second year. Guilt about my casual attitude to studies hit me like a firestorm. I wished I had done more reading. I wished I knew more about what I was supposed to know.

I lacked the confidence to read up on the French Revolution. I didn't think I had the capacity or intelligence to create a lesson that would pass the test. I knew I couldn't stand up in front of the class and say something sensible. Even today I am in awe of teachers who face a hostile group of kids and teach. My fears overwhelmed me and, in a state of absolute wretchedness, I broke down and fled the school, never to return. That was it. I knew then that teaching was out of the question. Everything seemed so surreal. My head swam, and clouded thoughts streamed through my consciousness. The world looked different, splashed in a wash of garish colours. I couldn't think clearly, and as I rode my motorbike home, I felt such despair at the future that I thought I should kill myself. The career I believed I could pursue had become an impossibility. Teaching was not my vocation. I was trapped in something I had neither the skill nor the will to accomplish.

What was ahead of me? The hope that had got me to university, that had helped me forge a new life away from home, was crumbling. I relinquished my studentship. I dropped the Education subject, enrolled in another History subject and changed my plan. I would pursue a straight degree without the Diploma of Education. I went into damage control but had no idea what I was going to do when I finished my studies.

Meanwhile Dido had completed her PhD at the end of 1974 and went to Canberra to take up a job with a government department. It was difficult with her so far away. Robbie and I continued to live at Warrandyte and finish our studies but now that I had relinquished my studentship, Dido offered to support me while I finished my degree. This kindness was integral to her character. With the support of both Dido and Robbie, I did finish in 1975 and graduated with a Bachelor of Arts. This was an interesting year in many ways. Robbie was doing Honours, with a view to doing a PhD. Labor Prime Minister Gough Whitlam was dismissed from parliamentary office after a collusion of the conservative forces. I remember the day well – 11 November 1975, Armistice Day. Robbie came rushing home from the university to tell me of the dismissal. I was writing an essay on 'Reform or Revolution' for my Marxism subject – I was advocating revolution. Whitlam's dismissal reinforced my view that it was the only way to bring about radical change, to contain the conservative forces protecting the power of the bourgeoisie. In those days I believed this was possible.

Finishing my degree did not provide a happy ending. I did not sail away into the sunset with a career and a future I could look forward to with optimism. Throughout my years at university a shadow had been lurking in the back of my mind, a faltering of my thought patterns. Besides the lingering melancholy that haunted me, always, I felt an unease with the world and with myself that laid me low. My confidence had drained away. My job applications were pathetic. I didn't believe in myself or my abilities. I had no skills to offer an employer. I have thought of myself as 'work shy', as someone without 'a good work ethic'. I don't understand why motivation was such a problem for me – a problem that dogged my life at school too – though on the sporting field I was and remain highly motivated. Was I work shy, or was it something more fundamental that dispirited me? I often felt like an incapable and incompetent person and this became a self-fulfilling prophecy. I was loath to take on responsibility. I felt overwhelmed by the prospect of having to make decisions.

By early 1976 I realised I was not going to get a job. I went on the dole and back to university part time. By remaining a student, I could continue to live without all the responsibilities of normal adult people. Robbie began her PhD and Dido returned from Canberra. We lived together again in our small but charming Warrandyte home. But by the end of that year the person Robbie and Dido thought they knew became a stranger.

Part Three

Bats in the Belfry
1976–1993

I am always with myself,
and it is I who am my tormentor.
Leo Tolstoy

SATAN'S WHORE

Throughout 1976 my behaviour was erratic and full of contradictions. I had enrolled to do a part-time economics degree. For me university was a sheltered workshop – something I could do while on the dole. I had already studied history and sociology, and now I wanted to complement those subjects with something that would broaden my understanding of the world. I was interested in economics and the rationalist view of the world it offered. But as the year progressed, I began quietly to unravel. I neglected my studies in the second half of that year. I would sit in my tutorials and have no idea what was going on, what the tutor and other students were saying. It all floated over me as though I weren't there. I was full of self-doubt. And riven by voices.

Satan's whore! Slut! Trollop! Stupid bitch! Scum! Trash! *railed one voice.* Look, they hate you. God has a secret mission for you, saviour, *continued another voice.* No pity for you, evil bitch, if you expose us, *they both warned.* You are the keeper of the eggs. Collect them from the chooks, *they commanded.* Caress them, turn them around in your hands, discern their cosmic importance, organise them in the fridge, number each egg, put them in cartons, alphabetise the cartons. Such important work, only you can do it. *I have been touched by God's will. I am a cosmic messenger, a saviour sent on a mission to arrange eggs.*

Yet, the world is disparaging of my work, it ridicules me. If I don't adhere to my calling, I'm liable to be punished by God. He is a dark force and I have to appease Him. Eggs and God go hand in hand.

My mind was wrestling to comprehend incoming cosmic messages that proclaimed me the keeper of the eggs, whore and saviour. There was a wild inconsistency in my thoughts about myself. How could I be both saviour and whore? What did all this mean? Deep inside I felt evil, and a danger to the world.

I had struggled with myself and my dark side for so long. Any confidence had eroded and an emotional paralysis had crept upon me. I couldn't find my way into the workforce and doubted I had the capacity to do even menial tasks let alone more demanding work. I was aimless and angst-ridden, empty and aching. I lived in parallel worlds which I sometimes couldn't distinguish: there was my daily life where I went through the motions and seemed to be coping, and then there was my secret world of voices and strange thoughts which I managed to hide from everyone.

I was playing in an inter-varsity hockey tournament, with teams from universities all over Australia, when things really began to go off the rails. It was September of 1976. My sleep patterns had become erratic: I hadn't slept for the entire week of the tournament. Irrational thoughts flooded my mind: thoughts that grossly inflated my sense of importance. Sleep-deprived and physically exhausted, I was functioning on adrenalin. At the tournament I became involved with a woman; her name was Laurel. She had a boyfriend she had been with for a few years, and I was still with Robbie and Dido. After the tournament Laurel and I continued to see each other. We decided we were going to leave our respective relationships and begin a life together. In October I told Robbie and Dido. I knew, as soon as I uttered the words *I'm leaving you for another woman*, that

I had made a catastrophic mistake. How I was to wish I could take back those words.

I was a car hurtling downhill with no brakes, unable to see the next corner. Yet I felt invulnerable. I thought that no matter what I did, it was going to be of cosmic significance. The world revolved around me, me, me. Everything fed into the fantasy in my inner world which further clouded my judgement and understanding of the outside world. That world existed for no-one else: I was the centre of everything. (I now know that delusions of grandeur are common in schizophrenia – and wonder what is more egocentric: having a psychotic episode or writing a memoir!)

I continued living with Robbie and Dido while I waited for Laurel to make arrangements to leave her partner. However, in early November Laurel told me on the telephone that she had changed her mind. She had decided to stay with her partner. In a trance I walked back from our neighbour's house where I had used the phone, strange voices chattering and laughing in my head. *Loser, loser, loser*, they laughed. *You're on your own, bitch!* My disappointment in losing Laurel's affection magnified the confusion in my spiralling mind. She, like everyone else, had unknowingly been caught up in its convolutions. No-one realised the extent of my mental disintegration, least of all me. Muddled and paranoid, I succumbed to the madness that had been hovering around me like a pair of dark wings.

Forces are gathering against me. Robbie and Dido give each other guarded looks coded with meaning. A voice warns me: You can't trust them, they want you destroyed, bitch. They are sending secretly encoded messages to God asking Him to punish you. *I won't tell Robbie and Dido of my mission; they might try to take over. The eggs have a universal importance that only I understand. Robbie and Dido's looks are getting to me; they must know something. I'm not safe with them. Those looks threaten me.* The knife on the sink is your only protection, grab it! *says a voice. I grab it and slash the air.*

They try to stop me; hurl me into the kitchen bench.

Laughter? Where is the laughter coming from?

Everything around me is in a murky pall. Objects are moving around in random ways. Things don't seem as they were. Pictures move on the walls, furniture has a life of its own, doors contract and expand, the floor seems to be floating. There! Behind the bookcase – the Devil! I must pull the books out. And there – a witch in the window! I snatch up a cricket bat to shatter the witch's face. Robbie and Dido grab me; they push me onto the couch and stand over me. Now I know they are my enemies. Everyone is out to get me: God, the Devil, the witch and Robbie and Dido.

The night is long and sleepless. I pace the room. There are witches and devils everywhere. My task with the eggs is the only reality I have. The mirror casts back at me an image of a vile witch, a she-devil, and she is me! Is there someone behind the mirror? Get away, go!

Morning. Sleep deprived and wrung out, I drag myself through the day. The constant surveillance by Robbie and Dido inhibits me. I look to my eggs and see they are all right. This afternoon I have a cricket match and I am determined to play, despite the long night of the witch and voices.

I go to cricket, angry and fearful. How am I going to get through the match? I can tell by the faces of my team-mates that they can read my mind. My cranium is made of glass. There is no need to talk. The exposure is ghastly. I grab a bat and go out into the middle of the oval. Out here no-one can touch me – it's just me and the ball and I have a fighting chance. But what if the ball is an agent of God too? I have to get away from the gaze of everyone.

My return to the eggs is a homecoming. They are still there, tucked away in the fridge in their boxes, numbered and ordered perfectly. But no matter how hard I try to appease God with the eggs, I feel a failure. Robbie and Dido have locked the doors. Home is treacherous. I'll curl up on the couch to plan my escape. I cannot stay here where I cannot avoid the witch and the plans of the Devil. I feel sad. I'll whisper a prayer to myself.

I am running for my life. I burst through an unguarded door. The bush calls, its tangled spaces protective. I rest in a womb-like hole surrounded by trees and shrubs that give me cover. Time stops. I am a frightened animal, crouching in a hole, fearful and restless. A voice shouts at me: Your rotting body is poisoning the world. Hide yourself! *Day is becoming night and I am so terror-stricken. I have to get away. Away from where I am.*

There is a bus stop nearby. A bus pulls up. I get on. The driver knows me! I can tell by the way he looks at me. He was expecting me. I'll move as far away from him as possible and sit at the back of the empty bus. My mind is awash with suspicion. I can't keep track of all these thoughts.

The whole city is a dangerous place. The lights are all trained on me – the shop lights, the neon signs, the traffic lights – all pinpoint me in their glare. And now I can see that everyone has a knife in their hands. Where can I be safe from these lunging assailants and piercing lights?

I'll catch a tram to Sue's; she is the only friend I can trust. Maybe she can understand these cosmic forces. The tram is crowded, stifling, each person threatening to crush me. I can't wait to get off. What's the time? What day is it? I don't recall much, but I do remember how to get to Sue's. I hope she is home.

Please, someone answer the door, I need someone to answer the door before the Devil finds me. I have left my eggs, abandoned them. Who is this ushering me in the door? I'm thankful but cautious. Sue is not home. Rushing upstairs without speaking, I fall into Sue's room. I'm tired. Books and papers are everywhere, scattered on the table, chairs and the floor. These must be for the Honours thesis she is writing. I lie on her bed, a mattress on the floor. My mind is racing. A voice pronounces: The world would be a better place without you. Cringe and cower, slut. You're such a fucking loser. *Even here I see the witch and flashing lights. The room is alive with ghosts. They want to infiltrate the minds of people and make them capable of great evil. Like me – I am the personification of evil.*

I'll sing to myself. That might clear my mind. There are thoughts to be thought that are important, that no-one else will ever think, but they crash through my mind so quickly I cannot stop them long enough to know what they are. My mind leaps but my body is torpid. I lie immobilised, waiting.

Time passes and I haven't moved. Have I been here long? Sue finally comes home but I can't talk to her. I know she can read my mind through my eyes so I mustn't make eye contact. I'll lie on the bed, sheltering myself from her gaze. I hear her talking with others in the house. Mutterings are all about around me, in the air, cursing my evil presence.

I get up from Sue's bed and stagger out of the room. I feel woozy. Sue's housemate's room is next door. I see her bed and it beckons me. I take off my clothes – nakedness is honest – and fall onto the mattress. A voice has told me: Spoken words are meaningless. *So I shall not speak. I shall write notes. Then a voice declares*: Food and drink are the Devil's food. *So I have to fast. I am not worthy to live. Another voice shouts*: Scum and shit, lie in this bed until you die! *Where are these voices coming from? I give up wondering. I think only of the eucalypt tree under which I wish to be left to peacefully die.*

I am shattering into a thousand pieces, imploding, in this strange bed, in this strange world where I'm not allowed to eat or drink. My mouth is foul. I am weak; my limbs are like jelly and I fear they may become detached. A monstrous thought is planted in my mind by a voice: You are the repository of immense cataclysmic potential; the Devil has planted the seeds of the world's destruction in your heart. *This is my own Annunciation. How long have I been here in this bed? A day? Three days? A week? I don't know. Time has stopped. Terror stops my breath. Everything grows huge around me. My hands and legs are tingling, my face is hot. I'm dying. Who are these people around me? Sue? Robbie and Dido, where did they come from? Someone is lifting my limp body, carrying me down the narrow stairs . . .*

The hospital lights are bright. A young doctor is looking at me. I cannot understand the questions he is asking me. I don't understand the language he speaks. But it is me who is the alien. He is looking at my naked body; it is covered in lines. I had to draw these on myself in the ritual compelled by my cosmic journey. A sheet partly covers my inscribed body. Why is the doctor touching my breasts? He says he is examining me for lumps. There is something wrong with this but my words of protest are lost along with my language. He must know that I am evil. He leaves.

Another doctor comes to see me, an older woman. She says she is Dr H and she is a psychiatrist. She also asks me questions. This is like a game, but I don't know the rules; I am not sure what she wants me to say. I suspect she already knows the answers. Can she read my mind too? I mustn't speak. To avoid her looking into my brain, I'll write her a note. It says: Take me to the eucalypt, and let me die peacefully beneath its canopy. *Although my mind is crammed with a thousand thoughts, I cannot utter them. Writing notes to the doctors is the only way I can communicate, the only suitable way.*

Dr H says she will admit me to her ward. She seems kind. I will go anywhere with someone who shows even the smallest kindness. So they take me to the psychiatric ward. How did it come to this? The eggs seem a distant memory. I am wheeled in a wheelchair down a long, pale corridor, passing doors and equipment, people and trolleys, on my way to a world of the lost. And all the way the maniacal laughter of God trills in my head.

My father's accusatory words to my mother catapult around in my mind: You're mad. You need to see a fuckin' psychiatrist. *I am ashamed. Only mad people come to places like this. I shall not speak to anyone. But, still, they will read my mind. Who to trust?*

And so it went, this, my first meeting with madness. I don't know when the voices started. They began slowly and mutedly – a whisper here, an odd sound there. By the time they started shrieking at me I had become accustomed to their presence, as if they had always been with me. I couldn't tell anyone about them because they were a secret that they themselves commanded me to keep. Nobody guessed I had these strange folk upstairs. I hid them very well.

When I reflect on my first bout of madness, I see how compelling my voices were. Suddenly everyone was my enemy, even Robbie and Dido. The voices that had commanded me to arrange the eggs had urged me to flee from Robbie and Dido. The bus trip into Melbourne was horrendous. I found my way to Sue's place where I collapsed in a physical torpor while my mind spiralled. For seven days Robbie, Dido and Sue watched me lie immobilised and mute. They washed my soiled, limp body but could not coax me to eat or drink. There was nothing else they could do. I was weak and disoriented. They were so worried about me that they had made the difficult decision to take me to a hospital where I would be safe. Their decision was hastened when I had a panic attack. My breathing became erratic, my limbs were numb and I thrashed about thinking I was dying. I was visibly upset and disturbed. They carried me down the steep narrow stairs and bundled me into a car. I thought this was the end: I am being taken to a rubbish dump where my body is going to be discarded like a piece of old furniture. We drove through the traffic-choked inner suburbs and ended up at the Queen Victoria Memorial Hospital, an old dark red-brick building in the heart of Melbourne. All I remember is signing the admission forms – because Robbie and Dido's expressions were so fraught and worried and they told me I didn't have a choice. I was admitted as a voluntary patient to the psychiatric ward.

Here I Sit

Here,
surrounded by the sterile relics of sanity,
lost in a labyrinth of refracted thought,
I sit
where life becomes a burden
and where the burden becomes the loss of life.
What is this confusion,
this confusion of the spheres,
this unyielding perplexity
that determinedly withers my countenance
and renders me helpless?

S

A FRACTURED MIND

November 1976 was the beginning of a long and arduous struggle with the monster of madness. None of us had seen mental illness before, so when it came rampaging into our lives, we were unprepared and confounded.

I spent a month at the Queen Victoria, not knowing what had gone wrong, why things had gone awry, wondering where I was going to end up. I was acutely aware of where I was: a madhouse! And this frightened me. I hadn't spoken, eaten or drunk fluid for a week. Friends showed real loyalty by visiting me even though I wasn't very communicative. Gradually I started to drink and eat again, with coaxing from the nurses. But I still refused to speak and communicated by writing notes. It took a few more days of coaxing before I started to speak again. The words came back to me in a quiet way. I felt their power when I uttered my first word; yet my voice sounded alien to me, as though some stranger were in my body making unfamiliar sounds. It was a fellow patient who had the kindness to say what a nice voice I had, and this encouraged me.

To communicate again was a profound lesson in the power of language. Bergman, in his film *Persona*, has an actress whom a crisis has rendered mute. Like me, she had no will to express herself, as if fearing words might reconnect her to a reality she dreaded. Language does connect one to others, I found, when I took those first tentative steps back into the spoken world. That month was a relearning to be in the world – how one needs food and sustenance, to speak, to care for oneself. It was as if I had to be shaken out of my strange state of dissolution and regression to innocence, and had to acquire again in a matter of days all those life skills in order to live in the world as the adult I was supposed to be.

I would like to know what the medicos thought was wrong with me, because it was all so indeterminate and confusing at the time. I have tried to access the files kept on my case at this time but, unfortunately, when the hospital was closed down, all the files for this period were sent away, and then destroyed after fifteen years. Although now I do have some capacity for objectivity, I am still left with a void of understanding about those first experiences of going mad. Then, I believed the medical staff thought I was just someone who was being difficult and behaving badly. I felt very uncomfortable with the doctors, insecure and anxious about saying the wrong thing. I covered my insecurity with an awkward arrogance. The fact was that I was terrified of psychiatrists. My father's words *You need to see a fuckin' psychiatrist!* were never far from my mind. I could not imagine how psychiatrists could really help people who were as disordered as I felt.

And sinking into the turbulent waters,
I am drowning in a sea of madness,
lashed to the mast of the sinking Ship of Fools.

I have no knowledge of any diagnosis made of my condition in the month I was at the Queen Victoria Hospital. I believe that I was treated with high dosages of Valium to alleviate my extreme anxiety. Dr H was the older woman doctor I had seen on admission and I felt she was someone I could relate to, talk to, with whom I felt I might be comfortable enough to relax my guarded emotions, maybe even defy the voices and tell her about them.

Meeting the other patients with their various illnesses was a revelatory experience. I had no idea such conditions existed. I remember one young woman who was confined to her bed and not allowed to get out of bed until she put on weight. She had to do everything from there: eat meals, use the bedpan, see friends. I thought that was strange and even unjust. She seemed quite normal to me and I wondered why she was there with all the *mad* people. I found out she was suffering from anorexia nervosa, a serious eating disorder with often drastic consequences. She didn't even look that under-weight to me, but I never saw her out of her loose pyjamas.

Then there was the man who had theories about science that didn't make sense. I thought if someone would just sit down with him and teach him the correct information, he would see the error of his ways. I didn't know about delusions and how they grip you, how one cannot be dissuaded by logic or reasoning. I didn't know he had schizophrenia until much later, when I understood my own condition and could see some of his symptoms mirroring my own. Another patient was a middle-aged man suffering from bipolar mood disorder. He would wake us all at five a.m. with a vigorous shake. We had to be up and out of bed so we could begin the day with him and his manic energy. He exhorted us: *Get up! Get up! We've got to see the sun rise and get busy. I've got to plan the extravaganza. Mick Jagger is waiting for me!* His relentless, surging energy was an awesome gale from which it was difficult to escape.

A young woman called Trish made a strong impression on me. She had come to the ward suffering from post-natal depression. She was withdrawn and distant from everyone, including her husband and her newborn baby. Her dark thoughts made a wall around her, immobilising her, keeping her inside and everyone else outside. She could not wash herself or eat. I watched her husband try to talk with her and encourage her to eat. He was trying to find a way in to her, and I admired his patience. For much of the time there was little or no response from her, but gradually he began to connect. She was given electroconvulsive therapy (ECT). This appeared to work for her, along with the antidepressant medication she received. I watched her with an eagle eye, almost clinical in the way I observed her, even though I sensed that I was in my own deep hole. I felt engaged with her struggle and wondered, when I went to sleep each night behind my yellow curtain, how she would be in the morning. I waited for the day when she would be able to look with loving eyes at her baby. And one morning she did. Seeing Trish recover her ability to relate to her husband and baby gave me hope that there was a chance for all of us to get better, including me. Even though I was muddled by madness, I was still able to feel compassion and concern for this young mother. Madness may have swamped me in confusion but it had not robbed me of empathy.

DIAGNOSIS

In early December the Queen Victoria Hospital discharged me. They were scaling down the ward for the Christmas break and those patients able to go home were allowed to do so, while those most in need of critical care stayed on with a skeleton staff. I felt wretched about having to go because I was still vulnerable and distracted. I felt abandoned by Dr H who I was beginning to trust. Now I was left with my voices and no-one to help me fight them. I couldn't go back to Warrandyte with Robbie and Dido because I felt so bad about what I had done to them. In my mind it didn't seem right. I didn't know what was right or wrong or what I should be doing or where I should be living or who I wanted to be with. But I was dreadfully afraid to be alone. Dido asked Ken, a good friend of hers with whom she had been to university and done a lot of bushwalking, if I could live in his attic. (I had always had romantic images of attics and struggling poets sitting in the little upstairs room quietly reading a classic novel.) He kindly agreed. Robbie and Dido helped me pack some of my things into Robbie's station wagon and together they moved me into Ken's attic in his house in the inner suburb of Clifton Hill. Although it was a haven, I was alone there a lot of the time, with none of the companionship I was used to. Now I was scared of an uncertain future. I was scared of my own feelings, which were irrational, sometimes dwelling on suicide. Everything was clouded by a growing paranoia in which the villain was me. I was a towering figure of evil.

Within a few weeks I was unable to cope with my melancholic, discordant thoughts and the admonishing voices. In an agitated state, I contacted the Queen Victoria. I had an interview with my older woman doctor. All I could say in answer to her questions was a plaintive: *I don't know*. She suggested I be admitted to Parkville Psychiatric Unit and sent me there with a letter of introduction. My walk there is still vivid in my memory.

The December day is warm and close. The walk to the hospital from Ken's is a long way, but it is a contemplative walk and I have things to think about. The voices of my parents are telling me I am shit, putrid, evil. My evil is a threat to the world. As I tug my old duffle coat around me, I realise I look odd on this warm day. But I pull my beanie down closer over my ears because I need to keep the world out. The light-blue coat is a security blanket covering my thin body. I am sweating, but I feel safer. I need a barrier against the invasive presence of everyone around me.

But I am sweating now with anxiety; each step is a step closer to an unknown outcome. I carry a letter from Dr H. I probably shouldn't have steamed it open, but I did. I was curious to know what she was thinking about me. I need to know what is wrong with me. The letter was in the handwriting of a doctor. It was hard to understand.

Queen Victoria Memorial Hospital
10-12-1976
The Admitting Officer
Parkville Psychiatric Unit

Dear Dr J

This is to introduce Miss Sandra Jeffs.

Miss Jeffs was sent to this hospital about a month ago because she had been fasting (? absolutely) for a week and would not talk although she would write notes in answer to our questions. Over the next four days she again began to eat, drink and talk. She is prone to intellectualisation and game playing in interviews but that is gradually improving and I feel that she has potential for growth. However she needs more intensive, more immediate treatment we are unable to offer at the moment and expressed an inability to cope without it. If you feel for some reason that she is not suitable we have made it plain that we are happy to have her back.

Thank you for seeing her so soon,

Dr H

Did I really intellectualise and game play? Yes, I had fasted absolutely. Would they really have me back if this doesn't work out? Maybe they hadn't dumped me as I thought they had? No, I'm sure they wanted me out of the ward because I was spreading my evil all over the place.

The sun is bearing down on me. The streets go from asphalt starkness to tree-lined laneways that are quite pleasant. The hospital is in the inner suburb of Parkville surrounded by exotic and native trees and shrubs. The way into the grounds is shaded and cool. It looks serene but what lies behind the facade, what is behind these benign red-brick buildings? I'm not sure where to go. I peer at a few doors before finding the right entrance. Does anyone know I am coming? I see a receptionist. I tell her where I have come from. I give her the letter. I wait. I am even hotter in my coat now and just have to take it off, although I shudder to expose myself to the glare of the world.

A doctor steps out from a room and invites me in to it. The voice of my father interjects: She is such a bitch. God will punish her and her Devil-worship; we know how evil she is. Everyone hates Sandra. *My mother's voice comes from nowhere*: Sandra is a virgin's heart. She is a fortune teller. *My father growls*: They despise her, she's a whore, she's the Devil's semen. *My mother responds*: Sandra is the emanation of divinity. *My father is railing*: She eats shit and her breath stinks. She's a rotting corpse.

Does the doctor know all of this stuff about me? He asks questions and I answer perfunctorily, distracted, afraid to show any emotions. Everything is a blur, and all that I had thought on my way here is lost. My answers are jumbled. Words are disappearing, stolen from my mouth as they are about to be uttered. Yet, in what feels like a few seconds, I find myself admitted to the hospital, not knowing why or wherefore, or what is going to happen to me. So easily have I given myself up to this madhouse.

13/12/76 Patient background. In October 1976 Sandra began to feel that she was in some way an evil influence and dangerous to those around her and at the same time she was being threatened by the two women with whom she was living. On one occasion she felt so threatened that she picked up a carving knife to protect herself and when the others tried to reason with her, rushed off to the bush and wandered around for the night. The next day she wandered about Melbourne in a frightened state believing that passers-by were looking at her and carrying knives to stab her. She began to hear voices in her head telling her that she was evil. At times she believed these to be the voices of her parents discussing her in the third person. She then developed a curious compulsion to walk into the bush and find a particular eucalypt tree which she had visualised vividly in her mind, to lay down under this tree, and die peacefully and be enveloped by the bush. For one week prior to her admission to the Queen Victoria Hospital in November 1976 she lay on her bed refusing to speak or take food and water. She did this as she felt she was evil and should let her body die and become rejoined with the bush.

Was that really me? Was I truly that ill? The records of my admission to Parkville Psychiatric Unit offer a clinical view of me at that time, and I sometimes wonder if I am the same person those records describe. I was in a confused mental state and, anyway, none of us recalls everything with accuracy. It was a only few years ago that I decided to obtain my records from the mental health authorities, facilitated by the Freedom of Information regulations, in the hope that they would help me understand all that has happened to me. I had no trouble getting my records from either Parkville or Larundel, the other hospital to which I was to have many admissions. I find these records useful in recalling dates and places. They may be an approximation of some of what I said and did, but as I think about them, I wonder how objective a view they provide of me and of my behaviour. They are, after all, only one individual staff member's interpretation of my words and actions. They are shaped by that person's relationship with me, and by the changing practices of psychiatry. I am aware also of the dangers of reconstructing my memory of these half-glimpsed parts of my life story from these reports.

Perhaps the most puzzling aspect of madness is the loss of insight into one's self and condition; it is this that makes me think of my mad self as a stranger. It was the conclusion of this report that finally put a label on my confused state:

> Management and Progress
>
> Her mental state remained as above although on occasions she reported auditory hallucinations, usually the voices of her parents arguing about her in the third person and she described experiences of derealisation and depersonalisation as well as fluctuating level of anxiety. After two weeks it was considered she was suffering from an acute schizophrenic illness and treatment was started with Trifluoperazine increasing the dose to 45mg/day.

I had finally told someone about my voices. Dr T had persisted with his examinations of me and eventually made me feel safe enough to confide in him. It was a relief to unburden myself but I worried that the voices might punish me for exposing them, which they invariably did. I was shocked and bewildered when the diagnosis of schizophrenia was made.

Western society has always had a troubled relationship with madness and over the centuries has treated mad people with disdain and derision. From the village idiot pilloried in the stocks to the madwoman locked away in the attic, from the witch burned at the stake to unfortunate mental patients lobotomised in asylums or murdered in Nazi camps, there has been a history of neglect and abuse of those called mad. And now here I was mong the incarcerated. Would I become a hapless mental patient in madhouses for the rest of my life?

Ironically, though, at that terrible time when I was suffering madness without understanding what was going on, I found that the label *schizophrenia*, and the medical model that uses that label, were helpful to me. For me the word *schizophrenia* at least explained my bad behaviour to myself, and to my friends. It validated the fact that I was ill rather than a bad person doing bad things. It gave meaning to my strange and inexplicable conduct, and hope that if it were an illness there would be treatment to deal with it. I was open to any sort of help I could get because of the terror I felt. I didn't care if it entailed labels or drugs if these could help alleviate my symptoms. When you are desperate you accept such help, along with the whole gamut of medical practice and research behind it.

THE STELAZINE STOMP

> 26/12/76 . . . complaining of slight tremor of hands - same noticeable? extrapyramidal side-effects. Duty Doctor notified. Cogentin 2mg orally - same given 11.30am.
>
> 2/1/77 Extrapyramidal reaction to Stelazine, has been experiencing akathisia for past couple of days. After lunch visited by friends, came and reported to staff - marked dystonia of neck muscle and some swallowing difficulties. Duty Doctor notified. Cogentin 2mg i.m.i - same given 1:50p.m.

Even though I was open to taking medication, there was a part of me that was reluctant to do so. There was something forbidding about the medications used in psychiatry. The fact that they altered one's cognitive functioning was itself a scary thing. We don't have the same suspicion about the medications used to treat heart disease, cancer, diabetes and the like.

The first antipsychotic drug I tried was Stelazine, notorious for causing extreme restlessness. At first, my hands developed a tremor; then I found myself pacing the floor. I couldn't stay still and was constantly stomping up and down, even as I tried to resist the urge to move. And when I sat down my legs jiggled like a floppy marionette's. This condition is well known in the psychiatric scene; the technical term for it is 'akathisia' but my fellow patients called it the 'Stelazine Stomp'. One of the most terrifying side-effects of Stelazine I experienced was what is termed a 'dystonic' reaction (the extrapyramidal side effect referred to in the case note), in which neck muscles and tongue start to cramp, twisting and contorting you so that you cannot swallow and your neck is involuntarily bent downwards. It's painful and alarming enough to make you think you are dying. I recall the relief I felt when I was given an injection of Cogentin, a drug used to stop this happening, not realising then that even antidotes had their problems.

> **25/12/76 Continues to be unable to make herself understood, appears to be more distressed & embarrassed by this, tries to participate socially with co-patients but is unsuccessful & then tries to maintain contact by an embarrassed laugh.**

My stammer, which was much worse in my school years, became severe and disabling under these drug treatments. I couldn't utter a word without falling over it into a tangle of syllables. It was frustrating and embarrassing not to be able to express myself. I'm sure it was the effects of the medications that made me drowsy and slow, made me stumble in my speech, because when I had my dosage reduced, and my brain and body were used to the drugs, my speech returned to its normal pattern. My earlier experience of muteness, and then the severe stammer, left me acutely aware of what it is like to be unable to express oneself. Deprived of language we become powerless – we are nobody.

When I first arrived at Parkville it was somehow different from the Queen Victoria. Parkville was bigger and more threatening because the patients seemed 'madder' and sadder. I was immediately struck by the languor of many of the patients who sank into old vinyl-covered armchairs arrayed around the edges of the day room. Cigarettes dangled from their trembling nicotine-stained fingers. Other patients paced up and down the corridor like caged lions, heads heavy and eyes fixed giving a sense of quiet desperation. Many of them shuffled. Their hands shook and their bodies were hunched and stiff. I wondered why they were so slow and cumbersome in their gait. Many were young people, and it alarmed me that they looked so old and frail, as if afflicted by physical disability. They couldn't get up and walk off briskly; it was as if they were dragging a ball and chain behind them. The term for this is 'Parkinsonism' because it looks like Parkinson's Disease. Parkinsonism is a reaction to Modecate, a drug given by injection. It is a long-acting preparation – I can still see the thick sesame-oil medium in the ampoule with a viscosity that allows it to stay in the body's system for a long time. This means that you can be treated by injections every two weeks or monthly, so staff don't have to rely on you to remember to take tablets. I learnt from my fellow patients the intricacies of the 'Modecate Shuffle'. There are medications that supposedly reduce the severity of these side-effects but in my experience their efficacy was minimal, and they often had their own side-effects, like blurred vision.

The so-called 'typical' antipsychotic drugs used in psychiatry at that time, 1976, were pretty crude. These medications made us dizzy, drowsy, restless, constipated, caused our mouths to over-salivate and dribble or dried them up, made us lose our sexual functioning, blurred our vision, gave us tremors, stiffened our muscles, caused our eyes to roll back, made us sensitive to sunlight, disrupted our menstrual cycles, caused our breasts to lactate, turned our walk to a shuffle. The doozy of them all must be the side-effect known as Tardive Dyskinesia where your body jerks uncontrollably with repetitive movements, the arms and torso writhing and the neck and head jolting back and forwards.

Features of Tardive Dyskenesia may also include grimacing, tongue protrusion, and lip smacking. There is no cure for this frightening condition. As you can see, the medications for mental illness could be worse – and definitely more stigmatising – than the illness itself.

I also noticed that the faces of some fellow patients looked like cardboard masks – blank and featureless, without smiles or frowns, without emotion. Their manner was bland too; they had lost the capacity to respond with any animation to what was happening around them. They were socially withdrawn and remote, isolated as if in a bell jar. I didn't know then if the medications were causing this, or whether it was their illness. I have since learned that this blankness is attributed to what are called negative symptoms that have nothing to do with medication, it is simply another symptom of schizophrenia. It is very distressing, even tragic, to see how it isolates a person.

INMATES

Psychiatric institutions have a particular culture: at Parkville Psychiatric Unit it revolved around an *us-and-them* mentality. We were in a madhouse and felt the eyes of the world upon us, with all its discomfort about mad people. When we went on an outing as a group we could feel the stares. I guess we must have looked odd, with our Modecate Shuffles and Stelazine Stomps, with our shakes and tremors, our faraway looks and glazed eyes. I learnt about stigma and what it felt like to be an outcast, even if much of it was in my own mind.

I learned a lot in the madhouse. Patients were influenced by the behaviours around them and often there was a domino effect. When one patient became aggressive or distressed, this would set off a chain reaction and others would follow suit. People were easily upset because they were very fragile. I'm sure my symptoms and behaviour were intensified by what was going on around me. It is probably what would be called being *institutionalised*. I saw people throwing tantrums and being violent, being difficult and non-compliant and refusing medications. I learned what to say to get more medication when I felt I needed it. I could feel myself being drawn into this world. Here was a sub-culture that society knew nothing about; a strange, unruly world yet one with its own rules. I was changed forever by the people I met and by my mind's inward journey. It showed me the possibility of other worlds and other ways of seeing the world. Suddenly there were many realities that didn't coincide with mine.

There was also a lively culture around cigarettes. Smoking takes on a life of its own in a psychiatric setting, where, it seems, the long draw on that last cigarette becomes a matter of life and death. According to one study (by Jablensky et al.), 73 per cent of men and 56 per cent of women with mental illness smoke. Often smoking is the only thing of comfort to someone in an emotional crisis. For many, having a cigarette is relaxing, and a legitimate way to take time out. Patients in psychiatric hospitals are often poor, on pensions and out of work. In the days when you spent weeks and months in a hospital, it was sometimes hard to buy cigarettes, especially if you were in the locked ward and unable to access a bank, or money was tight. It wasn't uncommon for the women in the hospital kiosk to give patients credit until the next pension day. Chatting with a nurse was often done while having a cigarette. (Psychiatric nurses themselves are among the heaviest smokers in these institutions.) Smoking with fellow patients was also relaxing and a time for serious and meaningful discussions. If someone couldn't afford but craved a cigarette, fellow patients were often generous. A subtle way of giving someone a cigarette was to leave one half-smoked in an ashtray for another to finish.

I myself have never smoked more than one puff. The idea of inhaling a foul-smelling substance turned me off at an early age. I was always appalled when my mother lit up a cigarette as soon as she got in the car to drive me to school. Being a non-smoker meant I had to suffer rooms of thick, billowing clouds, inhaling gales of smoke. In the locked ward it was atrocious. I was a captive in this mad smokers' paradise of overflowing ashtrays. In later years, smokers were encouraged to go outside to the courtyards. Although these then became littered with butts and ash, it was better than sitting in stifling interiors with the smell of burning tobacco and wafts of smoke in your watering eyes.

THE GIFT OF FRIENDSHIP

In the madhouse, everyone was in emotional turmoil, and therefore relationships of abnormal intensity formed between people who would not otherwise make a connection. One friendship I enjoyed watching emerge was between Fred and a Greek woman named Helena. They danced around the ward like a prince and princess. Fred would call longingly to Helena along the passageway and she would joyously call back, then they would laugh and chatter like new lovers. They sustained each other in their regal realm of madness. Such friendships, in the desert of mental illness, are oases of life-saving sustenance: mad people like everyone else make alliances to give each other the support needed to face the world. I don't know how many of those friendships would have endured once they had left hospital. I have one friend from my Parkville days, Gail, whom I still see and whose friendship, 33 years later, I greatly value.

When I met Gail, she was suffering from anorexia nervosa, just like the woman I had met at the Queen Victoria. Gail understands emotional desperation because she has been there in those desolate spaces of the mind. I have seen her go through many bouts of depression and anxiety that accompany her eating disorder. Gail was literally trying to eat her way out of Parkville, having been incarcerated because she had made herself dangerously thin. Over the years I watched her struggle with her anorexia, never really understanding her illness even though she tried to explain it to me. Her case illustrates to me how difficult it is to understand another's mental processes. Madness is like that.

Gail and I had picked each other as lesbians: one's lesbian 'gaydar' is usually pretty accurate. It was such a relief to find a soul-mate in an otherwise homophobic world. She was the only person in that environment with whom I felt safe talking about Robbie and Dido. Gail was self-conscious about her sexuality and once, when her partner came to see her, they experienced the homophobia of the hospital staff. They were sitting in Gail's room with the door slightly ajar when suddenly, a nurse in whom Gail had confided that she was a lesbian, flung open the door and announced: *We don't have the doors closed during visiting hours*. This horrified Gail and her partner. From that moment they always felt they were being watched. Gail and I were drawn to each other, not only by our sexuality but also by a passion for poetry and literature. I would visit Gail in her room when she was allowed to have visitors and we would talk about poetry and books we had read. We would talk about our lives and what we had done at university, what we might do when we got out of hospital. But Gail had to earn the privilege of having visitors by gaining a certain predetermined level of weight. Only when she had achieved this was I allowed to see her.

Because the doctors thought we were both too unwell to be out of hospital, Gail and I were unable to go home to celebrate Christmas with our friends. I was fixated in my delusional world and overwhelmed by my continuing feelings of being evil. I was also experiencing some obtrusive side-effects from the medications: my eyes were rolling back into their sockets, I was extremely restless, my blood pressure was low, making me sway when I stood up, and I was very drowsy. Gail was still too underweight to leave her room, though she was allowed to go the dining room just for the Christmas lunch. This wasn't a very festive season. The hospital was almost empty. We ate with a handful of ragbag patients, some visibly hallucinating, others talking to their voices, while others sat in complete silence. Just a few staff supervised us. For Christmas lunch we ate overcooked chicken and limp vegetables. For dessert we had red jelly and fruit. We drank orange fizzy drink. In the background we could hear the lions over at the zoo roaring for their food. The atmosphere was dank with disappointment. We marked the occasion with cursory acknowledgment of the day, before slinking off to our beds to sleep away our misery and the stifling effects of our medications. Gail and I often recall how tragic that whole episode was and recognise that we have survived, after all these years, to tell the tale with humour and fondness. She did eventually eat her way out of the hospital, gaining enough weight to be discharged a few months after me.

S

DARK AND INGLORIOUS DAYS

I spent two-and-a-half months in the Parkville Psychiatric Unit trying to sort through the web of delusions and hallucinations that had separated me from the real world. (These were the days when admissions were for weeks and months, if not years.) The Unit, in the middle 1970s, was *the* psychiatric hospital in which to be incarcerated if you were a student or inclined to the arts. The hospital was located near the University of Melbourne, which might explain why the patients seemed to be such interesting people – there were a lot of poets and 'alternative' types amongst them. While I could not forget for a minute that I was in a madhouse, I also found it a fascinating place full of memorable and creative characters.

One was a philosopher, Julian, who had schizophrenia. He was a gentle and peaceful man whose suffering was masked by his outward calmness, although he did have a slight tic. His eyes had a distinctive look about them: intense and piercing, fixed and distant. I saw many with eyes like his in my madhouse travels – the unmistakable eyes of madness! Four years ago, to my surprise, I met Julian again in a café and discovered he was suffering a side-effect of his psychiatric medication. He had developed the dreaded Tardive Dyskinesia. All eyes in the cafe focused on him, people gawping at him incredulously as his face grimaced involuntarily and his body contorted. He was like a marionette, with someone pulling and twisting the strings so that his torso and limbs went in different directions in a horribly perverse way. I felt so sad for him.

Julian remembered me and we talked briefly. He told me he had one of the worst cases of Tardive Dyskinesia the doctors had seen. I had actually written a poem about him not long after I left the Parkville Unit because he had made such an impression on me.

Julian
Gaunt, cadaverous,
blackened eyes,
stilted movements.
Body this way
now that way
grimaces and contortions.
What anguish that face exudes.
And those eyes!
Those glazed, crazed eyes
which stare.

That time of my life, in the hospital, is almost indescribable. I didn't know who I was. I had become a stranger in my own skin. I was preoccupied with my crazy thoughts and voices. As I walked along the long corridors, my father's voice would summon me: *Sandra, Sandra, come home. I want you to kill your mother*. I was alarmed at what he was telling me, probably because I *had* fantasised about killing her. Her alcoholism had disturbed me so much and I had felt so helpless that I still had terrible musings about releasing her, and us, from her alcoholic stupor. Even though it was only a thought, it was an awful thought to own up to. I told no-one about it. And now here was my father exhorting me to do it, as though he had read my mind. It was a terrifying experience. I had no idea how I was going to survive the next second, the next minute, the next hour, the next day. Anything beyond that was unthinkable. I wandered about in a state of limbo, wanting something to happen but not sure what.

> **23/12/76 Wandering about the unit appearing rather vacant at times.**
>
> **24/12/76 Wandering around unit like a lost soul.**

Robbie and Dido and other friends came to see me, but I felt only half there – a complicated jigsaw puzzle with many pieces missing. I was trapped inside my mind, unable to connect with the outside world. I could see it but not feel it.

The psychiatrists seemed to focus on the fact that I was a lesbian. Homophobia was alive and well in Australia in 1976. In the USA homosexuality was still categorised as a mental illness up until 1974, when it was taken out of the *Diagnostic and Statistical Manual of Mental Disorder* (*DSM*) of the American Psychiatric Association. I was aware the doctors thought my lesbianism was a possible cause or symptom of my mental illness, though they never said that to my face. Their unspoken, but very obvious, homophobia, made me feel more alienated than I already was. I wasn't comfortable talking about my relationships with Robbie and Dido and only reluctantly answered questions about my living arrangements. Besides, Robbie and Dido were not acknowledged as my primary carers, although they were. This meant that they were not kept informed of my progress in the hospital even though it was known that I lived with them, in what was noted in my records as a *lesbian menage-à-trois*.

The psychiatrists were quick to make judgments about my future, too. One psychiatrist said this about me:

> **12/12/76 Personality Profile. Walking contradiction, capable of many things, but of nothing. Enjoys reading, creative things like writing and sketching. Would like to be an artist - maybe presumptuous. Tends to be arrogant, tries not to be, likes to use words with precision.**

'Walking contradiction' – in writing this book I find I have used the same words to describe myself. Contradictions have become apparent in so much of my personal experience – in my yearning for a spiritual life and simultaneous dismissal of religion, in my need to be comforted while at the same time shrinking from human touch, in my humour and darkness. Was I really 'capable of many things, but of nothing'? Was I artistically presumptuous, arrogant? At the time I was exploring ways to express myself and any creativity was in its formative stage, but the psychiatrist questioned my ability to fulfil my creative dreams. I wonder which of us was being presumptuous? In this baffling setting, where one loses any confidence in one's identity, my abrasiveness and apparent arrogance masked my loss of a sense of self.

This, my first descent into madness, was a hellish journey. I learnt awful things about myself; I was amazed at the strange machinations of my mind, – what it manufactured in its madness – all from somewhere deep in my interior life. This torment, which twisted my thoughts and feelings beyond recognition, felt like what I can only describe as mental rape.

I began increasingly to look at the world through a darkening glass, the future uncertain. I was in a foreign place, where I couldn't understand the language, and the customs were alien. I felt like an outsider, but soon I adopted the language and ways of this world: I tottered and shuffled and paced the floor, mumbled through my cotton wool headpiece, dribbled here and there one moment, choked on a dry mouth the next. My career as a psychiatric patient had begun. My unquiet mind had been pierced by the steely shards of madness.

I remember that time
of dark and inglorious days
when the world whimpered
but did not cry
while my mind drowned in madness.

SLEEPING BEAUTY

I spent a total of three and a half months in the Queen Victoria Hospital and the Parkville Psychiatric Unit and during that time I had no idea what had gone on in the wider world: what events were shaping the political scene, what cultural happenings were defining our lives, what music was playing on the radio. Madness had cast a spell over me and I was Sleeping Beauty awaiting the kiss of sanity. Every day was a struggle but each day brought gradual improvement. The threads of my life hung in tangled skeins as I tried to unravel them, then weave them back together into a fabric of sense. I craved peace of mind. Every day a little bit of sanity pushed its way through my madness and each day I began to feel stronger and more in control of my thoughts. The voices were fading. The paranoia began to abate and my thoughts became clearer.

22/2/77 Follow Up & Prognosis

Sandra was discharged after two and half months in Hospital on Trifluoperazine 10mg mane, 30mg nocte, Cogentin 2mg b.d and Valium 2mg b.d. Arrangements have been made for her follow up at Larundel Hospital. Her prognosis is probably reasonably good as she has good

> **basic intelligence, a fair network of social supports and made an almost complete recovery from her first acute schizophrenic episode when treated with phenothiazines.**

After my discharge from Parkville on 22 February 1977, Robbie and Dido took me back to Warrandyte where they cared for me. Even now I cannot express enough gratitude for their kindness. They could easily have washed their hands of me. I felt like a burden. I was heavily medicated and don't remember a lot about those early times. I do know I was so glad to be home, to be with our dog and cats and my friends again. They looked after me: they cooked meals, made sure I took my medication, gave me somewhere to feel at peace and allowed me to just be. Having no income, I survived on sickness benefits.

Day after day I sat immobilised in a chair with my rambling thoughts drifting off into dream-like places, in a paralysed nothingness. I let much wash over me and didn't communicate much. My thinking was troubled by my uncertain future. Would I become trapped in that terrifying, tortured, mad world again? I feared this possibility but got on with life. I couldn't let myself sink into a hole and give up; I had to live as though I wouldn't be mad again. There were things that helped me through these months: friendship, sport, music, poetry, animals and humour. There was also something within my own character that refused to succumb to the poison. We may never understand what makes us mad but we can seek to understand what makes us well.

I decided to study Latin at the Council of Adult Education and there I found myself in a classroom with older, wiser and extraordinarily interesting people. In contrast, I felt dull and boring, with nothing to contribute in conversations. I began viola lessons in the hope this would make me a more interesting person. My friend Karen, who also lived with schizophrenia, was learning violin from a cultured European woman, Madame

Feuchtersleben. Karen took me along to see Madame who suggested I learn viola instead of the violin because she needed more viola players for her little orchestra. I wasn't fussy so I bought a cheap Chinese viola and started taking lessons. I finally had the chance to become a music-maker rather than just a listener. I remain grateful for that impulse. I later taught myself the violin and still enjoy playing folk fiddle with friends. Music is a source of immense enjoyment and I often stop and think of how privileged I am to have the opportunity to make music with other people. I think it *has* made me a more interesting person.

I needed to know more about schizophrenia, having passively taken on this onerous label. Ignorance was not bliss. I went to the library and read up on it. I was the one in a hundred afflicted by this illness. The word *schizophrenia* was first used in 1911 by the Swiss psychiatrist Eugen Bleuler. Its symptoms are delusional thinking, characterised as fixed, firm beliefs that are not based in reality, auditory and visual hallucinations, and thought disorder. Schizophrenia was seen as the cancer of psychiatry, an enigmatic and devastating condition that baffled those who observed it. For a long time, before the invention of anti-psychotic medication, there was nothing that could be done to help sufferers who were visibly terrorised by their terrible affliction. Even though there were treatments for schizophrenia in 1976, the prognosis for someone with it was poor. It was looked upon as a virtual death-sentence, one was thought by members of the medical profession as being doomed to a relentless deterioration into impregnable madness. I dared not look into the future, it was too terrible to contemplate.

I learnt that in schizophrenia everyday reality mixes with bizarre hallucinations. A sufferer may be able to watch television or read the paper yet see devils in the wall. There is a nightmare quality to the schizophrenic experience. It is not uncommon for people to have delusions of grandeur in which they see themselves as messianic figures like Jesus Christ or John Lennon. People may think God is speaking to them or is sending them messages, via billboards or television. Many think they are being watched by espionage agencies like the FBI, CIA, or ASIO, or that their home is bugged, or surveillance cameras are hidden in light fittings or in the walls. They may think that alien forces are controlling their minds. Voices, delusions and hallucinations have a surrealist quality: strange images are juxtaposed like a Salvador Dali painting. The bizarre stuff of psychosis is unimaginable, the repertoire of the psychotic mind is unlimited. My vibrant psychotic life was proof of this.

I also did a lot of general reading. I rediscovered D.H. Lawrence and found George Orwell, Dostoyevsky, Tolstoy, Virginia Woolf and many more. I read poetry and history, philosophy and sociological works, dipping in and out of books at my leisure. For all the reading, I'm not sure I took in much because my mind was blurred and preoccupied at the time, but reading gave me comfort. I felt I was doing something. I also started sitting in on lectures at La Trobe University. I wandered the campus trying to take myself back to the most carefree of my student days. It felt like a safe place. Yet I did these things without a lot of spirit; with little hope. I was merely going through the motions of my life.

I developed a fixation on the letterbox, one which l still have. Every day I would keenly listen for the postie, and on hearing his motorbike's whining engine, hasten to the letterbox hoping that it might contain a letter giving me the good news that madness would never touch me again. When this good news came it would change my life for the better and I would be like my friends. I would have a future I could look forward to in eager anticipation of achievements and successes. It seemed a reasonable thing to want, but as I was to find out, my wishes were beyond the constraints of my illness. The letter never came.

After some months I felt less emotionally burdened, and free of the delusions and the voices. I hoped I'd never have to listen to those abusive voices again. I began to think I was cured. Sleeping Beauty had awakened. I was still having unpleasant side-effects from the medication. My eyes regularly rolled into the back of their sockets, and even while sedated, I restlessly paced the floor. My doctor decided to take me off all medication. I had been free of symptoms for some time and he thought this, my first psychotic episode, might have been a one-off thing. Within twelve months, however, my mind was again filled with wailing voices: *You evil bitch, you evil bitch, we know who you are, evil bitch*. In the mirror I saw myself as a witch again, with dark powers, screeching. I was the bringer of evil to the world. Madness returned with furious intensity. I became lost in its dark labyrinthine passages, at the end of which awaited the Virgin Mary. Soon I was back in hospital. This time it was Larundel Psychiatric Hospital.

S

MADHOUSE ON THE EDGE OF TOWN

Larundel was a large madhouse. It had been built in the 1930s, at Bundoora, then an outer rural district of Melbourne. Suburban sprawl has since enveloped it. Larundel was a conglomeration of old and new buildings. The old part was characterised by dark red-brick, two-storey Tudor-style buildings. The administration, laundry, kitchen and social-work offices were in these, as well as A ward, a short-term, acute, locked ward, and B ward, which was an open ward. The newer north and south wards were uninspiring rectangular cream-brick buildings, built in the 1950s to accommodate the increasing number of psychiatric patients. I have been told by a former maintenance worker at Larundel in the 1960s that there were dungeon-like tunnels beneath the hospital grounds and buildings, where some patients were purportedly kept like prisoners. This has to be an urban myth.

Gardens and paddocks surrounded these buildings. There were rose-beds, exotic plants and plenty of big native eucalypts. I often strolled through the grounds lost in thought, breathing deeply before going back to the suffocating ward. Often I met sheepish couples covered in grass coming from the top paddocks, glancing at each other with knowing looks and trying to walk by nonchalantly. The gardens were a small fragment of asylum between the stifling wards. At night these same gardens were dark, and I was full of fear that an assailant could be lurking there. By day it was different and I looked forward to my strolls, to talking to the roses and sitting beneath the eucalypts for a peaceful moment.

In the middle of the hospital, next to the football oval, was a kiosk, to which people made afternoon pilgrimages to buy cigarettes, soft drinks, milk shakes, confectionary and other consolations for the atrocious hospital food. It was a meeting place where we caught up on hospital gossip. Sometimes our conversations were loose fragments tenuously held together by a flimsy ribbon of coherence, tragic reminders of how disengaged from the world we had become. The women who served in the kiosk were kind and helpful, never being too judgemental of behaviour that would have been frowned upon outside the hospital. They didn't growl at the person who refused to pay for their cigarettes, or when someone became angry because there were no ice-creams left. They humoured the person saying he was Jesus Christ and had come to save the world. They sometimes sounded patronising, but mostly accommodating and pleasant.

My admission notes said the following:

> 6/1/78 Mental State On Admission. A quiet, dark, long haired girl sitting in a school jumper, jeans and runners, speaking with her head hung low. Her sensorium was clear, orientation and memory intact. Her affect was flattened. There was no clear evidence of any hallucinations, but one got the feeling of a delusional mood. There was no formal thought disorder but there was certainly a poverty of production. She was aware that something was wrong but was not happy about coming to hospital.
>
> Diagnosis and Formulation. A 25 year old post-graduate girl, living in a lesbian menage-

> **a-trois, admitted for the second time with a relapse of her schizophrenia. The main features being her inappropriate affect, her autistic delusional thinking and nihilistic content.**

On this first admission to Larundel, I was taken to B ward, situated upstairs in part of the original hospital building. It was comfortable with single rooms and a large kitchen/day area, a nurses' station and consulting rooms. I quite liked it. But soon after getting there I was alarmed by bloodcurdling screams and slamming doors. It turned out B was directly above A, the locked ward, and those disturbing noises were coming from down there. Often the nurses on B ward would get a call and have to dash downstairs to assist with a difficult patient. Later, I would listen to people who had come from there telling spine-chilling stories of mistreatment, forced medication and seclusion rooms. I hoped I would never end up in that hell-hole.

I remember myself as shy and downcast on admission, a crumpled heap who sat miserably in the chair while everything drifted over me like a vapour. I hadn't the energy or spirit to engage with anyone, or the lucidity to comprehend my perilous position. My inner world preoccupied me and manufactured a grossly vivid life of its own. I heard voices babbling: *Bitch, bitch you will freeze in your evil. You are our messenger. You are our carrier of pestilence. Your evil emanations will suffocate the world.* The voices harassed me with admonitions and vile accusations: that I perpetrated the most heinous deeds and ultimately was responsible for every bad thing in the world. I became fixated on my extraordinary sense of having the capacity to contaminate anyone who came into physical contact with me. This power to contaminate others kept me to myself. I was oozing evil. I pulled away in horror from people who tried to hug or touch me. I kept my distance from everyone. I saw myself as a twisted, tortured soul, like the ones I had seen in Bruegel's or Bosch's paintings.

> **15/1/78 . . . conversing with a friend on her shoulder and she can see the Madonna on a cross in the glass of the door . . . feels depressed . . .**

In my hallucination, the Virgin Mary was fixed in a contorted posture to a cross. She had on a white dress and blue veil and was terrifyingly beautiful. A golden aura highlighted her perfect face and holy body. I related cosmically to her suffering.

My flirtation with Catholicism had embedded its symbols and rituals deep into my psyche and they surfaced in my madness. The Virgin Mary shone in my hallucinations – beautiful, but with the distinct look of the plaster statues you see in Catholic churches. Even though I had by this time rejected Catholicism, it was like a cloak I couldn't cast off. The fact that I now saw it as a religion riven by power and corruption didn't stop me hallucinating its symbols. In my journey through madness I was beset with feelings of profound evil and visions of the Virgin Mary. Perhaps, in another age, I would have been hailed as a seer, a saint, a religious ecstatic or a prophet. Or been burned at the stake as a witch or heretic.

Because of this intimate connection between religion and my madness, I now strive to stay entirely within the rationality of the intellect, to keep any irrationality at bay. When I rejected Catholicism, I rejected all religion. I am an atheist, having no belief in a God or spiritual transcendence. My mentor and friend, Werner, used to remind me that atheism and religion are alike in that proponents of both are intractable in their convictions: one believes there is no God and the other is just as convinced that there is. Werner's agnostic position proposed that we could never know the truth about God and must leave ourselves open to all possibilities. I wish I could be as open minded about it, but my pessimistic rationality always leads me to the desolate conclusion that we have nothing but our flawed material selves. In light of this, my spiritual nourishment must come from somewhere else.

I continue to find other people's religious devotion difficult to accept and uncomfortable to be around. Why? It is not only because religion feeds into my madness; it is also because other people's faith makes me conscious of my own unresolved search for answers and meaning. I feel a spiritual longing I am unable to satisfy. In acknowledging my dilemma, I know I can't risk religion. It's too dangerous for me. But for all this rationality, my delusions and hallucinations continued to feature the religious imagery that imprinted itself in my youth.

What power does one's culture, particularly its religious and messianic figures, have in influencing the manifestations of psychosis? Does a Hindu psychotic hallucinate Krishna? Does a Rastafarian hear the voice of Haile Selassie? Many people diagnosed with schizophrenia have strong religious beliefs. Some say they are in communication with God or other spiritual beings. Others declare they have a messianic mission to fulfil. I once got to spend time in hospital with three men who all thought they were Jesus Christ, simultaneously! Some report conversations with angels, saints or other deities. Others have hallucinations of iconic religious figures such as the Virgin Mary.

Religion can be a comfort for those who experience emotional disquiet. In the surging waters of madness, it is something to hold onto, to keep one's head above the tide. For as long as I have been mad and have witnessed madness around me, I have pondered the fine line between religious devotion and religious mania. When does one cross that imperceptible line, the hairbreadth space between comforting faith and psychotic fixation? My own religious inclination, and the way it has permeated my psychosis, showed me how profoundly immersion in the seas of religion and its symbols can penetrate the psyche. In a paper written for the *American Journal of Psychiatry*, S. Kapur suggests that 'since delusions are constructed by the individual they are imbued with the psychodynamic themes relevant to the individual and are embedded in the cultural context of the individual.' I am an example of this process.

Because I had a history of difficulties with Stelazine, the psychiatrists at Larundel decided to start me on Melleril, a slightly less potent antipsychotic drug. However, they used a massive dosage to treat my illness. It left me heavily sedated and in a drowsy and numbed state; I wafted through the ward like a shade from the underworld in black jeans and windcheater. But even with Melleril I had side-effects. My eyes rolled back into their sockets so frequently that I could have painted the Sistine Chapel standing up. This would happen at any time, and last from 20 minutes to several hours. It was bewildering for anyone with me at the time because I had to stop what I was doing while I waited for my eyes to come down. I found that tiredness or eye strain could induce a crisis. I discovered by chance, however, that if I watched television my eyes would stop rolling. It had something to do with relaxing my eyes and forgetting about them, because the more stressed I became, the longer they stayed up. Finally, after a couple of years of enduring this worrying condition, a nurse told me I was having an *Oculargyric crisis*. Just knowing this helped. I had a name for my mysterious and distressing affliction. But even taking Cogentin as an antidote didn't stop it happening.

During this admission I met Dr Y. She was to become my treating doctor for the next 27 years. I preferred a female psychiatrist because I related better to women. She looked after me during subsequent admissions to Larundel and continued to see me long after she had left Larundel to go into private practice.

She intrigued me because she was intelligent and had a self-confidence that gave me comfort. She appeared in control of things. Perhaps she could heal me? And for the first time I had someone on whom I could unload the traumatic memories of my unhappy childhood.

My fall back into madness in 1978 was a bitter blow. I had tried to live as though my insanity were an aberration that would never happen again. Now I had to countenance the possibility that it might be with me always. I admonished myself for being weak and pathetic. Couldn't I have done something to resist another episode? Could I have done things differently? This episode set the tone for the many that followed. My symptoms became more fanciful and I grew more miserable. It was difficult for everyone around me. I couldn't break the cycle. I became a classic revolving-door patient, in and out of hospital at regular intervals without ever getting on top of the illness. Rather, I felt it was on top of me, pressing and smothering me.

WILD PLACES

At Easter of 1978, we moved away from Warrandyte to a two-hectare bush property on the outer fringe of Melbourne on which we had built a small wooden house – a dream of Robbie and Dido's. They had bought the land and borrowed a small amount of money from the bank. In those days money was hard to borrow, especially if one were female and single. Dido had to dress up in her best clothes and meet with the bank manager, who would determine whether or not she was of good enough character as well as sufficiently financially secure to obtain the loan. She had to detail her earning capacity and job security. And just about promise her first-born to the bank to secure the loan! The loan paid for the building materials and for a builder to erect a frame. We built the rest with the help of Robbie's father.

In between my mad times, I did manage to live an interesting and active life. I had my music and intellectual interests, and there was also a ten-year period between 1977 and 1987 when Robbie, Dido and I bushwalked. Before we met Dido, she had trekked in the High Plains of Victoria and south-west Tasmania. I was hesitant when Robbie and Dido suggested the three of us go bushwalking. We started with easier walks in Victoria, but then they wanted to go to Tasmania where the walking is much harder. My physical health was very good but I feared I might go mad in a remote part of Tasmania, days away from medical help.

I knew how much they wanted to go, however, so I agreed.

Our first Tasmanian trip was in 1978 to Cradle Mountain – Lake St Clair National Park, a stunningly beautiful place. The walking was challenging. It required long hard days of continuous physical demands. The heavy pack weighed on my shoulders and by day's end was painful. The weather was changeable; sometimes snow would fall and the icy wind sliced our faces. At other times the sun seared our skin. In this harsh environment we were tested but I knew I was in good hands with Robbie and Dido. They were very good at map reading and had good bush skills. They in turn had confidence in me. They believed I could do it and were willing to take the risk.

Over the next ten years we walked often in Tasmania. Our most difficult trip was the South Coast Track: eight days of hard, relentless walking. We walked along beaches, through knee-deep mud on button-grass plains, climbed a mountain, crossed many creeks and rowed across a swelling river. The wind howled and the weather was bleak for much of that trip. But it was unforgettable; the terrain and vegetation were relatively untouched. After the walk I felt a sense of achievement and thought that if I could walk the South Coast Track, then I could do anything.

However, there was a downside to bushwalking. I found the pain from carrying the pack almost unendurable. But worse, the effects of my medication made me listless and fatigued. And because it made my eyes roll, walking was sometimes impossible. My eyes could roll several times a day and when this happened I couldn't see the ground or where to put my feet. There was pressure to keep going because we had to reach the campsite each night, which meant I stumbled much of the way as I tried to keep up. It was a combination of my eyes, and the pain, that finally made me decide to give up walking. I remember the moment. We were on a button-grass plain, up to our waists in water, trying to cross a creek on a submerged log, my eyes were rolling, and

I vowed to myself that I would never put myself in a dangerous position like this again.

I never went bushwalking again but I feel grateful for having experienced the simple joys of remote and wild places – to feel their 'sanity'. I consider myself a lucky madwoman.

I always felt Mother Nature was looking after me on these treks because even though they were physically and psychologically demanding, I never went mad. In fact, I felt saner in these wild places than anywhere else. Why? It is a mystery to me but the compelling necessity to survive drew on my instincts and allowed me to push myself beyond anything I thought I was capable of. My father always said I could be very determined.

S

SHE GENTLY BRUSHED MY HAIR

In July 1978 I suffered another psychotic episode. This time I found myself in the dreaded A ward in Larundel. It was the place I had heard such spine-chilling stories about, and from where the screaming had come. Now I was in that place. It was an awful, dilapidated bedlam with huge dormitories, primitive bathrooms and paint peeling from the walls.

> **20/7/78 Mental State On Admission. Presented as a rather mysterious young woman with long black hair giving a superficial impression of poetry and art personified. Underneath all this however, she was quite disordered and deluded, obviously preoccupied with her inner fantasy.**
>
> **Diagnosis and Formulation. Exacerbation of a schizophrenic illness in an intelligent young woman who is an arts graduate, unemployed and living in a lesbian menage-a-trois.**

Why was I *mysterious*? What did they mean by *superficial impression of poetry and art personified*? How must I have appeared to them? This was the second time a psychiatrist had commented on my poetic tendencies and on both occasions it was in a negative and judgemental tone. How could they know it was only a *superficial impression of poetry and art*? This was a cryptic note by a psychiatrist who didn't know what to make of me. Was I that unusual?

It was late at night when I was admitted and I was petrified. In psychosis your inner world is hostile. A hostile external world, such as the one I was now confronted by, only exacerbates it. Larundel seemed a dingy hell-hole and I feared for my life in it. The staff were keen to make me talk but I was unable to articulate my needs. I was more concerned about what was going on in my head. There were voices warning me: *They want to kill you. They hate your guts. They know how evil you are. They want to put you in a black hell-hole. They are going to take you away to a dungeon and leave you there to rot in your own piss and shit.* Then the voices chanted over and over: *Don't trust them, don't trust them.*

The nurses grabbed me. I resisted. I tried to protect myself. They threw me around the room and forced me into the bathroom. They pulled my jeans and underpants down and threw me onto a toilet. A jar was thrust between my legs. They demanded I give a specimen there and then. I couldn't. I sat there willing myself to piss. How long would I be a victim of these agents of the Devil? I wanted to be somewhere else where things like this didn't happen. My voices were laughing at me. Eventually I pissed and was allowed to get off the toilet. I was prisoner to these monsters. The doors were locked and I had no-one to protect me. The Antichrist was about to make an appearance. Everyone was in league with the Devil.

Do I trust the vividness of this memory? Is my imagination taking over? My memories of the times I have been unhinged stagger even me, but why would I not have memories of what happened? I was there, not some stranger. There is always the danger of creating a false memory. But I was terrified that night and I cannot forget that terror.

Soon after, I was sitting in the day room, distressed and weeping. The television was clattering in the background. A few of the male patients were laughing at me and saying *She's on drugs. She's a hooch smoker*. They were scornful, pointing their fingers and gesturing rudely at me. Suddenly, an old woman came up to where I was seated. She started brushing my long hair. She stroked my hair, gently pulling a brush through its matted strands. Only a woman could have done what she did. Her gentle, feminine hands holding the brush and patting my hair were for every woman who has ever been in a madhouse. Her face was serene. She whispered to me in a foreign language I didn't recognise. It was a poignant moment that showed how the kindness of a stranger could make all the difference, that not everyone was a monster.

I eventually went to bed and never saw her again. The nursing notes don't mention this incident (could I have imagined it?); all they say is this:

> **20/7/78 Had difficulty in getting Sandra into bed. She was crying and saying everything was "black" and that she was seeing the Devil.**

As She Gently Brushed My Long Hair

As the solid door closed behind me
and the brusque nurses led me to the locked ward,
I felt the world abandon me.
I felt myself abandon the world.

Before me were the forgotten people
who shuffled and gazed mysteriously into space,
and I was no-one, just another nutter,
just someone caught in a cosmic game
where sanity and madness are engaged in a bitter battle.

But something wonderful transpired
and through my barriers came the unexpected.
She spoke no English;
she spoke a universal language
that broke through all my sorrow and madness.
And sitting in the day room weeping
I was suddenly transported to a kingdom of love,
and a calm ensued
as she gently brushed my long hair.

I was discharged from A ward the next day after begging Dr Y to let me out. Maybe the trauma of being in there shocked me back to sanity because this episode of madness was short and sharp. Dr Y was happy for me to go home with Robbie and Dido.

There is a marvellous moment at the end of Tennessee Williams' play *A Streetcar Named Desire*, where Blanche DuBois, broken and lost, is taken from her sister's house by a doctor and nurse from the local asylum. After a forlorn struggle she stumbles to the floor. The doctor senses her despair and offers her a steadying hand. She responds with the famous words: *Whoever you are – I have always depended on the kindness of strangers*. There is a poignancy about these words that rings all too true for the mentally ill. Mad people have to suffer judgemental and dismissive gazes in trams, trains, cafes, parks, at the footy, in church, at the tennis club, next door or on the street. One nerve-wracking aspect of suffering schizophrenia is the uncertainty, never knowing when I am next going to humiliate myself with manifestations of an illness that does not obey the rules of society. There are countless moments when I have said and done things that are later as incomprehensible to me as to those around me. I have been seen muttering to the Devil, or in raptures at visions of the Virgin Mary. I have cried with the agony of being told I am evil, and have accused friends of trying to kill me. The crazy woman in the street could be me. The crazy woman in the street is me! I am constantly at the mercy of the kindness of strangers like the kind woman who brushed my hair that day or like the doctor who offered Blanche DuBois his hand.

I often think about the woman who brushed my hair and the other people I met in hospital. I wonder what happened to this cast of tragic-comic characters who paraded before me in all their guises? How many survived, how many suicided, how many got better? Psychiatric hospitals were extraordinary places, full of the most extraordinary people. Some were colourful, like Fred and Helena with their dance of madness; Patrick, the bipolar poet, who corralled people in a corner and read poetry at them; Christine, who wandered the ward talking incessantly to her voices; and Vicki, who shuffled around the ward calling me *lard arse*. Some were helplessly mad, they had to be carried in. Others were so extremely mad they seemed like a different species. I thought these patients could never recover their sanity, but they did. I saw others emerge from the depths of profound depression. They wrenched themselves out of their holes, out of the bog of their miseries, out of their impossible situations. Witnessing such human strength was a privilege. I may have forgotten some of the individuals but I shall always remember them as a group of remarkable characters all dealing with the biting pain of insanity.

SINKING DEEPER

> 19/7/79 Reason & Mode of Referral. . . 26 year old single girl who was admitted with a past history of schizophrenia following an overdose of Imipramine, 30 times 25mg. The overdose was taken in response to auditory hallucinations which told her "to go to sleep and go into the bushes". She also stated that she felt a strong feeling of being evil and that she was going to contaminate any person she spoke to or came in contact with.

I took my first overdose of tablets as a teenager in 1970. I made my second suicide attempt in 1979 with a botched overdose of antidepressants. Final rest beneath the eucalypt was an ever-present motif of my madness at that time – it was the mythical place where my voices compelled me to go and die. The overdose wasn't serious but it landed me in hospital.

My hands have disappeared again. What can I do without hands? Now I can feel again that chewing and gnawing and squirming of the maggots in my head. They never stop, they never rest. Even while I sleep they do their awful work. I know my brain is being eaten away because in the morning my intelligence has diminished. Yet there is a physical pressure building in my cra-

nium. I feel it is near a flash point, like a nuclear explosion. I put a bag over my head to catch the exploding pieces of brain tissue. My voices are at me again: Evil bitch, scum, shit-faced abortion. *They laugh at me.* What a fool, what a fucking, stupid fool you are. Don't lick your lips with your vile tongue, you'll contaminate the world with your saliva. Go to the bush and die, slut.

The memory is backed by the record:

> **26/7/79 Sandra can feel maggots in her brain squirming and chewing. Her hands are intermittently 'disappearing' so that the cardigan sleeves appear just to end abruptly and she has the overwhelming feeling that the bush is calling her to embrace it and die – reinforced by voices which say 'go to the bush'.**

After this episode, Dr Y decided I should apply for what was then called 'the invalid pension'. Up until that point I had either been on sickness benefits or the dole. I guess this was an acknowledgement that I was unlikely to be able to work. Even though I felt bad that I was incapable of earning my own living, it was a relief for me to not have to worry about trying to find a job.

Now, in my later years, I feel I can contribute, can give back to the community, by raising public awareness about mental illness. I fulfil my mutual obligation with my advocacy work. If I can change the attitudes of GPs and health workers, if I can change the public perception of mental illness, if I can help a school student understand what it is like to have schizophrenia, then I feel I have earned my pension. But back then, I could not see the potential for any of this. Neither did the social worker who was assisting me to complete the paperwork for the pension. As I was signing the pension papers, she turned to me and said: *You know it's the end of the line, don't you*. The *end of the line*, I thought, the *end*? She is saying I have no future and nothing to offer society. Do I go outside and jump in front of the first car I see, and get it over and done with? For a long time I saw myself as she saw me: at the end of the line with nowhere to go, a failure.

The social worker
thought I was cactus
a dead loss
a blight on the world. . .
I festered and oozed
and sealed the pus of my madness
in the scab of my life's retreat
which had reached the end of the line
so the social worker from hell said
condemning me to another hell
which had nothing to do with being mad.

The pension wasn't the end of the line for me; rather, it gave me the mental and physical space in which to gather myself together. It gave me the time to read and write. It gave me the opportunity to construct a life around my illness and all its demands. I had space away from the working world in which I did not have to function as a *normal* person. There I could learn to live with my voices and delusions in private, and to develop what talents and capacities I did have. If a society sincerely wishes to help the mentally ill live worthwhile lives, it needs to make such space for them.

CRAZY WOMAN

Each day at home I battled with my morbid thoughts, while Robbie and Dido went to work. People were talking to me over the radio; they could read my mind; voices were telling me to kill myself. *You are the most hideously evil person in the world*, they would convince me. I feared this mind of mine, this unconquerable fortress. It sat in my skull in all its majesty, waging war on me, pushing me further to the brink with every episode of madness. Many times I contemplated suicide to release me from its terror. I had three admissions to Larundel in 1980, 1982 and 1984. My records of those admissions provide a bleak picture.

> 28/5/80 History of Present Illness. Over the previous weeks she had felt very depressed and had considered taking her life. At the same time she heard voices telling her 'she was evil'. Occasionally she felt 'people were talking about her on the radio'.

> 22/5/82 History of Present Illness. She had non-specific paranoid feelings and an increase in the intensity and unpleasantness of her auditory hallucinations which I believe she is never free from. These voices were apparently telling her to harm herself and she believed that she had hurt her sister. The day after

admission she said that she felt she was going to be taken to a firing squad because she was evil. At that time she also described her auditory hallucinations as making her hands go numb and interfering with her concentration. She also felt others could read her thoughts.

27/5/82 Sandra remains quite disturbed. Is delusional about her head being gone and complains that it feels like it will explode. Maintains other delusions that she is evil and will contaminate others - protests when others touch her - tells them to be careful.

8/10/84 Mental State Exam. On admission Sandra presented as a restless young lady, had poor eye contact, her affect was blunted. She was orientated for time place and person and her memory was grossly intact. She seemed to be experiencing auditory hallucinations within the context of disorders of perception, and the stream of her thought was broken and inconsistent and the content seemed to have a depressive quality, thinking about death and dying. There was also marked poverty of thought. Her insight was nil.

11/10/84 Restless this evening at times sitting by herself looking involved in thought. Peering though several windows at times and in conversation, asked whether nursing staff can read her mind. Stated that a 'time bomb was in her head'.

12/10/84 Still very withdrawn and appears apprehensive and frightened. Still appears to be experiencing auditory hallucinations and believing that her mind can be read by others.

During these admissions to Larundel, I spent a lot of time in ward North 5. Inside its walls were stark rooms with lino-covered floors and second-hand furniture placed around the edges of the rooms. The faded curtains were stained with years of cigarette smoke wafting through the threads of cotton. The upstairs bedrooms had no heating or cooling. Each room had four beds and cupboards, arranged to give a semblance of privacy. I had the feeling these rooms had not changed from the time they were built, that no-one knew or cared how awful they were. A piano on which people sometimes desultorily tinkled sat forlornly in the day room. But once a week we had sing-alongs with Dr J; he was a keen musician who vamped at the piano with passion. I found respite from my inner turmoil in singing *Darlin' Clementine* with hillbilly gusto, or *Puff the Magic Dragon* dreamily. I sang *Over the Rainbow* just like Judy Garland, longing to wake up where the clouds were far behind us, where my troubles might *melt like lemon drops*. We sang songs from all the musicals – *My Fair Lady*, *South Pacific* and *The Sound of Music* – at least the first few lines, after which most voices trailed away, leaving only the few who knew all the words singing on. Some sang as if their lives depended on it while others sat deep in their own thoughts, unable to join in. A few danced, in an uninhibited carnival of their own. Picturing myself singing in Mrs Anderson's front room, I forgot for a short time where I was. When I was ill, music often reached into my soul when nothing else could.

An old pool table stood in the day room, its green cloth frayed and dotted with cigarette burns. Many a game of pool had been played on it by a psychotic or depressed patient with none of the customary aplomb of pool-players, sometimes hitting the balls with anger, sometimes with resignation. But it offered respite from boredom. Once I played a game with Paul. He thought he was a messenger from God with prophecies about the impending end of the world. We played a rambling game of eight ball, with Paul stopping mid shot to deliver his message: *God will turn the earth into a fireball and all will be cleansed*. Turning to me he shouted: *You will perish with everyone else!* He dashed the cue down and walked off. He returned minutes later to have his shot and continue his prophecies. From my perspective, these balls moved of their own volition and the cue looked bent. The table was possessed. Neither of us showed any interest in the outcome of the game. We were going through the motions of playing pool, simply filling in time. Curiously, I have played my best pool while psychotic: on regaining my sanity, my deftness with the cue always left me.

During my admission to Larundel in 1980 Dr Y decided that I needed the big-gun medication, because Melleril wasn't enough to deal with the psychosis. Dr Y started me on fortnightly Modecate injections, and Serenace tablets, two powerful drugs that were commonly used for the treatment of schizophrenia. It was a dynamic cocktail. The rolling upwards of my eyes got worse and, to my horror, I started to shuffle, just like the people around me. I felt befuddled. My head was filled with cotton-wool, my thoughts were slow and bland, about nothing. Thankfully the shuffle abated after a while, but my eyes continued to roll. I was to be on these drugs for the next 15 years.

When I wasn't in Larundel I would go to the GP every fortnight to have my Modecate injection. These injections had to be given slowly and carefully because Modecate was a thick preparation, and most GPs had little experience of giving them. My bum felt like a dartboard so I especially appreciated a doctor who could give a painless injection. I even endured the inappropriate behaviour of one particular GP because he didn't hurt me. He would always ceremoniously slap me on the bum after he had given me my injection. He was sleazy and made me cringe, but I didn't make a fuss. My passiveness was a measure of my low self-esteem and spirit. My life was punctuated by these appointments; they became its signposts. I knew when I fronted for my injection that two weeks had gone by and that two weeks were ahead of me before another was due. Nothing else I was doing at the time seemed to measure the passing of time as routinely as these fortnightly jabs.

My sister brought my parents to see me during one of these hospitalisations. She thought it was time they saw me; why I don't know. I had seen my parents infrequently since the middle 1970s. I hadn't wanted them involved in my life, let alone in my madness. They came and spoke with Dr Y who told them *Sandra suffers from a mental illness. She hears voices and has delusions and visual hallucinations. She is very ill with what we call schizophrenia and needs treatment*. She was at pains to explain the intricacies of schizophrenia but I could see it was going over their heads. When asked if they had any questions, my parents were silent. Did I have anything to say? I was silent too as I sat with my eyes downcast. What could I have said to them? There was too much to say and yet nothing could be adequate. It was a painful moment where all my past converged in this hospital room and my mind swam with anger, frustration and jumbled emotions. The encounter was filtered through the lens of my madness so that the picture I was getting was distorted and blurred. Was anything achieved from their visit? I don't think they believed Dr Y, or that their daughter could possibly be mad. Afterwards, just before they were about to leave the ward, my father turned to me and said: *Ya don't believe what them psychiatrists say, do ya?*

Even though I was addled with madness, the irony of my father's words didn't escape me. For years he had mocked my mother with the accusation she was mad and needed to see a psychiatrist. Now it was me who was mad and in the hands of a psychiatrist and my father couldn't accept or acknowledge my plight. Were his words of denial simply disbelief or were they coming from a sadness he felt for his youngest daughter? Or were they from an ignorance that clouded his understanding? I didn't know what was going through my father's mind, how it felt for him to see his daughter in the grip of madness; the daughter he once thought was capable of doing anything with her life. But he had never been able to express any emotions other than anger, and all I had wanted was a show of love or compassion, however clumsy or awkward. His blankness and coldness drove a wedge into my heart. As for my mother, the puzzled look on her face, and her silence, made me feel a welling sadness that she, too, was unable to show me the love I craved. I wished it could have been different. I didn't blame them for this stony coldness because I, too, withheld myself. None of us reached out to the other; too much had happened in our family life to allow any love to flow.

The disappointment I felt at not having achieved anything with my life was considerable, and for my parents to see me in a madhouse was further cause for me to feel a failure. Their reactions to my situation reinforced my belief that they would never understand me, not only because they couldn't accept my mental illness but also because there was so much about my life I couldn't share with them. The distance between us was greater now than ever before.

S

INSIGHT NIL

In the admission notes for 8 August 1984 the psychiatrist noted about me *her insight was nil*. Whether or not someone has insight into how they are functioning in the world is a determining factor in the assessment of their mental health. Normally we take reality for granted, because it is affirmed, validated and verified by those around us. To lose insight and not know how we present to the world is to lose the ability to see that our reality is at odds with that of everyone else. I value very highly the reflexive ability I developed as part of growing into adulthood, but I can reflect only when I have the capacity for insight. In fact, no-one likes to be told that their behaviour is inappropriate because it puts into question the essence of who they think they are and how they think they are presenting to the world.

The question of whether 'reality' is knowable causes endless philosophical debate. Some people argue that we can never know reality because it is socially constructed through meaning, and everyone has their own interpretation of the meaning of experience. For what is reality when there are so many different ways of seeing the same event? We can never know the subjective experience of anyone else, except through their interpretation. We can never know other people's thoughts or see how they see the world. However, the fact that I can communicate with people through speech, that you can understand my words, suggests a shared reality. When I go into those veiled spaces of madness I become obsessed with my own inner world. I do not see myself as others do. I cannot share the basics of a normal conversation and social interaction. I cannot stand outside myself. My madness compels me to listen to its voices, see its hallucinations, smell its perfumes and taste its poisons. I go into a world that cannot be shared because its words and images reveal themselves to me and only me. When I claim this to be reality and insist everyone share this world view, I have lost insight.

Although madness disconnects me from the world, another part of me is surprisingly attuned to what is going on around me. I still have my mind and my senses giving and taking messages from the stimuli outside me. On the one hand my senses go haywire with an overload of information I am unable to filter out. On the other hand there is still another part of me that can absorb what is happening around me. I don't know how to explain this contradiction except to say that I might look distracted, but my mind is still working; that alongside the insane delusions I still see and hear everyday realities. I remember the things people say and do to me, the asides they make to each other, the comments made, the doctor turning to the nurse in an interview and saying in a whisper *She's very disturbed*. I recall much with great clarity: the stale rooms full of smoke and body odour. Seeing people unravel before my very eyes, or get better. The loss of dignity, the bad treatment. But also, out of the dim madness shine clear memories of kindness and people who helped me along the way. Many of my friends are astounded at what I remember, given how distracted I am. My friend Felicity, for example, thought I would have forgotten that once when she was trying to restrain me from running off, she chased me down her driveway wearing nothing but a pair of pink gum boots.

Of course, the collective may also lack insight into reality. Our society has its own unruly madness: an economic system based on the fantasy of infinite growth, an escalating paranoia about terrorism that threatens to become a self-fulfilling prophecy, the systematic destruction of the environment we all depend upon. The world that labels some of us mad and lacking insight sometimes seems to be itself living in its own metapsychosis. Nonetheless, given a choice, I would rather have the personal insight to know the world was mad than be locked up in my own deranged self-absorption.

When people are trying to be sympathetic, they have also said to me that *all of us are a little mad*. However, in my experience, although there are degrees of madness, there is a line you cross into madness. There are times when I am anxious, depressed or over-excited, but this is still within a shared reality; when I am insane, no-one else experiences that reality, as I realise only afterwards. Although Robbie and Dido claim they can tell I am sliding into madness by the lie of my right eyebrow, I am never certain. When the voices and delusions assail me, they are more real than anything in the world. I have not the insight required to know they are merely imagined.

THE CHRONIC YEARS

Between 1984 and 1991 I had no more hospitalisations, yet during these years I endured chronic, low-level and persistent illness. My symptoms were sometimes controlled, sometimes not so controlled. From time to time I relapsed into the more florid symptoms and strange delusions, but I managed to stay out of hospital. Robbie and Dido were sometimes able to work at home and look after me. If that wasn't possible, I was able to go to the homes of friends and be cared for by them. I was monitored by Dr Y with phone calls and I was taken to see her when needed. She would speak to me on the phone to make an assessment and then ask Robbie or Dido what they thought. It was a good arrangement.

I started to attend lectures at La Trobe University again. It was a way of stimulating my thinking and keeping in touch with current thought on subjects ranging from sociology and philosophy to literature. I tried to keep up my reading as well. I developed an interest in reading about artists and writers who had experienced madness. To know that others had been to the depths of madness and yet had the capacity to give their experiences meaning and voice was inspiring. I read about Van Gogh and his luminous paintings, Schumann and his music, and Nijinsky and his expressive dance. I discovered that Baudelaire, Hölderlin, Dürer, Lewis Carroll, Leonardo da Vinci, Bosch, Nietzsche, Newton, Descartes and Mendelssohn had all suffered madness in some form. Being in the company of all these geniuses is also daunting. It raises expectations of the relationship between genius and madness. I feel short-changed: I am mad but I am not a creative genius. I also know that there has been a tendency to romanticise madness, genius and creativity. My father's proclamation that *genius and madness are related* is a popularly held belief. Yes, some significant artists and writers have suffered madness. But think of the millions of mad people who are not creative, or geniuses. Mental illness touches many people, some creative and some very ordinary. In fact, madness usually makes people less functional than they might have been had they not been ill. I have found that as madness isolates and overwhelms me emotionally and physically, there is no room for creativity or productive thought. Yet I can understand why people think there is something creative about madness. It surely exercises the imagination, producing lavish delusions. We can conjure strange linguistic associations and extravagant flights of fancy. Madness is like a fantastic work of esoteric art, and this inspires awe in people.

During these years I became fixated on Virginia Woolf, whose struggle with madness was widely discussed. She was my role model, someone whose artistry I wanted to emulate. When I read her novel *Mrs Dalloway*, I was moved by the way she was able to describe beautifully and knowingly the insane world of Septimus Warren Smith. From her descriptions of his madness, I knew she had experienced those moods of despair and had heard voices. Because she had been artistically creative in spite of all her madness, she was a beacon, someone whose artistry with words was compelling and ennobling. I wished in my dreams that I could create wildly wonderful words that would speak to others in the way she spoke to me. Yet ultimately she succumbed to the terrors of her mind. In her suicide note she told her husband Leonard: *I feel certain I am going mad again. I feel we can't go through another of those terrible times. And I shan't recover this time.* With the fear of her madness encroaching onto her life again, she could not live through another bout. Suicide is an agonisingly real possibility among the mentally ill. Mental illness is, after all, a life-threatening condition with devastating consequences.

Throughout these chronic years of my madness another voice talked to me, but it was not the voice of my madness, nor that of the great writers who I was reading about. It was my own voice and it was one to which I was compelled to listen. Its language was poetry. From some dark, distant part of my unconscious poems emerged, trailing onto blank pages with their own lively patterning. But for a long time I just left them in a drawer. While I do not have the abundant fertility of a Baudelaire or Virginia Woolf, I have felt the inspiration that creativity can bring to all of us. It may not cure us of our madness but it can give us a window through which we can peer into ourselves to understand our own complexities. It is also a way of piercing the remote world of others who have been touched by madness. Poetry, art and music, which are already on the margins, are safe ways of exploring the marginalised mad experience, and the artists who have done it well have spoken for all of us in an articulate and unique way. In poetry we utter the unutterable, speak the unspeakable, say the unsayable, express the inexpressible and sense the insensible.

My hope for humanity lies in the creative impulse. I have faith that there is a poem in every heart – even in George W. Bush's. Our dreams suggest that there is a creative and imaginative flair in everyone, but unfortunately most people don't have the confidence or encouragement to realise it. I have great faith in the healing powers of creativity. My fellow sufferer Brian, a visual artist, has described the way his creativity carries him through bad times. His work gives him a sense of being an artist. His paintings record his emotional ups and downs and express his feelings when he is unable to communicate. They are a window to his mind.

I believe this despite the fact that I am by nature a pessimist; I have habitually expected the worst, so that I can be pleasantly surprised when something nice happens. For me, poetry has been that wonderful surprise; it has manifested hidden potentiality, revealing aspects of myself that I never knew. As I hug rationality to protect myself against the irrationality that besieges me, poetry is the one place where my rationality and irrationality can engage. In completing a poem, a moment of transcendence occurs and something of my self becomes incarnate. This is as close to a spiritual experience as I have come.

I longed for intellectual stimulation and joined my first discussion group in 1985. It was an interest group that sprang from Sociology lectures I had sat in on at La Trobe University. It was through this group that I met my dear friends Lynne and Felicity. Long after the Sociology discussion group folded, my friendship with them continued. I joined another discussion group in 1988 which met once a week at Healesville, a small town in the Yarra Valley not far from my home. It began as a University of the Third Age group and I was by far its youngest member. In 2009, after 21 years, we are still meeting once a week to talk about everything and anything. Over the years some members sadly have died and new ones have joined. Werner Pelz, the founder of the group, became my mentor; it was he who taught me so much about poetry and thinking. He died in June 2006 and I miss his wisdom and eloquence. In this group I feel able to express myself openly and honestly. I have learnt so much about poetry and literature from these wise and interesting people. I look forward to Tuesdays when we explore the world of thought through poems, books, and whatever else inspires us to think.

I kept my sport going by playing midweek ladies' tennis. I played to the best of my ability but was impeded by the side-effects of my medications. I didn't hide my mental illness from the women with whom I played, who were always patient with me when I couldn't play and accommodated my sometimes eccentric behaviour. I think the women respected my honesty and persistence. In fact, I taught them a lot about schizophrenia and the difficulties of living with this illness, and they said that by knowing me they were better able to understand it. I wasn't an ogress or a she-devil and I wasn't a monster, I was somebody from their own community who played tennis but who also happened to live with schizophrenia. I was for them a human face for the label.

By doing these things – writing, reading, playing tennis – I was trying my best to stay sane, but it was hard to keep a grip on my sane self when I was uncertain about who I was and what I was supposed to be doing. I sometimes stayed in bed all day. I was either sedated or just wanted to sleep away the bad feelings. I saw my friends achieving and getting on with their careers and lives, while I stagnated. I was now into my thirties and felt that the time to do anything significant with my life was running out. If I was going to achieve something, I thought, I had better get on with it. But I wasn't qualified for any jobs and the thought of work still terrified me. I drifted from day to day, year to year, and time crawled. It became clear to me that life had moved on and I had not moved with it. I realised I had missed significant parts of the growing up process: I was unadventurous, shy, lacked self-belief. I remember Dr Y saying *Just do whatever makes you happy*. So I played tennis, read, wrote poems and visited friends, but felt I wasn't contributing anything worthwhile to the community. I felt conflicted by the gulf between what I was doing and what I thought I should be doing.

My mood tumbled me down an endless tunnel. Emmylou Harris sings of this experience in her song 'Red Dirt Girl': *One thing they don't tell you 'bout the blues/when you got 'em/you keep on fallin' cause there ain't no bottom/there ain't no end*. In my depression all was nebulous, grey and dull. The sun didn't warm, the flowers were dull, the day was empty. I was unable to feel anything at all, as though my emotions had gone into hibernation for a long and barren winter. My life seemed worthless.

When day succumbs
to the nightly shroud
and I rest my head
upon a beckoning pillow,
body wracked from the day's demands—
not physical, but the ever repetitious
banging of my head against the gate
that keeps me from that longed-for place—
how tired my self is,
how utterly spent I feel
with the mental pain that
throbs and throbs and throbs
and throws back my head
with an anguish that never relents.

Melancholy had been with me since my teenage years, varying in intensity at any given time, but it turned to depression during those chronic years. My diagnosis was sometimes set as *schizophrenia with depressive symptoms*. During the 1984 hospitalisation my depression was so deep the doctors were intent on giving me electroconvulsive therapy (ECT). ECT was once the treatment used for patients with psychotic illnesses and depression, but now it is used only in the case of deep depression that cannot be ameliorated by antidepressant medication. Although heavily regulated today, and much safer, medical scientists still don't know exactly how it works, and it remains an enigmatic and feared treatment associated with side effects such as memory loss and other cognitive problems.

I had heard horror stories about this controversial treatment, often referred to as *shock treatment*. People I met in hospital told me it was given as punishment for bad behaviour, that it had destroyed their minds, or caused irreparable memory loss. Yet Wendy, a woman I met in Larundel, acclaimed it as her saviour, saying it brought her back to the world and restored her ability to feel joy when all she had felt for the previous twelve months was dreary immobilising sadness and suicidal thoughts, and I had seen it work on Trish at the Queen Victoria Hospital. But the thought of electricity being pulsed through my brain was too terrifying, no matter how down I felt, and I kept refusing to have it. Thankfully I never had to risk it: my mood eventually lifted with antidepressants and the passing of time.

During those slow and muddled years of the 1980s, I wavered between incipient madness and uncertain sanity. Robbie and Dido would leave notes prompting me to do the dishes, to get some bread and milk and the paper from the milk-bar, to feed the chooks and make sure the cats and dog were looked after. They had to make sure I had a task to occupy my mind, so I didn't drift aimlessly through the day. I was incapable of doing more than one task in the day without getting too stressed. I took on the chore of the dishes and performed that particular duty assiduously, seeing it as justification for my existence. I did little else. It was a time of inner reflection when I had to take stock of the fact that I had a psychiatric disability and its impact on my life. I excused myself from a compulsory normality.

S

MY TWO DEMETERS

No matter how constant my friends are and no matter how much they try to be helpful and supportive, there is a part of my life they can never enter, a part of my madness they can never touch. A lot of the time I felt like I was in a glasshouse, looking out at all the people who were trying to break the glass with a hammer to reach me. My perceptions were coloured by whatever was going on in my mind at the time. If I was paranoid then everyone hated me and I was a carbuncle on the world that must be expunged. If my voices were reinforcing my evilness then I was a dangerous contaminant.

We live in a society that is quick to mark those who are different or who have disabilities. Being crazy rips your self-esteem away like a piece of Velcro, and it hurts. When you are low on self-esteem you take on stigma. Stigma is defined as *a mark of disgrace, a stain on one's reputation*. I saw myself as a nutter, a loony, a crazy, schizo, psycho, loopy, a basket case. I was marked like Cain with the labels *incapable* and *useless*. I often feared I would end up a bag lady on the street with no home and no friends, drinking from discarded bottles, rummaging through rubbish bins to find scraps of food, seeking a bed from the Salvos.

It was difficult for Robbie and Dido to have to watch as I slept most of the day and did little towards the running of the household. It was difficult for me as they watched. I had no opinions of my own, tending to defer to theirs. Because I became ill in my early twenties, I didn't have the opportunity to consolidate an identity. My childhood experiences had left me fragile and vulnerable, and with the onset of mental illness, I was unable to work or build a career, often significant to most people's sense of identity. Even though I had managed to complete my studies and was in a significant relationship, the illness had its impact. What little sense of self I had was stripped relentlessly away by the schizophrenia. I was awkward in social settings. I hated being asked: *Hello, what do you do?* I didn't have a job, I lay in bed for long hours, and I heard negative voices. There was not a lot I could say in reply.

Feeling comfortable with ourselves helps us in our relationships with others, which in turn allows us to validate ourselves in the eyes of our friends. The more fragile we are the more validation we need. Yet mental illness may cause us to lose those people around us who can give us that validation. Fellow-sufferers of mental illness have told me of the despair of not knowing who they were because, in losing friends, they had lost this crucial way of constructing themselves.

Having a strong sense of identity facilitates communication and sociability with others around us. It fosters a healthy confidence. The more positive you feel about yourself, the friendlier the world looks. The more self-confidence you have, the more you do. But if you feel useless and worthless, you cannot, and don't, do much. The less you do, the worse you feel about yourself. It becomes a self-fulfilling prophecy. Voices reinforced my sense of failure by droning: *She's useless, she's a useless hag. See, the bitch can't even get out of bed*. I walked in the shadow of others and cast none of my own. I was invisible. Getting out of bed is an act of hope; I had no hope; I couldn't face the day.

So how did I survive and exhume from my madness the capacities that led me to become a poet, an advocate for fellow-sufferers, even to write this memoir? The story so far is a grim tale and it's not over yet, but there were signs that my life was not on the scrap heap. For a start, I managed, as I had done all my life, to gather friends around me who were loyal through this long, unending journey. Many people with mental illness become strangers to their friends and end up lonely and isolated. I know all too well how difficult we may become for our friends, yet, thankfully, I managed not to alienate mine. Somehow I remained conscious throughout that I had to look after them too.

In Greek mythology, Demeter was the earth mother. Hades, lord of the Underworld, kidnapped her daughter, Persephone. Demeter grieved so hard that she neglected her duties as the earth mother. The earth was dying, the land grew barren, and the animals and humans lost interest in reproduction. And mortals stopped their sacrificial duties to the gods. Zeus sent Hermes to the Underworld to negotiate with Hades for Persephone's release. Hades reluctantly agreed. Before Persephone left, however, Hades tricked her into eating pomegranate seeds. Because she had eaten the food of the dead, she was obliged to return to the Underworld for one third of the year.

Robbie and Dido were like two Demeters holding onto their Persephone while madness tried to drag me into its Underworld. But no matter how vigilant they have been in their efforts, the seeds of madness are in me and my visits to that world are preordained. When the time comes, I am compelled to go. But Robbie and Dido wait for spring to bring me back. They have stuck by me through the deepest winters of my madness, through long seasons of chronic withdrawal. They have been through the lowest times and most acute crises, the many hospitalisations, always giving me their hands to hold. Even when they took me to hospital against my will and incurred my anger, I realised afterwards that they had done the wise thing. They have done whatever was necessary to keep me here in this world with them.

Lynne and Felicity, whom I have known for 20 years, have also been crucial in helping me survive. Their friendship has enriched my life immeasurably. Along with Robbie and Dido, they are my family. They have been with me many times when I was mad and talk about being loyal to the well person they know I can be. When I have spoken to carers at conferences, I emphasise this notion of loyalty to the wellness, rather than illness, of their loved ones, for I know it gives them the comfort in doing the things they must.

The pets that have shared our home have also been significant to our family. When I felt evil and unable to let people touch me, I could always let Bluey, our first dog, snuffle my hands and nestle her head in my lap. She was able to break through barriers that people simply couldn't. And just being able to cuddle and pat the smooth fur of the cats was a comfort when everything else was so difficult. Their presence has always been able to transcend what was going on my mind, as though they had special dispensation from my madness not to get mixed up in it.

WHEN IN ROME . . .

Robbie and Dido were keen to do some travelling overseas; so we all went – in 1987, 1989 and again in 1992. Over the course of the three trips we went to Britain, France, the Outer Hebrides, Italy and Cyprus. We chose to travel knowing I could relapse any time, declaring we couldn't let ourselves be captive to my madness. Like the bush-walking, it was a risk we were prepared to take. There is dignity in being able to take risks and Robbie and Dido allowed me that dignity. Of course they had the right to their own pursuits, and a holiday in Europe was something they really wanted. My condition had already taken its toll on their lives – their careers might have been different had they not been constrained by my situation. Yet, they say caring for me has given them the chance to see life differently and more widely, has enriched their lives. For all of us, the window of my madness has shown us life in all its glory and agony. So we travelled to Europe together.

When in Rome you naturally want to take in the grandeur of the Vatican, St Peter's Basilica and the Sistine Chapel. The chapel offered a spectacular display of religious art, including Michelangelo's inspired work. The ceiling's rich but menacing characterisation of the Last Judgement is a masterpiece. But for me, it was like one gigantic visual hallucination: I became wary of my reactions there. The Virgin herself could easily have made an appearance. But something worse awaited us.

St Peter's, the apotheosis of Catholicism, is an enormous and opulent cathedral. Even though I had dumped Catholicism by this time I sensed the potent symbolism in every corner of the building, but the shameless display of riches and magnificent works of art crowding the caverns and grottos were overpowering. Michelangelo's *Pieta* – Mary cradling the dead Christ – shone with unsurpassable beauty. The statue sat behind a glass wall, having been damaged by an Australian man in the grip of psychosis some years ago.

We walked around the marble floor, stood before the enormous altar. We went down into the crypt and saw the sarcophagi of the Popes, and other religious relics. We then decided to go up to the cupola, the very top of the dome. On the way there we passed the biggest trinket shop I have ever seen. There was a flock of nuns, speaking a babble of different languages, serving behind the counters. I bought a little St Christopher medal. It was very cheap. We joined a queue and made our way along a set of dark, narrow, stone stairs that wound their way up between the skins of the dome. We eventually came out at the top, to a spectacular view of Rome. On the roof there was yet another trinket shop. After taking in the view, we decided to go back down. I opted to take the lift. Robbie and Dido said they would use the stairs and we would meet at the bottom. I said: *Fine, see you down there* and made my way to the lift.

There was a delay at the lift. When I eventually got down to the level where I thought I was to meet them, they weren't there. Where were they? I ran around St Peter's in a blind panic looking for them. I had no money and had no idea of the name of our hotel. I had visions of being stranded alone in the rambling, cluttered spaces of Rome. After searching every nook and grotto of the main basilica, I went back down to the crypt, then up again to the basilica and back to the lift. It crossed my mind that Robbie and Dido might have worried that I had been overwhelmed by this Catholic religiosity and gone mad. This made me run faster. But there was nowhere to run except around the huge cathedral and back down to the crypt. I didn't think to just go to the front door and wait: that was too rational and sensible.

After about half an hour, Robbie eventually found me standing in the queue, in front of the trinket shop, waiting to go back up yet again to the cupola. I have never been so relieved to see Robbie and Dido, or they me. I couldn't believe the bad luck of getting lost in, of all places, what my father might have called the biggest Mickery in the world!

DEATH OF THE FATHER

My father died on 19 February 1990. He finally succumbed to the heart disease which had plagued him for many years. He was 69. I don't remember much about his funeral. But what I do recall vividly was my mother's refusal, after the wake, to climb into my brother's car to return to her empty house. It was awful to witness her agony. Finally she got into the car, sobbing, her face awash with tears. I guess for her, loneliness seemed far worse than living with my abusive father. My inability to comfort her left me feeling a terrible guilt and sadness: I was a bad daughter.

I had anticipated my father's death. I had longed for him to be out of my mother's life. He had maintained his rage against her. I thought it would have burnt out in his old age but well into their sixties he had continued to beat her, once throwing her down the passage so violently that she broke her hip. He despised her, and she blunted his ravings and brutality with alcohol. I had thought I wouldn't care when he died, but that was folly: I stewed in a mixed-up, tearless, emotional wilderness. How do you grieve for the father you hated? How do you grieve for an event you wished had happened years before? How do you grieve for your own twisted feelings? Twelve months of tangled, tortured grieving took its toll, and in 1991, a month before the anniversary of his death, the delusions and voices returned.

The Prime Minister is talking to me over the radio. I don't know why. What has Bob Hawke got to do with me, and how does he know I am listening? Sandra, Sandra, you are contaminating my society. Get rid of yourself now! Stop poisoning my country! Stop your evil spreading through Australia! Kill yourself now! You evil bitch! You fucking slut! *It must be true. He's talking to all of Australia; everyone will want to kill me and they know where I am. The antidepressants and Lorazepam will do it. I'll take them all, I don't care what happens to me. I have to do this. I have to do it now.*

I took the antidepressants and Lorazepam and quietly went to sleep on the bed. I didn't fight the wave of death as it washed over me. I wasn't afraid. It seemed peaceful. I abnegated all responsibility for myself and left myself in the hands of the potion, never expecting to wake from it. Robbie and Dido came home early from work that day and found me unconscious. They called an ambulance. As I lapsed in and out of consciousness through the journey, I could hear the siren wailing, so things must have been serious. At the Maroondah Hospital they tried to push a tube down my throat and I clenched onto it with my teeth. They poured a charcoal substance into my mouth which absorbs the poison. I fell unconscious. When I woke, I had wires and tubes in me and on me. My mouth was dry and black with the remnants of the charcoal.

A psychiatrist interviewed me.

Doctor: Count back from a hundred in sevens.
Me: 96, 85, 60, 51...
Doctor: I'll give you a street name and number to remember later: 43 Station Street. Meanwhile what does this proverb mean: A stitch in time saves nine.
Me: God needs a needle to stop the Devil.

Doctor: Do you know where you are?
Me: Hell.
Doctor: What is your name?
Me: The Virgin Mary.
Doctor: What was that street name and number?
Me: I've lost contact with the owners.
Doctor: Who is the Prime Minister of Australia?
Me: Me!

I failed the sanity test. My fatal mistake was to say I was the Prime Minister of Australia. (This is a cautionary tale, in case someone ever asks you the question!) I was taken by ambulance to Larundel, my mind in delusional ecstasy at the notion that I was not only the leader of the country but also the Virgin Mary. The logic that they were different genders, let alone people, did not seem to bother me. Yet, all the while, I was persecuted by the voices: *You stupid cow. You piece of shit. Don't tell them we are here. Don't tell them about our secret. You are the leader of the world's people. Go to Uluru and sacrifice yourself. Bob Hawke wants to exterminate you!* I was certified insane and made an involuntary patient.

16/1/91 History of Present Illness. She is described by her friends as having become depressed and irrational over a period of some weeks prior to admission. She was expressing belief that she was evil and that the Prime Minister wanted to exterminate her because she was contaminating Australia. She has little insight into her condition.

Treatment & Progress. . . was admitted initially to a locked ward . . . She continued to be actively hallucinated and delusional for some weeks on the ward. She did improve

> slowly but even some weeks after admission was reported by the nursing staff as looking up funeral directors in the yellow pages so that she could organise her own imminent funeral.

The admitting doctor observed the following:

> This patient has a past history of schizophrenia and was referred on as an involuntary patient from Maroondah Hospital after a large overdose of Dothiepin and Lorazepam. On admission was agitated, restless and demanding to be released claiming there was going to be a terrorist attack. Guilty delusions that she was evil and was going to be punished. She believed I could read her thoughts. Admitted she felt terrible. Patient requires urgent treatment in a secure environment.

Once again I found myself admitted to A ward, but at least by 1991 it had been renovated. It was carpeted, and had modern, comfortable furniture, although the walls remained typically institutional white with pale yellow. It had a pool table. There was an exercise bike in an alcove off the main passage, on which, later, I was to work off pent-up anger and frustration. However, a certain level of paternalism characterised the ethos of A ward. On admission, our clothes were labelled by the ward assistants because they did all our laundry. Our jewellery and valuables were taken and put in a safe. In short, we were fed, accommodated, washed and cleaned and medicated in this world of a bygone era. I didn't mind this level of care. I felt safe even if there was only one door in and out that was always locked. The constant rattle of keys in locks, as doctors and nurses came and went, as visitors were let in and out, harrowed me, a percussive accompaniment to my madness and reminder of the loss of freedom and privileges.

In mid January 1991 the first Gulf War was raging in the Middle East. I was certain I had caused it. Terrorists were after me. They knew I was in Larundel and were going to blow the place up. When I looked out of the lounge room window, I expected to see a fleet of helicopters land and armed men rushing towards the building. My death was imminent. And if the terrorists didn't get me, I would kill myself when I had the opportunity. Either way, my death was a certainty.

I feel so restless. I pace the room, the corridor, the bedroom. The Virgin Mary looks beautiful standing on the windowsill. This clatter in my head is unrelenting. Don't talk to me. Go away and leave me alone. Fuck off! I'm not what you think I am. You think I'm scum. Why? What did I ever do to you? Where are you hiding? I can hear you, I can hear you. Why am I evil? Fuck off!

I have tried leaving the room and shutting the door, but the voices come with me. The nurse is giving me some medication. She says I'm muttering to myself. She's giving me devil's tablets and devil's juice. I don't want it, it makes me feel like cardboard. I'll keep walking this floor until I drop dead. I won't take the medication, it makes me constipated. There, in the mirror, is a harridan, an unkempt, grimacing, snarling, terrifying woman laughing at me. The witch has returned. My ugliness frightens the other patients. I am both a terrifier and the terrified!

Everyone can read my thoughts. But I cannot look into their eyes. I must look at the floor. My soul is dying. I'll ask the nurse to help me die. I need an exorcism. I have to get the Devil out of my heart. I'm carrying the Devil's child. Abort it! Abort it! I can't go to bed because the Devil is waiting to rape me again. His hair was in flames. I can't go to bed unless the nurse pulls the covers down to show me the Devil is not waiting for me. I'm dead! I'm dead! Put flowers on my body.

> **22/1/91 Spoke this morning of being raped by the Devil last night and also of fears of being pregnant. Appeared to be hallucinating.**
>
> **31/1/91 Still believes however that her bed is possessed. Needed reassurance.**

Every night for weeks I feared being raped and would ask the night nurse to go into my room and pull the sheets down on the bed to show me the Devil wasn't there waiting for me. I was weak and fearful, twisted and gnarled in my psyche. I was violated, dirty. I was pregnant to the Devil and had to rid myself of the evil growth that was consuming my womb. I was going to give birth to an evil and repulsive child. This evil oozed inside me and I had to have it removed. I was desperate to have an abortion.

I asked the Catholic priest to exorcise me. I had to be saved from a dark and terrifying fate. He said: *Are you a Catholic, my child?* When I said, in a pathetic voiceless whisper *No,* he apologised saying: *Sorry my child, but God will help you.* I wonder what would have happened if he had exorcised me, whether it would have made any difference. These feelings of evil *are* reality; I feel evil with a biblical intensity. I was cursed by evil, and felt I was the most hideous person, physically and psychologically. Yet I was also endowed with supernatural powers that could destroy others with a touch of the hand or whisper of my breath.

Yet, there were humorous moments in this dark place. When the Virgin Mary appeared to me I thought her veil looked shabby. Mary can't go around with a shabby veil, I thought. I stood at the only door into the ward and asked people who were visiting their loved ones whether they would like to give a donation so I could buy Mary a new veil. No-one gave me money.

12/2/91 Required encouragement to attend kiosk, Sandra fearing the cracks in the pavement which, she says, burn her like hot coals.

I have to avoid walking on the pavement, yet they drag me to the kiosk and make me walk. Why are they doing this to me? The pavement is searing my feet; the heat is burning though my shoes. They don't understand my peril, what danger they are placing me in. They don't care about me.

My father's eerie presence perturbed me. I heard him playing the Devil's Trill on his saxophone. It was loud and had a harsh tone. I was sure he was trying to contact me from his wall in the crematorium. His ashes had had life breathed into them and he was now haunting me, tormenting me with his cacophonous music. On the anniversary of his death a strange mood overwhelmed me.

19/2/91 Became agitated and sat in dining room alone. Today is the anniversary of her father's death one year ago. Sandy sat and cried while watching the time get closer to 3:15 p.m. Spoke with me about her feelings of anger for her father and how her 'breakdown' at Easter had been marked by the voice of her dead father calling her to join him.

On the dot of 3:15 – the time of his death – I wept, and said to the nurse *He's gone*. For the first time since his death I felt free of his spectre, which had wracked me for the past twelve months. This moment transcended my deluded state. To feel released from the shackle of my father was a godsend. I was now left only with my madness. The two had been a destructive mix and I could now fight the madness with a renewed vigour; I could walk through to the other side of the dark wood.

The nursing notes remark on my constant stream of visitors. After each visit I felt more relaxed and less preoccupied by my voices and hallucinations. My friends were able to distract me from what was going on in my head. Their company broke the boredom of the ward, where there was nothing to do except watch television or play pool, both difficult when your mind is a whirlpool. The days dragged even more as I emerged from the psychotic fog and could see the world more clearly. My friends were my link with the outside world. I noticed many of the other patients didn't have a lot of visitors, and how lonely they looked. I was locked up with a fevered mob of people – terrified, confused, psychotic, manic or depressed.

Robbie and Dido had learnt from my early hospitalisations that how I looked, what clothes I wore and having visitors were very important factors in how the doctors and nurses treated me, and so they always made sure I had clean clothes and was well groomed. Those who had no visitors were usually dressed in ill-fitting hospital clothes and never seemed to emerge from their madness; they were forgotten by everyone.

Like most wards at Larundel, A ward was shared by males and females. I always felt uncomfortable in these mixed wards, especially when I was locked in. On this admission I was stalked by a male patient. He threatened me several times. I reported him but the staff did nothing to make me feel safe. I'm not even sure if they believed me. Perhaps they dismissed it as one of my delusions. Then there was the streaker who ran through the ward with his penis erect. I have been told by many sources that in the 1960s it was thought better to integrate wards because the presence of women would calm or socialise the men. What an extraordinary piece of social engineering: to see the role of mentally ill women as ensuring psychotic or manic men are better behaved! My own preference would have been a single-sex ward, away from men whose behaviour was sometimes threatening.

Other women have told me mixed wards were an issue for them because in their past they have been victims of sexual abuse. For them, being locked up with potentially dangerous men placed them yet again in a vulnerable and powerless position. I shared their feelings.

I saw burly nurses manhandle patients, inject them with a sedative as they held them by the arms and legs and then throw them into the seclusion room. The seclusion room was frequently used to subdue violent patients or corral people who were distressed and needed to be closely monitored, but it was heart-rending to hear the panic-stricken cries of these poor people who had no understanding of what was happening to them. I remember one poor woman who lay on the floor and screamed through the grille in the door to the feet of passers-by: *Sneakers, sneakers, don't go! Sneakers, help me! Help me!* It was disturbing to witness the terror of people incarcerated there, yet I have to admit my sense of relief when violent males were put in seclusion. How can we treat with greater compassion patients so disturbed they have become dangerous to others?

I was a danger to myself rather than to others. Because of my suicidal threats and the fact that I was still very psychotic, the consulting psychiatrists decided I should be kept in A ward. This meant I had to go before the Mental Health Review Board to be assessed as to whether I was to stay an involuntary patient. As the day of my review neared, I demanded to be let out of the locked ward. I was determined to kill myself because my voices were commanding me to do it. My madness and misery had drained me of my life-force.

The Board was a panel of three people I had never seen before. They sat behind a long table. The room was bare, apart from the wooden furniture. They asked my treating psychiatrist and nurses about my mental condition. Robbie and Dido had also been called to the review, and were asked what they thought about me. They asked me some questions too. I stared at the floor and answered in monotones, fearing the outcome. I left the room with Robbie and Dido and waited while the panel deliberated. They determined I was to stay in A ward as an involuntary patient. I had been certified a second time. I was disappointed with the decision and angry with Robbie and Dido who I thought had colluded with the doctors to keep me locked up. Robbie and Dido were relieved with the decision because they knew I was still very ill and needed to be restrained. Looking back, I can see it was the right thing to do. If I had been released from a secure ward I have no doubt I would have harmed myself.

My medication regime had been upgraded to a high dosage of Modecate, Serenace and antidepressants and as a consequence I was shuffling and dribbling, in a continuous state of numbness. My thoughts tumbled out in garbled speech, laced with the darkness of my delusions and input from my voices. But after about five weeks the medication did eventually take hold of the psychosis and turn it on its head, negating its power and consigning it to the outer limits of my waking thought. I started to see the world through a mind more at ease with itself.

As the psychosis slowly began to subside my symptoms grew less and less disturbing. Each day I took a small step towards recovery. I had some good days and some not so good days, but I was coming out of the tortured world in which I had been trapped. The voices were becoming less pressing. I was more engaged with people, less introverted, and better able to understand conversations. Thoughts of suicide dissipated. The seven long weeks I had been in the locked ward seemed like years. Now I was being transferred to B ward, which was the first step to going home. I felt glad to escape the threat of male patients, to have freedom again, to regain some control of my life again. There was, however, an anxiety about being free and responsible for my own behaviour. The locked ward had been like a womb, and after being there it was hard to face the outside world again. It almost seemed easier to stay in psychosis and not have to face so many pressures and expectations. Yet something in me wanted to engage, wanted to make the effort to come back to my friends who had waited.

I spent the next few weeks in the open ward, flat, depressed, still coming to terms with my suicide attempt and all that had happened to me since. B ward had a balcony that opened out to a courtyard. I sat on this balcony with the other patients who often came out there for a smoke. We would discuss our moods and hopes and aspirations, sometimes in great detail, sometimes in coded messages only we understood.

. . . sitting on the balcony,
consumed by a dreadful scourge,
we show our sorrows to those looking on.
And we are such a motley lot!
Some madder than others.
Some more drugged than others.
Some more distressed.
Some more acquainted
with the way of the balcony,
where the life skill,
the sharing of one's madness with others,
is an art form . . .

I was finally discharged after 80 days in hospital, a long admission impelled by confusion over my father's death and by my own morbidity. My nights had been filled with nightmares and devils, and days with voices, the Virgin Mary, imminent terrorist attack, and plots for suicide. Clambering out of all that had left me exhausted but I was no longer in a constant state of terror, and I felt calmer and more accepting of the world, more in control. But as I gained insight, I could see clearly how I had once again succumbed to the ruthless spooks and phantoms of my mind. My discharge notes say this:

> 5/4/91 After a slow recovery she was referred to an open ward where her antidepressants were discontinued on the grounds that her risk of overdose made it unwise for her to be placed on them on discharge. When she was fully recovered she was returned to her normal living accommodation which involves a shared residence with two female friends of long standing who had been very supportive to her in the past and continued to look after her.
>
> Recommendations For Future Treatment. She should remain on neuroleptics for the foreseeable future. It is possible that future depressive episodes may require antidepressant treatment but this should be considered in the context of her risk of overdose. Hospitalisation may well be necessary.

THE STRANGE FOLK UPSTAIRS

What is it like to hear voices, these 'strange folk upstairs'? Hearing these voices is an unearthly experience, difficult to describe, and so giving an account of their moods and mutterings is not easy. The voices are persecutory and abusive. I have likened them to abusive, unforgiving parents who relentlessly chastise their child. The voices can be random and rambling one moment, poignant and pointed the next. They can be secretive, persuasive and cajoling, warning me not to tell anyone they are there: *Don't share our secret. Listen to us! Listen to us!* They say salacious and threatening things: *You are a sex slave to the Devil. Show us your tits. If you don't stop eating now, we will smear you in shit*. They deride the things that normally give me pleasure, like playing hockey. *Your hockey team hates you. You're an ass at hockey. The coach is sending telepathic messages about you to Condoleezza Rice and George W. Bush. They hate you, bitch!* They are monotonous, repetitive and boring. They say the same things over and over like a twisted, maniacal mantra. They are imperious, compelling me to obey them. And sometimes the voices have a theatricality, like actors carefully projecting their lines. More recently these voices have taken on a posh persona, having developed a newfound eloquence. I am convinced they have done elocution. They would be able to give a much better poetry reading than me! Yet they are inconsistent because they can be as foul-mouthed and crass as I am when cursing and swearing. My use of bad language is a bad habit, though I like to think I have turned it into an art form. So I suppose it is not surprising then that the voices would echo my own language.

I have two voices, a male and female, who engage in a running commentary on what I might be doing, talking about me in the third person. They mock me. They pick on the fact that I have concerns about my body image. Here's an example of their dialogue:

> *Voice 1: Her tits are so huge, they hang like huge pendulums.*
> *Voice 2: And her nose is so gross with its horrible shape.*
> *Voice 1: The bitch's bum is hanging like a sagging bag.*
> *Voice 2: And her flabby stomach is hanging out like a fat cow.*
> *Voice 1: Yeah, and look at her thighs.*
> *Voice 2: And she talks crap.*
> *Voice 1: The bitch is a liar.*
> *Voice 2: She's scum. She's Satan's whore.*
> *Voice 1: She's hideous to look at, everyone's laughing at her.*
> *Voice 2: The bitch should kill herself.*
> *Voice 1: Yeah, the bitch should do it now.*
> *Voice 2: What a joke. What a laughing stock.*

And they will laugh at me uproariously. At other times they simply rail at me with their vitriol and revulsion. The voices are unassailable and inviolable. Their assault generates paranoia and self-loathing. And even when their ravings cease I think maybe they are right, maybe all they say is true: I am as bad and vile and ugly as they say.

At other times an androgynous voice whispers into my ear with an eerie authority. I can almost feel a hot breath on my cheek. It wants to make me suspicious of my friends. One day I was having a meal with my friend Lynne, and she served pumpkin soup and bread. The voice whispered: *It's poisoned, it's poisoned, don't eat it, don't eat it, she's trying to kill you*. I could smell poison coming from the soup. I announced I wasn't eating the soup because it might be poisoned. Lynne's response, knowing I was ravenously hungry, was one of almost childish anger. She poked the bread with her finger and said: *There, I've poisoned that too. Now eat it!* I was so shocked by her outburst that I ate the soup and the bread. Lynne was responding to the silliness of my delusion with her own foibles and insecurities. But the whisper continued: *Hide yourself now. If she knew you, she wouldn't want to associate with you. Bitches like you don't deserve friends. She's laughing at you, big arse. She thinks you're shit*. I slunk away from Lynne, viewing her with apprehension, not knowing if I could trust her. I withdrew into my inner world which beckoned me; it was the only thing I could do to protect myself.

That whisper could be dangerous. One day I found myself stopped in a busy intersection in Melbourne, standing in front of my white Toyota Corolla, too scared to get in and drive it away because the voice had told me: *The car's possessed. It's your enemy. Don't drive it. Get out of it now. It's going to kill you*. Cars were tooting at me with their horns, drivers were cursing me with rude gestures, and I felt immobilised with fear. Eventually I got back in the car and took off, nearly hitting a pedestrian. I had to get rid of the car. I tried to offload it on Lynne and Felicity's grown children for ten dollars, but they declined my generous offer. I then offered it to some other friends telling them I'd give them two hundred dollars to take the car away.

Every time the voices call me *Satan's whore*, *trollop*, *slut* and *scum of the earth*, I feel the shame of Bruce and what he did to me.

The voices punish me for my failure to protect myself and I relive my horror over and over. Are they from my unconscious, from my deep-seated feelings of worthlessness that stem from this awful time? Are they harking back to my feelings of guilt and loss?

Every time I hear their persecutory chatter, I feel a deep anxiety, and wonder at how they seem to delight in what they say to me. I am becoming more certain that the voices draw on the lived experience of the mind in which they rest. They sit in the imagination and the unconscious as part of the emotional baggage and represent the deepest secret thoughts. It makes sense that something that affects someone so drastically can later become part of the inner world expressed in psychosis.

My madness is a tale of terror and persecution from voices that seem to want to destroy me, reminding me of my shame and powerlessness. But in a horrible twist, these voices mimic my father's abuse of my mother, only it is now me who is the victim of his vitriol. And like a battered wife who protects her abusive husband, I am reluctant to disclose my voices and their content to the wider world. But why do the voices delight in making me a victim all over again? Why would thoughts from my own mind turn on me and persecute me? Perhaps I could hire an electrician to repair the faulty wiring in my brain.

Hearing voices is not like hearing the voice of your conscience: one's internal recognition of right and wrong in relation to one's actions and motives. These voices are not simply lingering thoughts, wishes, remembered shame; they are as real to me as someone talking directly to me in a conversation. I cannot just walk out of the room, shut the door, and leave them behind; they go wherever I go. Sometimes they appear quite randomly: it feels as if some fiend has put a small radio in my brain, then delights in turning it on and off, and changing stations to give me scrambled messages. My mind is invaded by auditory spam, or worse, a virus which paralyses my capacity for rational thought.

It is a crowded house and some nights I have to hang out the *No Vacancy* sign.

Indeed, the voices are the opposite of conscience. They wrestle with my superego for control of my moral compass, turning my internal world upside down, urging me to do things that work against my conscience. They convince me to think bad things about my friends, to withhold information, to do things against my better judgment, to be secretive and tell lies. They make me into a person I neither know nor like. They are like an anti-conscience. The malevolence of the voices are evidence that they are immoral agents who themselves lack a conscience, heartless conspirators who toil to bring me down.

I have another way of describing the voices. They are parasites. My mind is their host; without it they couldn't exist. They feed on my turbulent internal world and my mind's vulnerabilities; they feed on my soul using its pain to initiate a vexatious attack on my character.

Many people with schizophrenia have strategies to deal with their voices. Some people develop the power to summon and dismiss their voices. Others listen to Walkmans or iPods to distract them. Sometimes watching television can be helpful, or reading a book. If my voices are at me when I am home alone, I put on loud music to try and drown them out. When they come at me at night as I am lying in bed trying to sleep, I try to ward them off by doing mental arithmetic to keep my mind occupied: 2x2=4, 72÷8=9, 4x9=36. The evangelical fundamentalist Christians preach that an empty mind will be invaded by Satan. For me, an empty mind leaves me open to my voices. Listening to Beethoven on my MP3 player is an important distraction. (What a godsend this piece of technology is for those of us who hear voices! It offers respite from the chattering by overpowering the voices with the sound of music. In fact, I think everyone who hears voices should be automatically given an MP3 player by mental health authorities.) In my madder moments, though, I talk back to the voices, and argue, or whisper to them, hoping to appease them. When the voices are railing at me like possessed banshees, I just wish my cranium would shatter to let them float into the ether and give me some peace.

In fact the voices have never entirely gone away. They may hibernate for a week or two, but then they will reappear, unannounced, as if they are hiding in a cavern in my mind awaiting their moment to assail me. I don't know where they come from or where they go, but I have had their intermittent transmissions for so long now that I am resigned to them. Are these monsters a creation of my imagination? Because only I hear them, and because they reveal something about my inner world, there is something seductive about their presence. It is a complex and contradictory love–hate relationship. I struggle with my acceptance of them, given how destructive they have been, yet I can't imagine them not being there; I might miss them.

Whisper, my friend, you are the only reality I have.
When you beckon I cannot ignore your commands.
You give power and a purpose
in our secure world of shared secrets.
Whisper, my friend, tell me your stories,
tell me in your charming, seductive voice.
You are my creator and my lover,
you belong to me and no-one else
and I belong to you alone.
Together we resist the outside world
and toil to make a harmony of disorder.
How you move my senses with your power.

They try to take you away from me
because of the secrets we share,
but only we know the truth of us,
only we can communicate with honesty.

No-one will ever separate our beings
because we are each other.
Even though there were times when you betrayed me
and told false and deceitful lies,
I forgave you because you always forgive me.
Whisper, my friend, I have no choice,
I am entwined in your briar arms
that caress my withered soul.

Hearing voices has been documented as far back as the Bible. In the gospel story of St Mark, Jesus comes across a man possessed by *unclean spirits*. He asks the man his name. *My name is Legion: for we are many*, he answers. I interpret the *many* as a gaggle of voices. And like me, this man is entangled in and beguiled by the voices which have become an indivisible force. He even asks Jesus not to send them away. But Jesus bids the voices leave and they enter the swine which then hurl themselves into the sea. The man is cured. If only it were that simple.

The *Legion* in my head have maintained their abusive nature over the years they have been with me. Not only are they abusive, they are also punitive, berating me for resisting them or telling on them. I have even incurred their wrath for exposing them in this memoir. Most times I am able to recognise them as part of my illness and so can deal with them or ignore them; but too often these days I fail in this and become their victim. They are uncompromising and intransigent. The relationship between the voices and the delusions remains one in which the one perpetuates the other. Often the voices change, evolving as I evolve. When I think I have a handle on them and understand their agenda, they make comments and pronouncements on changes in my life with an alarming knowledge of me and my inner world. In an act of revenge I have decided to name these voices Tweedledum and Tweedledee. By mocking them maybe I can steal their thunder and diminish their power.

RECOVERY

Can you recover after such a meltdown of the mind? William Anthony from the Centre for Psychiatric Rehabilitation in Boston sees recovery as *a deeply personal, unique process of changing one's attitudes, values, feelings, goals, skills and/or roles . . . as one grows beyond the catastrophe of mental illness*. The more profound the illness, the deeper it has shaken the roots of who we are. The fact that I emerged from my psychotic episodes shows that I haven't deteriorated into impenetrable madness many others thought I was condemned to. The meltdown hasn't been comprehensive. Climbing out of the madness has been a process of self-discovery and renewal. It has been a transforming, enlightening experience, going forward two steps only to fall back one, or three. Many times I thought I had made no progress at all. I went back to the place where I had started. One important part of my recovery has been to acknowledge that the enemy is not the world, or Robbie or Dido, or my friends, or my doctor, but mental illness itself. Accepting that I cannot deal with my illness alone, that I need the help of others, has also been important.

When the label was first applied to me I saw myself only as 'a schizophrenic', because my life was so limited and so affected by the symptoms of the illness. Part of my recovery was to see myself more clearly and more positively so I no longer think of myself as 'a schizophrenic' but as someone who lives with schizophrenia and all its moods. I can now think beyond the label of the illness to all the other things that make me myself, that constitute my identity – like my relationships, poetry, humour, and potentialities.

Recovery does not necessarily mean being cured. In *Recovered, Not Cured: A Journey through Schizophrenia*, Richard McLean takes the reader on a fascinating journey through his madness, from his careless youth to another world where voices and delusions ruled his nights and days. He concludes by saying: *Nowadays, I say that I am recovered, not cured.* Most textbooks will tell you that schizophrenia is a treatable condition, but because its causes are not known there is no cure. Some people have one psychotic episode and never another, while others are forever locked up in a psychotic prison. But generally the illness is episodic, like mine. Schizophrenia is like living with a bomb in your mind; you never know when it might go off.

Mental illness is as unique as the individuals it touches. Because we all have our own imaginations and life-experiences, our madness will express itself uniquely too. There are as many kinds of madness as there are mad minds in the world. And there are many theories about the causal factors in schizophrenia – from viruses to dysfunctional families. Likewise, recovery is an individual process, a different journey and destination for each of us. Recovery can begin with something as simple as just being able to get out of bed in the morning, being able to wash yourself or walk to the letterbox. Recovery for another might be finding full-time employment. My creativity too has been my path to recovery. Writing about my life in poetry has allowed me to release many of my demons. Recovery affirms and validates my dignity. Recovery also means others acknowledging my strengths, and me acknowledging them myself.

Some people recovering from schizophrenia go into meditation or try alternative healers such as naturopaths or homeopaths.

Others embrace religion to find the spiritual fulfilment that helps their healing. My fellow sufferer Graham found great comfort in his church, feeling that the beliefs and fellowship of the religious community give meaning and stability to his life. The companionship and support he finds in the church community sustain him though his bad times.

Historically, much has been done to the mad that was cruel, dangerous and sometimes fatal in the course of finding cures. These things were done out of a bewildering fear of madness, or perhaps because doing anything seemed better than nothing. This attitude allowed the proliferation of preposterous treatments in the twentieth century to purge the mad of their untamable furies and make them *normal*. Perhaps those who promoted these were well intended but some, like lobotomy – a surgical intervention in the frontal lobes of the brain – had dire consequences. This controversial treatment was pioneered in the USA by Walter Freeman. *The New York Times* called it *surgery of the soul*. These days, I might be assured I would not be subjected to a lobotomy, a needless hysterectomy, or some other outlandish experimental treatment that rendered me fevered, frozen or drenched; we have more sophisticated drugs and programs to help the mentally ill. Yet on our streets walk many homeless, suffering souls, for whom recovery from mental illness remains elusive.

I am glad to live in a time when we are able to benefit from the new drugs, called 'atypical' antipsychotics. In comparison to the old drugs, they have fewer side-effects, but they aren't perfect. Weight gain is a significant and distressing side-effect of Olanzapine, for example. My breasts lactated and grew larger as a result of one medication I was given, Risperidone. Medication *is* an important tool in the armory of psychiatry, but for me it is only a key that unlocks a door. Behind the door is a person with emotions, sensibilities and sensitivities, someone who needs friends and a strong sense of self to aid the recovery process. If a sufferer is well medicated yet living in substandard accommodation, with no friends or social network, no job and no hope, she is unlikely to recover the sense of self that inspires strong self-esteem. A combination of treatments, rehabilitation and stable accommodation is important for a person's recovery because emotional health brings stability and stability brings emotional health. Treatment needs to be more than just medication: besides balancing the chemicals, the whole person needs to be nurtured, including spirit and soul. One needs dignity and hope for some quality of life.

WHY ME?

I was consumed by the question *Why me?* Why had this impossible mental illness been imposed on me? I initially blamed my parents. I was already angry with them and my mental illness added fuel to the fire. Blaming the parents for the child's mental illness was a popular theory in the 1960s and 70s, proposed by the anti-psychiatry movement led by R.D. Laing. Laing famously suggested that madness was a sane response to a mad world. In *The Politics of Experience and the Bird of Paradise* he writes, "to the best of my knowledge, no schizophrenic has been studied whose disturbed pattern of communication has not been shown to be a reflection of, and reaction to, the disturbed and disturbing pattern characterising his or her family of origin".

Laing was building on ideas first put forward in the 1940s by theorists who saw the family as the breeding ground for psychiatric disturbance. Mothers in particular were singled out for blame. It was the psychoanalyst Frieda Fromm-Reichmann who coined the term *schizophrenogenic mother* to describe the mothers she thought were the cause of mental illness in their children. Subsequently, throughout the 1950s, 60s and 70s the schizophrenogenic mother was often portrayed stereotypically as a harridan who terrorised her children and drove them mad. By the 1970s 'dysfunctional' families were widely believed to be implicated in the schizophrenia of their children – particularly mothers. What about fathers? How did men escape such scrutiny and blame?

Mental illness continues to appear in many families, some happy, some not. Argument about the respective roles of physical and social factors in mental illness – nature or nurture, the medical or the social model – remains a robust debate even now, though most thinking people in the field have agreed that both physical and emotional causes are implicated.

When I first became ill, however, it was the middle of the 1970s, and families were still perceived as the monsters who damaged their children. I had distanced myself from my parents when I escaped home to go to university and was adamant I didn't want them to know I had a mental illness. They only found out because my sister told them. I was tantalised by the notion that my much-loathed parents might be the cause of my madness. I needed reasons for my bewildering condition, and doctors had shown interest in exploring my childhood experiences as a possible reason for my schizophrenia. But although I had wanted at first to blame my parents for what had happened to me, I began to realise that my anger at them was driven by disappointment with my seemingly lost future. I was looking for scapegoats and they were an easy target.

Dr Y believed my parents did not necessarily cause my illness but that they contributed to my melancholic disposition and made my life more complicated than it might have been. It seems I had a predisposition to getting schizophrenia that was exacerbated by the stress and damage of my disturbed family. But ultimately the illness had a life of its own, regardless of my upbringing. Dr Y has asked whether I thought there might have been an underlying pathology in one of my parents. She wondered in particular if my mother's alcoholism masked an undiagnosed mental illness. I don't know, but I didn't see her manifest symptoms of mental illness, and I feel her alcoholism was more a response to disappointments, and then her awful life, rather than pathology.

I often wondered why I became mentally ill and yet my siblings did not. I presume that only in me were the chemicals so poorly balanced. Yet, although it was me who went mad, I have survived our disturbed childhood in ways my siblings haven't. In spite of the machinations of my mind, I have had more stable long-term relationships and a settled lifestyle. I don't ask *Why me?* any more. It doesn't ease the illness or the symptoms; it doesn't change anything to lay blame or be bitter and angry.

LIFE BEGINS AT FORTY

My mother died in 1992, a year after my psychotic episode associated with my father's death. She was 68. My sister and I found her semi-conscious in her bed. We rang an ambulance and she was taken to hospital. The doctors found a growth in her colon that had caused an obstruction. It perforated and she died a day later of septicemia. We did not sit by her hospital bed to comfort her. She died alone, abandoned by her children and her friends. Even before her death we had abandoned her, leaving her to sit in a ramshackle armchair in a hovel that reeked of cigarette smoke and stale beer. She had nothing except the television and alcohol for company. When the ambulance had taken her, I looked in her fridge; it was bare except for a few bottles of beer and an old carton of Red Rooster chicken. After watching her descend into alcoholism and a pitiful loneliness I could not ameliorate, her death was a release for me. At her small funeral, no-one shed a tear for her. I shed no tears either. My mother had never heard the words *I love you* from me because I couldn't say what I didn't feel. Did she ever tell me she loved me? I don't recall hearing her say so. Yet, after a time, her death did move me, and I was able to grieve for her in a more normal fashion than I did for my father. Her death did not send me into a spiral of madness as my father's had. In my mother's case I mourned for the different life she might have had.

No Tears

No tears for you, Mother.
No weeping into soggy handkerchiefs
by the gathered few
who view your elevated coffin
festooned with perfunctory flowers.

No tears for you, Mother
who drifted out of our lives years ago
when you abandoned the world
for a ramshackle chair set in the corner of
the stale room you barely shadowed.

No tears for you, Mother.
No great wails of grief.
No weighty outpourings
to mark your passing.
Death snatched you long ago.

But much has changed.
Emotions have swelled enormously.
Thoughts of you filter through my mind
moment after moment.
So deep and compelling that
the tears have more than been shed
they have flowed and flowed.
The dry eyes have become torrents.

I turned 40 in 1993. Nearly two decades had passed in which I had little recollection of what had happened politically, culturally and socially. I remained unformed as a person. The 1991 hospitalisation had been a crucial time: I had found myself in the loneliest place in the world, lost in the deepest caverns of my mind. I couldn't have gone any lower; the only way was up. And I was to emerge a different person.

The poems that had languished for years in yellowing folders in a drawer became my salvation. I had begun writing them when I was at university, often in lectures when I was supposed to be taking notes. When madness caged me I started to document my experiences and feelings in poetry. It was a way of understanding myself at a time when nothing much was making sense to me. I kept writing because it gave me a sense of achievement. I liked being creative; it was something I had wanted to be since those formative years at high school. My poems eventually found an audience when Susan Hawthorne and Renate Klein at Spinifex Press said they would publish them in a book. I was 40 when *Poems from the Madhouse* was published in 1993. It seemed like a miracle; suddenly my life had purpose. I saw myself differently, and other people saw me differently too. My life had new meaning and I felt inspired. I had a name for myself: I was a poet. All those years ago at high school, I had told the vocational psychologist I wanted to be a poet. A dream that had inspired me had come true.

Both of my parents died without seeing me achieve anything in a disappointing life. My bright beginning in sports had come to nothing, as had my degree. Why would this bother me? I suppose every child wants to please her parents, and so did I. Even though I distanced myself from them, I would still have liked to have shown them that I could achieve something; that they could be proud of their daughter. They never said they were disappointed in me, so perhaps I'm projecting my own sense of failure onto them. Sadly they had no understanding of my uneasy path in life. We never understood each other. We never tried. But I am sad that they didn't live to see even one of my books published.

What I did share with my mother was a love of cats, with a passionate affection. We always had a cat in the house and cats were encouraged to sleep on the bed, despite my mother being so houseproud. When I brought home a stray cat, it was immediately loved and fed. When I came home from school in the winter months, there was my mother, lolling back in the armchair in front of the open fire, feet up on the mantelpiece, and a cat on her lap. It was a picture of domestic harmony.

I adore cats too. Without a cat, I feel lost and alone. All my life there have been cats, big ones and little ones, black ones and white ones, young and old ones, moggies and well-bred ones, tabbies and motley ones. And each cat I have loved has been a way of loving my mother, a way of celebrating something of her that is important to me and an integral part of who I am.

Feline Love

When a feline beauty
curls its furred body
upon my lap
smooching its elegance
lounging languidly in the midst
of my curious enduring love
I think of you, Mum.
In every fickle feline sovereign
that graced my home
there has been a piece of you
an undying reservoir of love
that has overflowed with a raucous joy.
I have devoured your joy of cats.
This tiny morsel of you
affords a deep connection
to your lost soul.
I sit in the calm and stroke
the smooth fur of a purring majesty.
I draw your beckoning soul's
outstretched hand to mine.
I grasp this transcendence;
it is all I have left of
the wasteland that was you.

Part Four

Into the Sunset
1993–2004

So I find words I never thought to speak
In streets I never thought I should revisit
When I left my body on a distant shore.
T. S. Eliot

GATHERING STRENGTH

When my poetry was first published I felt at last that I did have some abilities, something to build on, to give back to the community. The sunset beckoned and I was sailing into its radiance, the worst years behind me, the future no longer a void. I had a glimpse of what might be, a newborn optimism. My creativity flourished and I derived a great sense of well-being from each poem that emerged from my heart and soul.

The publication of my first book had changed my life. I entered my forties with no future, identity or self-esteem, and left that decade with success, hope, and a much stronger sense of self. I had always been in awe of published writers. I thought they must be blessed with unimaginable talent and creative powers. I never thought that *I* would one day hold an edition of my own poetry in my hands. The first time I saw a copy of *Poems from the Madhouse* I couldn't believe that I had written it. I caressed it as if it were a newborn child and felt profound wonder that it had been born at all. I kept looking at it as if it were a foreign object, staring at the colourful cover, fingering the pages, carefully leafing through them, reading my words. I'd put it down and pick it up a minute later to make sure it wasn't an apparition. And then I worried about its life in the world and what might happen to it. I feared what people might say about it, whether it would be seen as a joke or taken seriously. My fears were allayed when *Poems from the Madhouse* became runner-up in two poetry prizes. Since then people have told me how much the poems moved them, how they offer a small window into the world of madness. Carers have been amongst my most loyal supporters, saying how much they value the poems. This first book gave me courage and inspiration to write more but I never thought there would be other books. Each of the five books I have written seemed like a gift from a benevolent angel.

As more books were published, I was beginning to believe in myself as a poet. And I found myself becoming a public face of schizophrenia, sharing my story with many others who lived with mental illness or cared for someone who did. Robbie and Dido foresaw this career blossoming, and for a birthday gift one year gave me a lovely leather satchel, a mobile phone, a business card and an email address to help facilitate my new life.

After years in a haunted wilderness I was finally getting myself together. The seed of poetry planted long ago had germinated, and allowed me the hope of imagining who I was or could be. This creative impulse continues to sustain and enrich my life. I no longer await with trepidation the question: *Hello, what do you do?* I am at my best when I am creating, at my happiest when I produce a final version of a poem. Poetry has taken me on a wondrous journey where I have found myself crying with angels, singing with gods and writing words that attest to who I am.

Writing about my madness has enabled me to retrieve a sense of purpose and meaning that seemed forever lost. It has allowed me to delve into darkness, to return with truths and lost dreams, and turn them into poems. The troubled mindscape becomes a palette. Using its textures and colours, I try to evoke the ravages of madness. Madness is my Monster, but it has also been my Muse. I have become the Madwoman who sings with a sane voice.

In a strange irony, madness, my affliction, has become my public identity and occupation. It informs my poetry and is the subject of my media appearances and public speaking. Having carved out a niche for myself using madness credentials, what would my life be like without it? What would happen if my madness should suddenly disappear? My life would certainly be less troubled, quieter and calmer. More conventional? Dare I say it, less interesting? Nor might I have had the opportunities afforded me because of it. What an odd silver lining my madness has turned out to be – even if to a cloud of blackest torment.

The absence of dramatic hospitalisations and medical intervention during these years did not mean that madness had been banished from my life. On the contrary, madness was always in the shadows, sometimes stepping out to waylay me with a wild delusion, or set its voices on me like a pack of marauding dogs. The delusions and voices remained unshakable, a constant menace in my everyday existence, sometimes horrifying; sometimes quite laughable.

One time I became sure my friend Veronica, who had just had a baby, had given birth to the new Messiah. I was so convinced, I wanted to put a full-page advertisement in Melbourne's major newspaper, *The Age*, to announce the momentous event. Veronica said she couldn't quite believe me but that we should wait a couple of weeks before we made a final announcement about it. It was a wise way to handle me because after a couple of weeks my delusion subsided. And she saved me a lot of money. I am also proud of myself that, in the mire of psychosis, I can have a feminist delusion – the child was a girl!

It was I who shot the albatross of Coleridge's poem *The Rime of the Ancient Mariner*. I fired the crossbow myself. The guilt was burdensome; I felt like Atlas with the world on my shoulders. Then there were two sublime weeks when I knew I was a genius. Beethoven had stolen those nine symphonies from me! There was no question about it, I was a brilliant composer, somehow composing these symphonies without ever having written a note of music. For two weeks I was in creative heaven and full of my own importance. It was marvellous. When I came back to reality, the facts that I had not composed the music, and I was not a genius, were truly disappointing.

When the Twin Towers collapsed in New York on 11 September 2001, voices told me that I was responsible for the terrorist attacks, and that I was a mind terrorist with the power to infiltrate people's minds and destroy their thoughts. This was a change from thinking other people could read *my* mind, as I had in the past. But I feared this power. I walked around with my head downcast, too timorous to look people in the eyes. Even God couldn't destroy people's thoughts.

I was Eve; it was I who gave Adam the apple. Therefore I was responsible for the human condition and all its failings. I felt compelled to apologise to God for what I had done. If I contacted the Pope in Rome, who at the time was John Paul II, he would be able to give me God's email address and I could email him my apology. I couldn't understand why I couldn't find the Pope's phone number in the Melbourne telephone book. (I can tell you that there are a lot of listings under 'Pope' in that directory, but none listed as being Pope, John Paul II. I have since thought that if God had an email address, it would be, God@heaven.com.uni). I have smelt God too. I had just been to the toilet, and when I stood up a perfume emanated from the bowl. It was the perfume of God's body. It was beautiful, fragrant and sweet. But when I breathed in the perfume, God laughed at me in a frenzied way, as if he too were mad.

Once I had a strange visual hallucination at the football. My team, the Demons, was going badly. Just before half time, I was horrified to see wires coming out of my heart. They snaked their way over the football ground, pierced the chests of the footballers of my team and penetrated their hearts. They seemed to slow down as they were running over the grass and this is why they were losing. It was all my fault because I was transferring my bad blood through these wires to them. In a panic I fled the ground, believing that if I weren't there they would at least have a chance of winning. But my team still lost, despite me leaving the ground. Because I fear such an episode happening again, I am reluctant to go back to the football.

My friends Lynne and Felicity have had to endure many of my mad moments, some of which have been hilarious. One night Lynne took me to a restaurant to have a meal before going to a movie. I had it in my mind that I had to deliver a message of cosmic importance to the other diners who were quietly eating their meals. It had to be delivered effectively, with drama. I began to take off my clothes and tried to stand on top of a table to deliver my message. I asked the waiter: *Have you had an orgasmic dysfunction lately?* Lynne was beside herself, urging me to put my shirt back on and get off the table. She ushered me out of the restaurant and into the movie theatre, where I sat hunched while Lynne watched the movie. I haven't a clue what movie it was.

On our way home, I was freaking out in the car, my voices saying: *She's driving you to hell. She's going to dump you in the rubbish tip. Fucking bitch, you didn't give your message. You failed.* As we were making our way, I noticed up ahead a booze bus and the police. My voices started: *They are waiting for you. They are going to drag you to a cell and throw away the key. They know you are evil. They are waiting for you.* I started yelling: *Don't stop! Don't stop!* Lynne had her arm across my chest to stop me from opening the car door. They waved her into the bay to breath-test her. I was trying to get out of the car. Lynne still had her arm across my chest. I was agitated. She wound the window down. The policeman leaned in the car, took one look at me and thrust the breathalyser in her face and said in a deadpan voice: *Just blow lady*. She blew into the machine. The policeman checked the reading and signalled for us to go. Lynne planted her foot down and off we went into the night. We laugh a lot about that eventful night. I can't remember, however, what the message of cosmic importance was.

The baggage of my childhood continued to weigh on me. In the recesses of memory still crouched images of things I would rather forget. My father's fist coming down, my mother slumped on the floor, both their mouths twisted with foul curses. Even today, the smell of stale beer sets off a trembling in me. My relationship with my parents was characterised by absence. There was the absence of love between my parents, an absence of a loving family, of a real family structure where I felt safe. I never felt I could have a proper human relationship with my family. The absence of parental love and security had somehow drained the relationships of us as siblings too. This feeling of being unloved is what drove me to seek out alternative relationships with people like Miss Vines who could only offer a limited substitute for what I needed. It is probably what drove me to Catholicism too. My confused loyalties of trying to love my parents, and knowing I couldn't, shredded my emotions and sent me into the world melancholic and troubled.

My parents' relationship was an awful example of marriage to my siblings and me. My sister desperately tried to create the perfect family she felt she never had, yet went on to much unhappiness in her own marriage. Like my mother, she married an abusive man and her own family was far from the happy one she craved. She is, however, a true survivor, weathering many waves in her own stormy life. I don't see my siblings much. They still live in Ballarat while I have long lived in Melbourne. None of us are close, even after all we shared. Yet I care about them enough to ring both occasionally to make sure they are all right. I want them to be all right, and more, I need to *know* they are all right. We suffered a lot together, and a lot on our own, and this has joined us in an unspoken pact that will always make me care for them and they for me, even if we can't show it.

In my book of poems *Blood Relations* I lay bare the wounds of this family life. I see now how this poetry is drenched in sorrow, longing and hurt; but writing it was like an exorcism, dragging out the silenced demons, binding the pain in my soul, soothing the sadness of witness to my mother's decline. Time and distance, hard thought, patience and therapy – all have helped me move to a place where the memories are less tumultuous and strangling.

In 2001 I went back to play hockey at the tender age of 48, rediscovering a passion for team sport. It was one of the biggest challenges of my life because I was playing with younger, fitter, faster, more skilled women. I had lost speed, agility and stick skills in my twenty-five-year absence from the game. Was I trying to recapture a younger part of me from those earlier years when sport was my passion and I was good at it? Whatever it was that prompted me back, it had a good outcome. Hockey provided me with one of the most unforgettable weeks of my life. In 2002 I played for the VicStrikers in the Sydney Gay Games. It was a week of revelry, fun, loads of laughter, socialising and lots of hockey. And we won a silver medal! We often reminisce about the high time we had. Now, in 2009, I play both midweek ladies' tennis and hockey, and I find the camaraderie of the teams exhilarating yet grounding. Being able to return to these vigorous and physically demanding sports has been a heartening indication of my physical well-being.

I wanted to live not in the past with its wrenching despondency but in this new present, and with an eye to the future. Yet, still, a recurring dream haunted me: *The corridor is long. I am running down its uninterrupted, tapering passageway. There are doors either side of me: some wide open, some bolted closed. I can see into the open cells as I rush past them. The same person is lying on each bed. It is me! Screaming and writhing. A crowd of people is standing around the beds. They are all Doctor Y. I walk around these people, wondering why I am on the beds. I can't utter a word of comfort to my distraught selves. My words float up to the ceiling as they come out of my mouth. I walk away from the noise and find myself talking to a bird in a cage. The bird is me and she tells me I am mad. Only then I realise I am in a madhouse from which there is no escape.*

WELLINGTON, NEW ZEALAND
12 SEPTEMBER 1999

There must have been 300 people in the room. I looked out at them in disbelief. Was this really me on the stage? I stood behind the podium thinking: *My God, this is huge, I hope I don't fall into a stammering babble*. I had been invited by the Schizophrenia Fellowship of New Zealand to speak at their biennial conference: all expenses paid. My friend Lynne had said that usually such invitations are extended to 'keynote speakers' but it was only when I found myself before this vast audience that I twigged I *was* a keynote speaker. I was sure that the paper I was about to deliver was a load of rubbish and I would make a fool of myself. I had called my paper 'Poetry, Madness and the Search for Identity'. I calmed myself and began. My words came out with passion and conviction and I didn't stammer once. There was a respectful hush in the room. I ended my speech with, 'To write poetry, after madness, is sanity'. I looked down, shuffled my papers and heard clapping. When I looked up, I saw that the audience was on its feet, applauding loudly. Tears welled in my eyes; I felt overwhelmed. I couldn't believe it. Could I be the same person who had for so long lived without hope or purpose? Was this a dream, or worse, another fanciful hallucination?

In the late 1980s I had begun to talk publicly about living with schizophrenia. The publication of *Poems from the Madhouse* in 1993 drew people's attention to me, and I became known in the psychiatric world as someone who could speak about madness. Since then, advocacy for the mentally ill and their carers had become, with writing, my life's work. As a student teacher in 1975 I had fled from a high school placement feeling I could never teach. I felt terror in front of a class of adolescents. Yet somehow, by the 1990s, I had gathered the confidence to stand in front of general practitioners, psychiatrists, medical students, community groups and school students and talk about what it was like to live with schizophrenia. I used my poetry to help the audience understand madness.

In 2001 my advocacy work was formally recognised when I was one of 250 women whose names were placed on the inaugural Victorian Honour Roll of Women for my work in mental health. A presentation ceremony was held in the Legislative Council chamber at the Victorian parliament where a citation was read and I was presented with a certificate. It was such an honour to be in the presence of women who had achieved so much. Was this the coming to fruition of doing *something important* my sister's friend had prophesied?

I have always had extreme difficulty in being able to celebrate or even acknowledge my successes. I cannot take a compliment without feeling total embarrassment or the necessity to deny the fact that I may have done something well. I learnt about this need for humility as a young girl in primary school when I had an experience so overwhelming it tainted the rest of my life. I was a ten-year-old in grade four when the wrath of my classmates fell upon me in a sustained and cruel way. I had won a foot race and in my delight had raised my arms in celebration. It was done with such innocence and naivety. The next day I started getting notes from the other kids in class saying how much they hated me for my boastful display. The notes kept coming for months and I went from being a popular kid in class to the most reviled. Being popular was crucial to me because it was my way of feeling accepted and loved in the face of the unhappiness of home. Kids stopped asking me to birthday parties; I became ostracised and an outcast. It was a painful year, and when I topped the class after the end of year tests, I didn't tell my parents or anyone else about my achievement nor did I allow myself to feel good about it. This was to become my pattern; to never celebrate success or feel positive about myself. And my voices tap into this self-admonishment by always bringing me back to earth with their scurrilous attacks on my achievements and my character. They are like the kids who mercilessly punished and shunned me.

In 2001 I became involved with a program called SKIPS (Supporting Kids in Primary Schools) which supports children and families affected by mental illness. My role is to talk about how mental illness has affected my life. I have found this work to be the most rewarding of all, because the kids are eager to learn and their imaginations are still fertile. Their questions are always insightful and reflective. I remember one eleven-year-old asking me if I thought my schizophrenia had a spiritual dimension to it. Given the way religion has informed my madness, that question is extraordinarily perceptive. Some of the responses of the kids are overwhelming. Here are a few:

> Today was the last day of SKIPS and Sandy who had schizophrenia came and told us about her illness and how it impacted on her life. When she talked it was very emotional because she was so sad about her illness but she was very inspirational.

> I was really touched by Sandy, a lady who had schizophrenia, when she was brave enough to get up in front of a lot of strangers and how she talked about her personal life and how the voices talked to her.

> I felt that if a trust or bond is made you can share things and learn from others. I felt the guest speaker Sandy was very brave in that she came out and spoke to us about her illness. I felt I became more understanding about it.

> It is easier to understand what people with mental illness go through when you actually listen to someone.

People said I was articulate but I was surprised when I realised they were talking about me, the girl who used to stammer. I would never have believed that I could do any of this. Since the early 1990s there have been many conferences and presentations. I always feel humbled that audiences find my talks moving. I see people crying. At other times they laugh. People tell me they have been enlightened by what I say. Such responses give me the courage to speak in the media for people with mental illness, especially for those who have been silenced. All of this has given my life purpose.

Was my sense of my self so fragile that it collapsed into madness, or did the schizophrenia fracture my sense of self so badly it could not hold together? Who knows? I know that I often felt broken into bits and pieces, my thoughts tumbling so fast I couldn't gather them into a sustained logical reality. At other times, I felt like a sluggish drone, everything about me being laboured, my thoughts stalling in a numbed haze. It was difficult to live with myself. In contrast, I now felt structured and connected. I had a sense of self, a sense that I could be my own person with my own strengths and ideas. While often the world itself may seem bewildering or meaningless, I grew confident that I could interpret it, and find purpose in my wanderings.

When sanity had given way
to reclusive imagination,
I walked tall and deluded.
Now I bask in the joy
of being at home, complete,
mindful of the capricious time
when my mind was pierced by
the steely shards of madness.

Part Five

Billowing Psychotic Fantasia
May 2005

Like one who on a lonesome road
Doth walk in fear and dread,
And having once turned round in fear walks on,
And turns no more his head;
Because he knows, a frightful fiend
Doth close behind him tread.
S. T. Coleridge

CRACKING THE CODE OF THE GOLDEN M

For 14 years I had managed to stay relatively well and functioning quite adequately. I almost believed I was out of the woods. Like the ancient mariner, I was sailing on a calm sea with fair winds, the albatross flying high as a good omen. Then I changed my medication and the white bird fell from the sky. The weight of its carcass remains with me still.

In December 2004 I became concerned that the medication I had been taking for some years was making me gain too much weight. I didn't like my podgy body. I felt like an elephant lumbering around the hockey field and tennis court. I asked Dr Y about changing my medication and she agreed to try something different.

Soon after taking the new medication, and at the same time reducing the old one, I began to experience chronic insomnia. It was a side-effect of the new medication but I thought it would pass. It didn't. There were other problems – nausea and severe headaches, exacerbated by withdrawal symptoms from the previous medication. For six weeks I experienced a mania: it was like someone had turned on a light show in my brain and I couldn't turn it off. I was loud, racy and agitated when I was with people, talking non-stop. I was very irritable, erupting at one stage into uncharacteristic rage. I had cooked a quiche and taken it to Lynne and Felicity's to share. It was on the back seat of the car and, on arrival at their house, Ruby, our dog, who was with me, saw their neighbour's dog in their drive, and leapt onto the back seat and into the middle of the quiche. I was enraged, got out of the car, ranted, raved and cursed the neighbour's dog and made a complete fool of myself. I had never raged like that before. The insomnia got worse and even sleeping tablets were unable to help me. I went for months on only a few hours sleep, when I had been used to a good ten hours every night. Lack of sleep and stress had always been a dangerous combination for me, and I should have been more alert to the signs.

Out of some corner of my mind voices began to whisper, and then to chatter interminably. The voices must have indicated their presence because Lynne asked me if I was hearing them. But they were saying to me: *Don't say, don't tell. Don't trust anyone.* And I didn't. The louder and more insistent they became, the more secretive I became about them. In early May 2005, the simmering madness erupted into a billowing psychotic fantasia.

2/5/2005

I am to do a poetry reading in Daylesford, a little township an hour's drive west of Melbourne. It is cold. The drive along the freeway is pregnant with the gathering forces. A voice says Keep driving, bitch. *I arrive at the house belonging to Gillie, a friend of ours, where I am staying the night. I see that Gillie's body is covered in words and letters. I'm trying to decipher their meaning. She mustn't know I can see them. Another voice says* Hide your face, bitch. *I go off to a pub to meet the organisers of the poetry reading and the other performers. We eat. I listen to the conversation. They speak like prophets, but* I *am the prophet – the prophet of doom . . . the doomed prophet! A voice whispers* Just listen, just listen, count the words before they spill. *It is unnerving me. I leave to make my way to the venue.*

The performance venue feels too intimate, too close and claustrophobic for me. Too many people. I am uncomfortable. I listen to the other performers. A voice tells me They are laughing at you. *The MC introduces me. I stand behind the microphone. I read my poems but they are alien to me. I have to get out of here. A voice tells me*: If you leave now you will never see the sun. I will crush you, and tell everyone to laugh at you. Leaving will only show them how evil you are. *My poems are falling. I am falling. I shudder when the words*, 'The Madwoman in this poem is me' *come from my mouth. The voices laugh. I tell the audience* I feel so bad tonight. *I press on. The voices won't let me leave. One of them says* Don't leave, bitch, you have to struggle. *I finish my reading with the lines*, 'Am I, Cassandra, the seer, mad again?' *A voice demands* Eat your words, slut. *The forces have taken me. I go back to Gillie's, stalk her lounge room, go to bed, sleep fitfully.*

3/5/2005

It's morning. I get up, read the newspaper and see that Rene Rivkin, the business man who has bipolar mood disorder, has killed himself. His suicide rips me apart. I leave Gillie's to run a poetry workshop at the community centre.

I am running the workshop. A voice distracts me: They don't know about the universe and scum like you. *I am detached like a leaf fluttering in the wind. The workshop finally ends. Another voice says* I watched while God raped you, *and laughs. I escape back to Gillie's and ring Lynne. I tell her* The volcano is erupting. *She asks* Where are you? *I answer* At Gillie's. *Lynne persists*: Where's Gillie, can I talk to her? *A voice warns me* Beware of false friends. *I lie*: She's working and can't come to the phone. *Lynne says* Ring me later, will you? *I lie again*: I can't talk, my phone is running out of battery. *I turn off my phone. A voice praises me*: You did well. *The clock says 2:30p.m. I say goodbye to Gillie, get in the car and hit the road.*

I am Thelma and Louise, just like in the film. Every car on the freeway is chasing me! Cars to the left of me, cars to the right of me, cars in front of me and behind me, cars everywhere. I can't escape them. There, in front of me, is a McDonald's restaurant. A voice barks at me: Break the code of the golden M! It's the Virgin Mary, it's Mary Magdalene. It's the golden M. *I pull into the restaurant. A voice commands me*: Eat a cheese burger, go to the toilet and meditate on the golden M. *I eat, piss and meditate, and take to the road. Up ahead is another McDonald's. A voice commands again*: Stop, be faithful to the golden M – the Virgin Mary and Mary Magdalene – eat a cheeseburger and go to the toilet. *The road is troubling me, it's too threatening, too many cars chasing me. A comforting voice offers a solution saying* Drive into Caroline Springs; it's a safe place. *The entrance to this satellite suburb is off the freeway to Melbourne. I drive around its neat streets thinking that perhaps God won't expect to find me here. Laughter. Who is laughing at me? At last I am in Melbourne. My car clock says it's 7p.m. I don't know how many McDonald's there were on the way here, but I have stopped at every one I pass between Daylesford and Lonsdale Street in central Melbourne. I feel sick, full to the brim with cheeseburgers. But I couldn't break the code of the golden M. A voice is chastising me*: You failed, slut. *I am to give a talk with Margie to the Lifeline telephone counsellors. Margie is my bipolar friend and we have given lots of talks together. Crazy women like us have to stick together. I can't let her down. The talk is at Lifeline's rooms at Wesley Church. The W is an inverted M, I think. Two voices are singing to me* Mary, Mary, quite contrary. *I climb the stairs and enter the building clutching a poem in one hand, my car keys in the other. Margie asks* How are you, Sandy?

Words are tumbling out of my mouth: I am possessed, the Antichrist is in me, I've got to go to the Bendigo show, have a spew in Kew and go to Footscray. Robbie and Dido are trying to kill me, they have the house booby-trapped, I'm going to the police station to report them. I've been raped by God. *Margie looks concerned. She is calm and comforts me*: Who would you like me to ring, Sandy? *I can't answer her because of the noise in my head. Where is that laughter coming from? The voices and laughter pause. I am whispering*: I trust only Felicity. *Then a voice commands:* Crawl under the table bitch, prepare to be reborn, bitch, prepare to be aborted, bitch. You are unsafe here. Sluts like you should have been drowned at birth. *I am curled up in foetal position under a table with my eyes closed saying*: I need to be re-birthed, I have to be aborted.

I open my eyes and there's Felicity. And Robbie and Dido are behind her. Betrayed! I don't want to go with them but there's no option. We are walking through the hall and past the audience waiting for me; they are still patiently waiting. They watch me leave with suspicion. I am defiant: I'm not going home, I know it's booby-trapped.

The car is gliding like a cushion. They are taking me to Lynne and Felicity's. The laughter is killing me. I am yelling Fuck off! *How can I stop the laughter? Time is in a warp; we are at Lynne and Felicity's already. The house is a cage. I can't sit down. I'm so scared. My sadness is overwhelming me and I am telling them* When God raped me, it was slow and methodical, slow and methodical. I am being raped over and over and over. I have to go to the toilet and abort the foetus because it's the Antichrist. *I warn them*: My vagina reeks of a foul odour, I can smell it! *They are trying to get me to take some tablets. They are stern and insistent. I know they are in league with God. I relent, swallow the pills, go to bed, sleep a short time, get up, go to the lounge room, sit on the couch, pull a blanket over my shoulders and look into the dark. I feel lonely. A voice chimes a mantra for me*: The mind is a clock, tick tock, the mind is a clock, tick-tock, *and tells me it's a gift. I am whispering it to myself while in the background the rhythmic tick-tock pulses from the kitchen clock.*

4/5/2005

It's morning. Everyone gets up. I'm still on the couch whispering the mantra. Robbie is ringing Dr Y. It's a short phone call. Dr Y says to go back onto the old medication and triple the dosage. She doesn't need to see me. Robbie and Dido are taking me home.

Home is not peaceful. I'm ringing the Royal Women's Hospital to get them to send out a midwife to rebirth me and abort me. The answering service is saying Press one for this and press two for that. *I can't follow it. I hang up. The phone rings. It's my hockey team-mate Kay, she is asking:* How are you, Sandy? *Maybe she can help me: I plead*: Kay, Kay, call the police, I'm being held hostage by Robbie and Dido! I'm in a prison. Ring the Women's Hospital, find me a midwife, God raped me, I'm desperate! *Kay says* Hang in there Sandy, take care. *The phone is my only way to get the message out. I'll ask whoever rings me for help. You never know, someone might be able to find me a midwife and call the police. A voice murmurs my name then says* I saw God rape you, slut.

Once the fantasia took hold, it billowed like a wildfire. I was floridly psychotic for the next few weeks. The only reason I didn't go to hospital was because Robbie and Dido and Lynne and Felicity rearranged their work schedules so that someone could stay at home with me. Other friends rang to see how I was and offer support. I was reeling with the effects of the increased medication. My mind was blancmange and my body was torpid. I felt I was writhing in a bowl of spaghetti, trapped and tangled in its messy strands. I had gone from relative stability to the shambles of uncontrolled madness, unloading my delusional thoughts on all my friends. My inner world had tumbled out unfiltered and uncensored, leaving nowhere to hide. How does one evoke something so wild and unimaginable? It is incomprehensible to anyone not in it. Perhaps the only comparison is a nightmare from which you cannot wake, with all its odd and surreal characters and out-of-kilter settings and distortions of the real world. It was as though my mind was in a macabre prison and the voices were its gaolers. It is not possible to make sense of it, or capture the terror and desperation it induces.

The monster of psychosis had crept from its cage. Getting it back in is one thing, but securing the lock is another. I recovered from this episode only to fall back into a psychotic state a month later. By mid-August I thought I had regained control of my mind, but the monster was only resting. It slipped from its cage at its whim. I wrestled with it, but it clamped onto my mind, twisting and knotting the strands of thought into *mind-forg'd manacles* of paranoia and fear. When it left me, I found myself alone with Melancholia: she trailed behind me in a dowdy gown. Seven months after the breakdown, I was lucid one week and in a fog of psychosis or depression the next. Suicide entered my thoughts on too many occasions. I never knew what mood lay around the corner.

My therapeutic relationship with Dr Y had stalled. After she had shown little concern for what had happened to me in the preceding months, I decided I needed to find another psychiatrist: someone I could talk to. I was scared of making such a big change in my life but it had to be done as I had become disenchanted with Dr Y over the last ten years. I had drifted through the latter part of 2005, still struggling with my voices and delusions, adrift from everyone around me and myself. But I couldn't make the final decision to change psychiatrists because of my fears and emotional paralysis. After procrastinating for some months, I finally plucked up the courage to find someone else. With the help of a friend who asked her therapist if she could recommend someone, I found Dr K. I began therapy with her in February 2006. She is someone to whom I could talk about my voices, delusions and spiritual bereft-ness. I have slowly regained trust in the therapeutic relationship which I felt I had lost with Dr Y. What I like most about Dr K is that she is able to say: *I don't know*. She doesn't feel the need to have answers for everything.

Finding a new therapist during this tumultuous year was crucial as I continued to experience psychotic symptoms. In August 2006 psychosis erupted again. My voices were overpowering me: *you bitch, you witch, you sluttish moll, cankerous leper*. In the mirror was the witch. She looked haggard and unkempt. Her hair was a tangle of incandescent wire. Her wrinkled face was angular and pock-marked with an odd-shaped bony chin. Her large collagen-infused lips were painted bright red, while her teeth were black with decay. Her nose was long and sharp. Her blood-red eyes pierced me like flaming arrows. From the mirror she screamed back at me; sometimes she laughed as though to mock me. I developed a morbid fascination with mirrors, constantly peering into them with an awful anticipation that she might appear again. And she did, over and over.

Who was this witch? Where did she come from? Was she the personification of the evil woman my voices talk about? Whoever she was, she made my skin crawl and I cringed with self-loathing. Around about this time I read Oscar Wilde's novel *The Picture of Dorian Gray*, and in my madness, I assumed the persona of Dorian Gray looking at his hideous, loathsome portrait which had taken on the evil of his soul. I was the root of all the evil in the world.

Dr K thought I needed to spend some time in hospital. Luckily I had private health insurance which meant I could be admitted to a private clinic. She suggested I go to the Albert Road Clinic where she sent her private patients. She said Albert Road was not at all like Larundel. And it wasn't. I had a private room with a million-dollar view of Melbourne. There was no garden to walk in, but the comfort of the clinic was asylum enough to let me feel safe and cared for. On arrival at the clinic I asked for the mirrors in my room to be covered to keep the witch at bay. As for the voices, they were mischievous and crass, and at the height of their powers.

I was four weeks at the clinic. My room was my haven and I spent most of my time in it listening to my MP3 player. As ever, music was my lifeline. Time drifted while I wafted from day to day, unaware of the outside world. My mind was swamped by paranoid delusions and voice-riddled mumbo-jumbo; Melancholia held me tightly in her grasp. The Olanzapine I had been taking no longer held my psychosis. Something had been unleashed in my mind that had a feral life of its own and taming it was not going to be easy. Dr K suggested I try Clozapine, a medication used when everything else has failed. It required assiduous monitoring and regular blood tests because of potential fatal side-effects. I agreed, and started the Clozapine with some reservation, not quite knowing what to expect. Almost immediately after starting the medication I became heavily sedated and lethargic. My speech left me and my stammer reappeared. I was physically burdened by a constant feeling of low-level nausea. In my mind I felt addled and emotionless.

Since then the struggle to retain sanity has been a day-by-day proposition. Suicide was never far from my thoughts. If only I could find a key that would lock the monster away securely.

S

MAD DOCTORS

The sudden relapse into madness has made me question everything. Could I be back where I began? Will the monster hound me always? If I hadn't asked to change my medication when I was relatively stable, would it have happened at all? Who knows? On many occasions I have blamed myself for events over which I have no control: for not being able to stop my father's violence, for Bruce's abuse, for becoming psychotic. Is this related to the feeling, common in my psychosis, that I taint the world around me, that I am responsible for evil things in it, regardless of my powerlessness?

Whatever the answer, I must accept that the madness *has* recurred and I am left with the aftermath. Something positive has emerged since the shocking episode of 2005: it has forced me to question psychiatry more rigorously, with its reliance on drugs, and along with that, the ways childhood trauma affect the content of my delusions. I also reflected critically on therapies and the therapeutic relationship. My ruminations have been painful but illuminating. They have moved me into a new phase of my life.

Therapy requires us to take the risk of trusting another with our inner life, perhaps even our soul. It is a minefield of difficult questions without answers. During my hospital experiences I have been assailed by many doctors asking questions. They expect me to trust them simply because they are the professionals. They must know all about my life, while I know nothing about them. I have sometimes felt it would be useful to have a recording of my life-story to play for these doctors instead of repeating myself endlessly. Maybe now I can just hand them this memoir. Trust is not easily given, even in normal circumstances. When I am mad it is difficult enough to talk to strangers, let alone trust them. Do I disclose things knowing I might never see that doctor again? Do I trust this doctor proffering medications because she is a professional and I am the patient? How can I know whether this treatment will help in my healing?

After meeting Dr Y in B ward at Larundel in 1978 I continued to see her for the next 27 years of my madness. Because she was my treating doctor on a number of admissions to Larundel, she saw me at times when I was very psychotic. I initially engaged in this therapeutic relationship for two reasons. First, I had a mental illness which needed to be treated. Second, I was desperate to talk to someone about my parents and reflect on the pall they cast over me and my siblings. In the beginning, Dr Y and I talked a lot about my parents and their destructive relationship. It was good to be able to explore the anger and pain my parents had caused me. She allowed me to be the hurt child, something I needed to do in order to be able to put my parents in an emotional place where I could deal with them. She spent time preparing me for their death because I expressed anxiety about how I would handle the aftermath. She helped me to untangle some of my puzzled emotions about them, and so manage my baggage better. This therapy lasted a few years, after which my sessions with her became much more like maintenance visits, to monitor medication. At one time Dr Y did express her concern to Robbie and Dido that she didn't want to delve too deeply into my dark world for fear of unleashing something that was too awful for me to deal with. But isn't that what psychiatrists do?

Was she protecting me or avoiding something she felt she couldn't deal with? But I had never given her, or anyone, a comprehensive exposition on what the voices say, or how they affect me. Not until now where, in writing this memoir, I have systematically dredged their murky foul-mouthed world to expose its horrors. They will castigate me for this.

Dr Y tried different sorts of therapy with me: drug therapy, talking cure, and Cognitive Behavioural Therapy (CBT). The CBT focused on making me recognise how my thoughts, feelings and behaviour were stuck in an unhelpful pattern. She tried this when I was delusional about Robbie and Dido and gave me some techniques to reality-check my beliefs. Sometimes she tried to point out the inconsistencies and illogicalities of my delusions by offering concrete evidence to dispel my false beliefs. I didn't find this all that helpful – perhaps I wasn't a very receptive patient, but also because, while the therapy softened the effects of my schizophrenia, it somehow failed to plumb the emotional influences. Over the years her focus remained on what the drugs could do for me rather than what patterns talking might reveal. I can see that the drugs do have an effect, and she was astute at times at adjusting the combinations of medications she prescribed for me, but sometimes my resistance and questioning exasperated her and she would say: *Just let me heal you!* as though she had all the answers. It is important for me to be able to question, rather than passively accept.

We did not explore much my religious contradictions and spiritual emptiness, nor the many other emotional tensions I have been living with. Western psychiatry has been a notoriously rationalist discipline, especially to those with a more spiritual world view. From the scientific viewpoint, treatment for madness is more about balancing chemicals than healing the spirit.

Dr Y's approach to me and to psychiatry changed over the years. Early on she was reluctant to engage with Robbie and

Dido. She was suspicious of their motives and wasn't forthcoming to them about my condition. Possibly she felt awkward about our lesbianism in the beginning. She did, after some time, accept them as my primary carers, I guess, because she had to recognise the significance and durability of our relationships, that Robbie and Dido were capable women who could stand up for themselves, and for me. In terms of treatment, she went from the *talking cure* to a reliance on medication. Her approach to treatment mirrored the changes that have taken place in the practice of psychiatry over the last 30 years. I changed too, going from frustration at her conservatism and unshakable faith in the medical model, with its heavy reliance on drugs, to accepting her method and trying to work with it.

My friend Lynne's experience of therapy was very different. She told me she went into therapy because she felt troubled about something that had happened with a friend to which she over-reacted. Lynne thought she was starting to unravel. She wondered if it might have something to do with her family and religion. Lynne saw her therapist as a personal private detective whom she engaged to help her find the missing pieces and sort out the puzzle of why she was behaving the way she was. She came from an empowered position: knowing what she wanted to work on, setting boundaries on what she was prepared to talk about. For Lynne, the therapeutic experience was very helpful and enlightening, and she came away with a much better self-knowledge and understanding of what drove her. Lynne says she cried rivers of tears with her therapist. When I told Lynne I had never cried with Dr Y, she was astounded.

It took me 17 years to raise the issue of Bruce with Dr Y. Why so long? Because it was a shame I felt too deeply to talk about with anyone, even Robbie and Dido. I had also pushed it to the back of my mind and convinced myself it wasn't important. I realised its significance as I watched a friend struggle with abuse in her own case. When I finally broached the issue and the effect it had had on me with Dr Y, she was at first more concerned that I was depressed and wanted to treat the depression with antidepressants. When I expressed shame and guilt associated with my memories, she suggested that I would have been a 'mature thirteen year old'. Did she mean that I was mature enough to deal with this twenty-four-year-old man, even though I was a thirteen-year-old girl, and drunk? Did she think my emotional reaction was unwarranted? Did she even believe me? Her response shocked and angered me, reminding me painfully of the abused, powerless little girl I was then, whose trust had been betrayed. Her lack of empathy made me wonder about how she dealt with other women who had issues of abuse. I didn't pursue the subject because I didn't feel safe with her. Nor did I challenge her; my inability to handle disharmony paralysed me. I internalised my anger and seethed for another ten years over what she had said. In my silence, I started to disengage from her.

Ultimately, I have felt stymied in my attempts to understand the content of my psychotic ramblings and their persistent patterns. I accept that the brain is an organ like the heart, kidney, or liver and is susceptible to illness. However, it is also the locus of the mind, and the interaction between the mind and brain is not well understood. Would it make a difference to the process of healing, I wonder, to explore the symbolism of my delusions and voices, and the innumerable set of contradictions I have lived with?

Recent research by a team led by J. Read looked at the relationship of childhood trauma to psychosis and schizophrenia. They found that 'reference to evil or the Devil was more common among those who had been sexually abused'. In the same review article it states that 'in people with psychosis, there is a marked excess of victimising experiences, many of which will have occurred in childhood. This is suggestive of a social contribution to aetiology.' Drugs only deal with the chemical side of me, and while they have kept me relatively sane, they have done little to help me resolve the internal contradictions and emotional trauma that fuel the content of my madness.

A psychotic illness like schizophrenia is a complex condition, determined partly by chemicals in the brain being unbalanced as well as the effects of lived experience. I believe psychosis does not manifest itself in a vacuum; it fixes upon content, just as nightmares must be about something already within a mind. My feeling is that the psychiatric treatment I have had concentrated on the brain and its mix of chemicals to the cost of exploring the mind. What I would say to psychiatry is this: you can medicate the brain but you have to engage with the mind. The word *psychiatrist* means *healer of the soul*.

Why did I persist with a relationship that had such limits to its therapeutic value? A relationship with a therapist has many aspects. Dr Y managed my psychotic symptoms well. I am also appreciative that during periods of illness she kept me home when another psychiatrist might have hospitalised me. She was prepared for me to stay on a disability pension because she understood the difficulties I have with work. She was of some help in coming to terms with my parents. She knew much of my story. We shared a long history to which I felt a strange loyalty. Perhaps the duration of our relationship bred complacency, where she thought she understood me perhaps better than she did. For me, our relationship bred resignation. I felt a certain powerlessness in it, being dependent on her for treatment for such tormenting psychosis. I clung to the hand proffering medication. I was paralysed by self-doubt, and summoning the courage to start all over again with this sorry story was a challenge. I was well aware of the irony of my situation. There I was speaking to audiences about managing mental illness yet my own treatment was seriously flawed.

Madness for me has been a roller-coaster, driven by a stranger seizing control of my mind and lunging from one delusion to another. If I could identify the stranger, would therapy help me accept her or incorporate her into my life? Or fear her less? Or banish her? At least help me establish a tolerable relationship with her? Is this stranger that part of me which Carl Jung would call the 'shadow', which personifies all I refuse to acknowledge about myself? If I could heal that damaged little girl, would the persecutory content of my delusions and voices diminish, and allow me to embrace her?

Have Dr Y and psychiatry failed me? I don't think so. I haven't descended into relentless madness, becoming unreachable and unreaching to the point of complete isolation, as others have. Medication has kept the symptoms more or less controlled. I have gained some understanding of myself through therapy.

Perhaps I am more equipped now, and more able, to begin a new exploration, so that I might arrive 'at the place I began and know myself for the first time'.

I have been afraid to attend some wounds for fear they might bleed too much and never heal. My poetry has been good therapy, a place in which I can explore and process a lot of emotional hurt, but it isn't enough. Writing this memoir has aroused harrowing memories I have suppressed for a long time, yet it has helped me make connections between my traumatic history and my incomprehensible symptoms, and this has been therapeutic in itself. Can I find my ideal 'soul healer' out there whom I can trust to illuminate with me this dark territory into which Dr Y seemed reluctant to venture too deeply? I think so. Dr K has been a revelation and I am hopeful we can form a good and productive therapeutic relationship. But there is a lot of work to be done and Dr K says she is in for the long haul. So am I.

SURVIVOR OF THAT TIME

I stand as witness to the common lot,
survivor of that time, that place.
Anna Akhmatova

Over the course of my journey into madness, and my return from that Underworld, I have seen major changes in the field of psychiatric treatment. The development of more effective drug treatments and the domination by psychopharmacology to the exclusion of more holistic therapies, is one significant change. But there have been many others worth recording. When I first went mad 33 years ago, no-one talked about madness. Now there are articulate people living with mental illness who speak out for themselves in forceful and challenging ways. Our emerging voices are a sign that change is on the way. This will remain difficult so long as the media continues with sensationalist and ill-informed stories about mental illness.

In recent decades there has been a sustained development of non-government services representing the mentally ill, and those caring for them, known now as Psychiatric Disability Rehabilitation Support Services (PDRSS). The PDRSS sector was set up to empower and support the mentally ill and their carers by educating them and teaching them the skills that enable them to cope better with their difficult circumstances. But in 1976, none of these organisations existed: the Mental Illness Fellowship (formerly the Schizophrenia Fellowship), SANE Australia, ARAFMI (Association for the Relatives and Friends of the Mentally Ill), Beyond Blue, the Victorian Mental Illness Awareness Council (VMIAC). These are just some of the many organisations that do enormously valuable work for the mentally ill and their carers, providing rehabilitation, mutual support and self-help, accommodation, advocacy, drop-in centres and transitional employment training. Most of these NGOs are funded by government to provide these services. Some, like SANE, are funded from donations and bequests which ensures they have an independent and critical voice. We need to inspire the community's compassion, and can do this by speaking out, gaining understanding, showing our human faces long shadowed by ignorance and stereotypes. There are also signs that clinicians are prepared to listen to the voices of those for whom they work, to recognise and value the lived experience of those who do care for the mentally ill. People with a mental illness are now employed as consumer consultants by hospitals in the state of Victoria, to work with inpatients in psychiatric wards. Carers are being employed as carer consultants in some hospitals as well. These are major steps but there is a long way to go before those who control our lives hear what we have to say.

People who have a psychiatric illness are now called *consumers*. Some of the other words used to describe us over the years have been *patient* and *client*, both of which have lost favour. The term *consumer* suggests that people using psychiatric services have a choice of care and treatment, which would certainly be empowerment in a system that historically offered mentally ill people no choice. Yet I do not like the term *consumer*. It was first used in North America, not surprisingly, and in using the language of the economic market, tends to reduce the ill person to someone who purchases services rather than someone who should receive human compassion and care. I like the sense of the term used by the Maori in New Zealand, who describe people with a psychiatric illness as *tangata whaiora*, which means *person seeking wellness*. I tend to call myself *mad* – so that I can defuse the vilification in that label. Reclaiming language that is used to stigmatise is an act of empowerment.

In the early years my lesbianism was definitely a problem for the psychiatrists and this was reflected in the language they used in their notes when writing reports about me. In an early note one psychiatrist said: *On admission was a co-operative though rather masculine looking girl*. Masculine? I have always had long hair and my breasts were always ample. It was always noted I was in a *lesbian menage-à-trois* but, by my last hospitalisation in 1991, the language around my relationships with Robbie and Dido had changed. In my discharge notes it was said I was living in a *shared residence with two female friends of long standing who have been very supportive to her in the past and continued to look after her*. Did this indicate greater acceptance? Or was it simply that I became stronger and more settled in my own sexuality, and that made me more impervious to stigma? I'm not sure, but my feeling is that society was changing in its attitude towards homosexuality and this fact was reflected in the way clinicians began to treat my lesbianism, and Robbie and Dido, with more respect.

* * *

In the early 1990s sweeping changes were made to the mental health system in the state of Victoria. There was a shift away from the stand-alone psychiatric hospitals to what is called '*care in the community*', or '*de-institutionalisation*'. This policy presumes the community *will care*, something which makes our voices especially significant, for closing the madhouses and moving the mad into the community has been a bold but flawed reform. The philosophy underpinning the notion of keeping the ill person within their home environment is that familiar places and less restrictive environments are more conducive to recovery. Thus, family and friends have become primary carers – a difficult and challenging role for them, without enough support. While there are case-managers and workers employed by government and non-government agencies to help with the rehabilitation of the mentally ill, their case-loads are usually too large to be manageable. Nor are there enough supported accommodation places, halfway houses or community-care units for people released from the acute psychiatric wards. When all else fails, however, it is family and friends who are left to care for their loved ones. Without the multitude of carers who, out of love and responsibility, care for the mentally ill, using their own resources, there would be a crisis in the mental health system.

The funding needed to make the policy of 'de-institutionalisation' successful hasn't been provided. Psychiatric hospitals have been replaced by small acute wards in the general hospitals. The gatekeepers to these wards are the Crisis Assessment Teams who go into the homes of the mentally ill to assess and treat them. It is very difficult to be admitted to an acute ward; one essentially has to be suicidal or a danger to others. My Parkville friend Gail, who works in one of these wards as a consumer consultant, says they are characterised by a culture of despair and hopelessness. An admission to the old madhouses used to be weeks, months, or maybe years. People used to say: *Never let yourself be put in a loony bin, you'll never get out.* And it was true. Now, the pendulum has swung the other way: an admission to these small, acute wards is on average eight to ten days. Thus the pressure on the small number of beds is intense, and results in a high turnover of patients. I describe these wards as being like a McDonald's drive-thru where you pick up a diagnosis and medication while the CAT teams are a home-delivery service. Not only is this fast tracking of patients endemic to the acute wards, private psychiatrists are also delivering what I describe as McDonald's therapy. People feel as though they are shunted out of the consulting room without having been listened to, with a prescription thrust into their hands as they leave. I call this new clinical paradigm *Fast*psychiatry.

I also sense that there has been a devaluing of the skill of psychiatric nursing since the closure of the psychiatric hospitals, which is reflected in how nurses are now trained. Psychiatric nurses used to be educated and trained in the hospitals over a three-year period; now the discipline has become a mere add-on to a general nursing degree. Psychiatric nursing skills are lost among the plethora of other more desirable or highly regarded nursing disciplines on offer. Who would want to work in the stressful environment of an acute psychiatric ward where there is usually an unremitting sense of despair and hopelessness? Yet I know I have been helped enormously during my hospitalisations by the psychiatric nurses who cared for me, with good clinical skills, empathy, compassion and kindness. With these nurses I was able to form a relationship because they, unlike the psychiatrists I only saw once or twice a week, were with me day and night, watching the different phases of my fluctuating illness. I always felt the nurses had a more realistic understanding of my madness and how it impacted on me. One cannot value enough the role of psychiatric nurses in the care of the mentally ill: their clinical and caring skills can make the difference between a good and bad experience of hospital.

We have lost the notion of asylum – a refuge where one has space and time to recover from trauma. It takes more than a few days to recover from a psychotic episode. And if you do get admitted, these hot-house wards, in which only the most acutely ill are cared for, cannot provide asylum. People experiencing psychosis are exposed as ill and out of control more often than even a few years ago because it is so difficult for them to access a hospital bed. This can only increase the stigma of mental illness. We don't leave people with broken legs on the street, or make heart-attack victims wait long hours in casualty wards. Healing can only occur in a space that encourages healing.

I am not, however, suggesting we go back to the appalling asylums of old; we must and can do better. Psychiatrist John Cawte in his book *The Last of the Lunatics* says 'the community is the proper resort of humanity, but it can also generate pressures that go beyond endurance for those who are vulnerable. Refuge – of a temporary kind – supported by sound medical care, provides one solution.' I used to dream of a retreat where I might be cared for sympathetically, fed good food, given appropriate medical care, art and music therapy, pleasant living quarters, gardens tended with love, and as much time as I need to find my balance. Then I might contribute, rather than be a cost, to my community.

It is said that a society should be judged by the way it treats its unfortunate. Our illnesses make us vulnerable and dependent, and at the mercy of whatever treatment and care we are able to get. We may have moved on from putting the mad into stocks, but mental health remains under-funded. There are not many votes in madness. Yet one in five people in Australia will suffer mental illness – that may be someone in your family, if not you yourself. Has the plight of the mentally ill in fact changed substantively? In a system that is struggling to cope, many of the mentally ill are simply discharged to the street. A 1998 report titled *Down and Out in Sydney* by Hodder and others found that, of the 210 homeless people aged between 17-87 years surveyed, 75 per cent had a mental illness, and 23 per cent of men and 46 per cent of women had schizophrenia. The 1999 Jablensky report found that the majority of people who live with a psychotic illness have lost essential skills and supports that provide self-esteem and meaning. Eighty-four per cent are separated, divorced, widowed or single; 85 per cent are reliant on welfare benefits; 72 per cent do not have a regular occupation; 45 per cent live in institutions, hostels, supported accommodation, crisis shelters or are homeless. Another report by Lambert and others in 2003 found that people diagnosed with schizophrenia can expect to live nine to twelve years fewer on average than those in the general population. More than two-thirds (72 per cent) of people affected by mental illness consulted for the first SANE Australia Research Report in 2005 said they felt lonely 'often' or 'all the time'. It has also been estimated that half the prison population in Australia has a mental illness.

These are sobering statistics that show compassionate action is needed. There are no easy answers to how best those with mental illness can be helped so that they might fulfil their potential for a good life which also contributes to the society. Extensive research is needed to unravel complexities of the issue, and humane wisdom to resolve them.

* * *

It is good that they have gone: the lunatic asylum, madhouse, loony bin, booby hatch, bug house, rat house, giggle factory, nut house and funny farm. People were locked away for years in these places in a drug-induced straightjacket, with nothing in their lives but the demented others with whom they shared their sad world. Their normal living skills were lost as a result of long hospitalisation, and their mental health often only deteriorated. Some have made it into long-term residences set up in the community. Many more have fallen through the cracks of the system and are on the street.

The closing down of Larundel began in 1990. Before the last ward was decommissioned in 1999, it was decided to have a ceremony. It was a hastily prepared function to which people who had worked there as nurses, clinicians, administrators, social workers, occupational therapists and maintenance staff were invited. Gail found out about it through her contacts and alerted me, suggesting I go along. I'm glad I did. I was the only person in the room who had been a patient there. I asked to address the gathering, some of whom I recognised as staff who had looked after me in my many admissions. I felt the weighty responsibility of knowing I was speaking for every mad person who had ever been in Larundel. I reminded them that Larundel existed only because of madmen and women like myself, and that we were standing on sacred ground still haunted by their anguished spirits. I suggested Larundel was like a church no longer in use, and a desanctification of it was needed, a blessing to release the souls of the tortured mad who had paced these grounds, captive to their minds' unease and society's neglect. I then read two of my poems: 'Sitting on the Balcony of B Ward' and 'As She Gently Brushed My Long Hair', both of which are in this book. It was a poignant occasion, and for me full of solemn memories.

With the closure of hospitals like Larundel a world has been lost. Yet Larundel had its good points too. My recollections of it are not all bad. The gardens were a comfort. I was fed, if with pretty awful food. I was housed in adequate accommodation. I sometimes felt cared for by staff. I could take the time I needed to get well. It provided me with a safe place. There was asylum of sorts while I was there. I also found the experience of Larundel salutary and instructive of the human condition. I would not have seen the full gamut of human behaviour in such minute detail, and with such clarity, had I not had my time in this unsettled sanctuary.

The once rambling gardens and rolling paddocks of Larundel are now a sprawling mass of houses and high-density living. Carefree cries of families oblivious to the history of these precincts now mingle with the ghosts of the mad who once wandered here. Will these old madhouses on the edge of town be forgotten? Will the sighs of the lunatic looking longingly to the outside world be remembered by anyone? Is what we do now better? Is today's catchcry for mental health, *care in the community*, a reality? We have closed the madhouses, but do the mad really receive more recognition, care, compassion? Perhaps, as a symbolic gesture, monuments ought to be erected on the sites of these former mad-houses to commemorate all those who witnessed the suffering, or passed through, or lived and died in madhouses like Larundel.

THE FAR SIDE OF MADNESS

For all the pain my madness has caused me, it has shown me life in all its beauty and grotesqueness. I have been to the end of the universe and seen the sun in all its glory; I have also seen the Devil. I have glimpsed aspects of the human condition rarely seen by others. I have seen people in the depths of despair lift themselves to touch the stars, people in the grip of psychosis regain their sanity. I have seen others succumb to their madness, their lives a shipwreck on the rocks of insanity. I have seen people care with compassion and self-sacrifice for those unable to be responsible for themselves. I have seen minds destroyed by madness, families torn apart and bereft at the loss of a child or sibling to suicide. My own callings to death's door have been compelling; yet I have turned away from this grim threshold and survived. I have witnessed such despair in myself that nothing can offer meaning for it. While I can't forget the effect my childhood has had on how I see the world and live in it, I have seen the future beckon. I have felt futile and weak, and also strong and purposeful. Sometimes I believe in miracles, for why have I been lucky enough to be helped out of the pit that has claimed so many lives?

When I have fallen, my dearest of friends have picked me up. I grasp my friendships and hold them in my heart, even when I know I have not always been such a good friend myself. The gift of friendship is one miracle. My two Demeters are two miracles. They are my reality check when I need to be grounded. They have said to me, when I stride in after a speaking engagement, over-inflated with self-importance: *Keep your feet on the ground and your hand on the vacuum cleaner*. They are my rock when I need to feel stable, my carers when I need to be safe, my source of strength when I feel weak. They are my IT troubleshooters when my computer malfunctions. They keep my place at the table; they keep me warm. And all this for someone who carries with her so much hulking baggage. When I look at what has happened in my life it reads like a soap opera. I describe myself as being *a hamburger with the lot*. Robbie and Dido have helped me make a life worth living – and this is as effective as any antipsychotic drug. If only others afflicted by mental illness were as blessed.

We have lived in the same house for 30 years in a place where we all say it is Christmas every day. It has been of great comfort to me to have the space and fresh air of the bush, a place where I love living, and which I believe helps me live a calmer life. But I do muse on the fact that when Robbie and Dido had a vision, they saw our home in the bush. Why is it that when I had a vision, it was of the Virgin Mary and I ended up in a madhouse?

Being mad again has intensified the uncertainty with which I see myself. I question my sanity all the time. I monitor my moods. I watch myself when I am with others. I ask myself: am I behaving appropriately? am I in control of myself? how are others seeing me? I am also aware that others are watching me, looking out for tell-tale signs of my state of mind. The scrutiny of my friends is the price I pay for being mad, but it is essential that they are able to do this because without their interventions my madness would destroy me.

With this latest ambush on my sanity I realise that the longer I live with schizophrenia, the more mysterious this illness has become. How can we know its workings? I feel its mystery cannot be explained fully by research on the brain and its chemicals. While I am no scientist, in observing my own life and madness, I am struck by the interplay of so many childhood and emotional experiences with a brain physiologically flawed. There is a complex relationship between the two yet to be fully discovered.

From the moment when my mind first fractured into madness, I have had to live with the truth about my own fragility. At times my mind has seemed so fragmented it was impossible to imagine again a whole self, connected to others in the world. In the end I was left with only myself, realising no-one else could know the internal hell of madness, only its undignified display of bizarre behaviour. I always feel as though I am ten minutes away from a complete breakdown.

Throughout the 33 years of my madness something has pulled me back from the void and kept me together. It may simply be that I have no choice but to keep staggering on; that I can never give up. I fight my madness. I fight my self-denigrating and destructive impulses. I fight to forge a sense of self based on a conciliatory acceptance of who I am. Schizophrenia has imposed limitations on my life; in acknowledging this I can live with myself. I find relief in accepting my flaws. After each episode of psychosis, I start uphill again, like Sisyphus never quite reaching the top.

Through all of my difficulties and discordance, the moments when I feel strongest and most alive are when I am creating. I hold these moments close to me because I know they are fleeting. Round the corner the voices can almost be heard.

There have been times when I forget what the sane me is like, that for much of the time I am a sane, functioning person. I forget that I can work in a disciplined way, as I have in completing this memoir. In many ways I am very down-to-earth and realistic about the world – perhaps a little too overwrought by politicians and their apparently cynical disregard of vulnerable and dispossessed people – but generally quite pragmatic, careful, balanced. I am not into what I would term 'spooky' things, like astrology, crystals, tarot readings or psychic healing. I am quite conservative in many ways. I am a sports fan and follow my football team. I watch sport on television but enjoy playing it more. I admit that I like to win, but more than winning, I love being part of a team and revel in the feeling of team spirit.

I have a strong sense of humour, if often countered by a morbid disposition – a black humour, I guess, but one which has on occasion had large audiences laughing uproariously. Black humour is one way of dealing with a condition otherwise unendurable. Grappling with the spectre of a psychotic illness and its consequences has to provoke a philosophical, sideways view of the world. I like the idea that I can write poems both dark and humorous; that I can make people laugh and cry. I want to bring angels to tears then revive them with hilarity. It was my sense of humour, among other qualities, that was recognised by an award bestowed upon me by the Australasian Mental Health Services Conference in 2007 for an exceptional contribution to mental health services in Australia. The citation reads: *In recognition of qualities of deep compassion and creativity given wholeheartedly towards the recovery of others and graced by a unique message of hope through poetry and humour*. Yet, in writing about the facts of my life, I have found this leavening humour has only occasionally been able to surface. My sane self spends a lot of time reflecting on my mad self because I can't escape her.

I have been described by my fellow sufferer Greg as *the sanest madwoman* he knows. The contradictions keep coming. People who haven't seen me mad cannot imagine the mad me. What they don't see is the constant wrestling between the mad and sane forces that takes place in the ferment of my own mind.

Peace of mind?
There is no calm
amidst the turmoil
or a friendly glow
to assuage the desperation.

Ignorance talks of the
comfort of madness.
I talk of the
far side of madness
and the flames of Hell.
No, I shall never be the same.

Since the sudden and dreadful descent back into madness in 2005, I have found a new psychiatrist and begun a more productive therapeutic relationship. I know I must try to understand myself more completely, if I am to live tolerably with the madness that may always lie in wait. I am thankful that I have my friends, my animals, music, books and sport to accompany me and keep me strong. I have my writing to carry into the future with me as well. Already it has set me on an expedition from which there is no turning back.

EPILOGUE

When I started writing this memoir, five years ago, I had no idea of the journey that lay ahead of me; what a roller-coaster, topsy-turvy time I was going to have; what highs and lows awaited. I didn't know that from the time of that catastrophic breakdown in 2005 I'd be fighting for my sanity nearly every day.

As I write, in February 2009, I have just come out of the Albert Road Clinic where I have spent five weeks. Hospitalised yet again. I have little recollection of how I got there. It had something to do with the microchip Tony Blair implanted in my left ear which had been programmed to systematically destroy my thoughts. When I awoke in the morning there was an empty space in my brain where my thoughts once were. I was driven to occupy my mind with mental arithmetic and music to keep the voices at bay. My morning mantra, which had been with me since 2005, was in full voice: *top myself? have brekkie? top myself? have brekkie?* At night, I was awakened routinely at 3:30a.m. to the wailing of a woman in great distress.

Who is this wailing woman whose grief is so profound, so raw? Are her tears my unshed tears? I have a sense she is doing something I am unable to do, that she is expressing grief I am unable to express. I have a sense she may be weeping for the little girl who is demanding to be heard and in need of healing. I used to think I needed to forgive her. Why do I blame her and, worse, punish her? Rescuing and caring for that little girl has become a priority. She needs love and kindness. I am now investigating her damaged soul more mindfully than ever before. I am looking more deeply into the part she plays in my emotional life. Acknowledging her, validating her experience, is an important component in her healing. But how do I begin to rescue her?

This new investigation is a crucial development for me and has come about through the agency of Dr K. Together we are examining my life and in particular the abuse of that little girl whose sadness is grave and relentless. Another reason for the admission to the clinic was to undergo a medication change. It was finally recognised that the Clozapine experiment had failed. When I developed a very rare side-effect to the drug, Dr K decided to wean me off it and put me back onto Olanzapine. My final medication regime will be a hefty dosage of Olanzapine in conjunction with an antidepressant called Lexapro. The irony of this medication change is that I am back to almost exactly where I was when the whole sorry medication saga began in December 2004. Except that during this time I found my way to Dr K and this, I believe, has put me on a more hopeful path.

Dr K has also referred me to a psychologist who may be able to help me deal with my voices by undergoing intensive Cognitive Behavioural Therapy. Because the voices have ruled my inner world for so long, I am finding the therapy challenging. The voices are finding it challenging too. Their existence and power rest in my continued helplessness. Empowering myself to negate, and ultimately dismiss, them and their destructiveness, can only be a good thing. It's like a war of words between us. I hope it will be me who has the last word.

My room at the clinic was in the adolescent ward because, on admission, there were no beds free in the adult ward. This gave me the opportunity to mingle with young people, all of whom were struggling with mental illness. How cruel of life to mess with the minds of people so young, so innocent. I looked at these teenagers and thought: you are me 30 years ago; I am you 30 years on. I hope your journey will be less painful than mine; that there are better medications and treatments for you. I hope you recover better and sooner.

Whilst these last five years have been sometimes almost unendurable, some wonderful things have happened. My poetry has been given the opportunity to engage a new audience. A young composer in the UK, Nirmali Fenn, who is doing a PhD in composition at Oxford University, is turning *The Wings of Angels: A Memoir of Madness* into an opera. In Australia, Russian-born Australian composer Elena Kats-Chernin and choreographer Meryl Tankard have been commissioned by the Joan Sutherland Performing Arts Centre to create a performance piece inspired by my poetry and life. It will incorporate dance, spoken word, song and music in a set of vignettes. The projected date for the performance is 2010. In early 2008 I was interviewed, along with a young singer-song writer, Heidi Everett, for a special edition of the television show *Enough Rope*, hosted by Andrew Denton. It was called *Angels and Demons* and it explored the torturous world of mental illness through the stories of those who struggle with it every day of their uneasy lives. It was watched by a million people and had rave reviews and, following from that success, Andrew Denton has asked Heidi, who is also a talented artist, and me to collaborate on a book.

And all this has come about while I have been in the midst of lingering madness.

* * *

As I was nearing time for discharge from the clinic I was allowed to go home to Christmas Hills for overnight leave. I was looking forward to the tranquillity of home, to patting the animals and spending time with Robbie and Dido, both of whom had recently retired, and were also looking forward to quieter times.

Of all the times to go home, I went on the day of the most extreme fire danger ever recorded in Victoria. It was followed by one of Australia's worst natural disasters – the 'Black Saturday' bushfires. Conflagrations engulfed entire towns; new fires sprang up before earlier ones could be contained, and Christmas Hills was under direct threat. Robbie and Dido were called out on CFA (Country Fire Authority) duties, and I was left at home to patrol the veranda for falling embers.

The wind was gusting ferociously and smoke was building to the north of us. On the CFA listening set I could hear that things were serious. I continued to patrol the house, filling buckets of water, making sure I knew where mops and buckets and knapsacks were.

I was alone there, holding the fort from the fire. So this was to be my respite from the clinc, my homecoming. Suddenly, my eyes started rolling upwards; I was having an oculargyric crisis! My voices came to the party, commanding me to: *Curl up in foetal position on the front deck*. I was fighting my mutinous eyes and trying to remain focused on what I had to do. I did. And I resisted the commands. I was so relieved when Dido came home,

Much changed during these few days. We survived our Paradise becoming the Inferno. A serendipitous wind change saved our home, but many were lost in our community. It is no longer Christmas every day for many families in our area who face rebuilding devastated homes and lives.

Things have changed for me too. The day of the fires has shown me a reservoir of resilience I didn't know I had, and a powerful sense that I might yet control if not cure the madness that remains part of me.

Part Six

Afterword to the 2024 Edition

HOMECOMING: AN AFTERWORD

Here then at home by no more storms distrest,
Folding laborious hands we sit, wings furled;
Here in close perfume lies the rose-leaf curled,
Here the sun stands and knows not east nor west,
Here no tide runs; we have come last and best,
From the wide zone in dizzying circles hurled
To that still centre where the spinning world
Sleeps on its axis, to the heart of rest.

Dorothy L. Sayers, *Gaudy Night*

Even as our hills were parched bone dry
by the ten-year Millennium Drought,
on that fateful February day,
after a long, blistering heatwave
had rolled across the landscape,
with driving, angry northerly winds lashing our faces,
we watched in horror,
as our Paradiso became the Inferno.
What a terrifying day it was—
its trauma carved into our collective memories.
As the whorl of the consuming flames
razed homes and scorched the earth,
with blackened, twisted twigs and leaf-ash everywhere,
and wildlife displaced,

it was as if the foretold apocalypse had come.
O how our hearts sank into a deep, deep trough.
And in the aftermath grievance,
as neighbour was pitted against neighbour,
and some, now uneasy in our fire-prone hills
having fled to the safety of the suburbs,
we wondered if our hills would ever sing again.

This is an excerpt from a long poem I have recently written called 'Christmas Hills Rhapsody'.[1] It is a celebration of where I live, about being connected to my home. The aftermath of the Black Saturday bushfires of 7 February 2009 was an awful reminder of how fragile communities are. As in a lot of traumatised communities, conflict threatened to tear ours apart. Those who were directly fire affected, and lost their homes, were pitted against those, like us, who were spared that adversity. It was unpleasant and distressing to see people in our community at odds with each other. That harrowing day turned our world upside down and people were dislocated and torn from everything that had held them together. There was heartbreak, grief and anger everywhere.

When I look back on that day of the fires, and how traumatic it was, I don't know how I survived it, given my mental state at the time. The recent disintegration of my mind into psychosis again weighed heavily. I had been so fragmented I didn't know if I could be put back together again. I needed all the support I could muster for my mind to settle back into a pattern of thinking that was unencumbered by delusional, wayward thoughts and intrusive voices. As ever, after a psychotic episode, I have to rebuild my self-esteem and confidence, to get back to doing daily things, to feel 'normal' again. Would I find my

1 'Christmas Hills Rhapsody' was first published in *It's All Connected: Feminist Fiction and Poetry* edited by Pauline Hopkins and published by Spinifex Press, 2022. Since publication, I have expanded and edited the poem. Some excerpts of the poem in this chapter are from the original published version, some are altered and some are new.

equilibrium after the double catastrophe of falling into madness and the ordeal of the fires that threatened our home? Would I, and our hills, ever sing again?

Thankfully, over time, the wounds began to heal and our community mended. My Christmas Hills anchorage, where I am grounded and sane, where we have spent 46 happy years, recovered:

> While the flames seared our skin,
> charred our land and disrupted Nature's order,
> like the immortal bird rising,
> we emerged from the Black Saturday ashes,
> and the undying bush choir once again
> filled our hearts with grateful gladness.

My mind also gradually eased back into a calmness where I felt integrated and whole. After witnessing how easily we could have lost our home, my connection to the bush and our home in the hills deepened. The psychotic episode was behind me, and with the support of friends and 'my Team', I re-joined the world and set about to again enjoy the things that had already been nourishing my life.

> These ancient hills will always console me,
> wrapping me in a sylvan rug
> where I am snug against the railing storms,
> where time is tamed briefly,
> and I can loaf and loiter without care.
> Just knowing I am in the midst of this eternal land,
> not having to step out amongst it,
> but to watch it from my window,
> gives me comfort.
> And to see the rainbow lorikeets and
> king parrots bluster around,
> to hear the magpies warble,
> and the jester-laughing kookaburras,

to feel the reverberating crash and bash
of chunky wombats wombling
through the dense understorey,
and the thud, thud of wallabies and kangaroos
leaping feather-light around the stately trees,
all a symphonic chorus that soothes my troubles.
I am forever moved to great emotion,
bigger and stronger than I am able to give to words.

All through this book I have talked about the importance of friends and having things in your life that give you hope, purpose and meaning; to give you a reason to get out of bed, which is an act of hope. What I realise I have done over the years is put in place Team Sandy, which consists of Robbie and Dido and friends, a place to call home, our pets – whose snuffling, furry cuteness and companionship gives me so much joy – my hockey teams, music, my doctors, my writing and my advocacy work. We all need a Team, and I am fortunate and privileged enough have one. I remember talking to a primary school class one day and I told them about Team Sandy and one little boy put his hand up and asked: Can we be in Team Sandy? It was so special, and I was touched and moved by his empathy.

I continued to see my psychiatrist, Dr K up until 2018 when, after a health issue, she decided to close her private practice. I was sad to lose her. We had had a good therapeutic relationship and I had hoped it would continue for as long as I needed to see someone. She referred me onto another psychiatrist, Dr R, with whom I have developed quite a good relationship. Sadly, in 2023 she succumbed to long COVID and scaled down her private practice. I now see Dr R every six weeks on Skype as she feels I don't need intensive psychiatric care anymore because I am more mentally stable. It's not ideal but it works well enough.

Meanwhile, I am still seeing Dr H, the psychologist to whom Dr K referred me in 2008 initially to try Cognitive Behavioural Therapy (CBT) to help me deal with my voices. CBT didn't work for me, and my voices continue to be a disturbing presence, but Dr H and I talk. I feel particularly safe when I enter her room which is a welcoming space away from the commotion of the outside world. The room is light, with paintings and prints on the walls, a bookshelf lined with books and journals and an outdoor area with green shrubs which are pleasant and contemplative. The room looks loved and that is important in creating an ambience of safety. It's somewhere where I can dump my baggage rather than dumping it on my friends. I keep both these worlds separate. I meet my secular confessor in a sanctified place. This is important to me. We are on the same political page and often solve the problems of the world with lively discussions. She is big however, on keeping her distance and not revealing a lot about herself. She says it is not about her, it's about me. I know there have to be boundaries in a therapeutic setting but sometimes I'd like to know more about to whom I am telling my inner discontents. Interestingly, Dr K and Dr R were more willing to share personal information.

What happens in the therapy room stays in the therapy room. This can be a strength because being removed from the noise of the outside world can give you space to examine yourself, hopefully with a non-judgemental guide. Its weakness is that this is an artificial environment which bears no relation to the real world. Who I am in the therapy room may not be the person I am beyond it. It can be a constructed relationship because the therapists don't see you and you don't see them outside the therapy room. What is more, they only know what I choose to tell them. I am aware of the transactional nature of the therapeutic relationship. They are all paid to listen. And I am not special; I am only one of many patients who they see at an appointed time for 50 minutes. It's very challenging when it can take you 49 minutes to work up to baring your soul only to be told *we have to finish now*.

I used to feel intellectually inferior to my first psychiatrist, Dr Y, because I felt an overwhelming power imbalance. I was much younger and had much less confidence and agency. These days I feel more equal in the therapeutic relationship. Luckily, I have had female psychiatrists who, unlike a lot of psychiatrists now, were comfortable doing talking therapy. They have given me a space in which to be vulnerable.

It seems there are two categories of people – those who do therapy and those who don't. I do. I wonder, am I a therapy junkie? I often ask myself what the years of therapy have done for me. The therapists have provided ongoing monitoring of my mental state and professional constancy in the midst of potential emotional disruption. My medication is supervised by my psychiatrist who can also arrange a private hospital admission if needed. Having both a psychiatrist and psychologist works for me as it does for some of my mad comrades. A therapeutic relationship, however, is like all personal relationships – who we get on well with is different for everyone. My therapists, with whom I feel safe, might be toxic for other people so I am loath to recommend them to others because it is too fraught with individual preference. In spite of all the limitations, in the end, my therapists are a safety net. They are adjuncts to my Team, part of the armoury enlisted to fight against my madness.

I can say that in 2024 I am in a much better place. I haven't had any admissions to a psych ward since 2009. And thankfully, I no longer wake to my morning mantra: *Top myself? Have brekkie?* But my wellness is not without unease or apprehension. On waking, I find myself doing an inventory of my thoughts to make sure they are still there because I have in the back of my mind a festering delusion that Tony Blair has implanted a microchip in my left ear and programmed it to delete my thoughts. Even though I know in the real world this cannot be true, in a strange, insidious way this thought stalks my sanity like a menacing shade, and the uncertainty bothers me.

My voices also continue to be a presence. In a bizarre twist, they have changed the way they speak. They used to hound and harass me with uneducated, crass voices, but in the past ten years they have done elocution and now sound very posh! Nowadays they lurk in the depths of my mind, waiting to pounce. And at nighttime they do, when the isolation and loneliness of the darkness leaves a void which is an open invitation to them. I go to bed to their sounds of persecution and denigration most nights. Bed is a battleground as I struggle with insomnia caused by the ambush of these uninvited intruders. Sleep is a lottery. I don't know when I go to bed if I am going to pick the sleep ticket or the sleeplessness ticket. It's like the wiring in my brain has been disrupted and gone haywire and it has forgotten how to sleep. My MP3 player and its miscellany of music is getting a serious workout as a distraction from the incessant chattering. In spite of all this, in spite of my nighttime disturbance and Tony Blair's microchip, there has been a steady improvement in my emotional stability and wellbeing. You may wonder how is this so, but I feel that the power of Tweedledum and Tweedledee has diminished and I live more tolerably with them. Daytime, at least, is quiet and relatively peaceful. Dr H sees the schizophrenia as lying dormant and me as a much better functioning person.

A more settled life has allowed me to expand on what I do these days, like playing more music. In the 1980s and 90s I had a couple of stints playing viola in the Maroondah Symphony Orchestra. It was fun to be in an orchestra surrounded by a multitude of instruments and to play the music of Beethoven or Mozart or Brahms or other great composers. But it was also stressful because there were always only a few violas and I felt exposed as my playing wasn't at the standard it needed to be. I left the orchestra and didn't play much viola after that until the Christmas Hills Orchestral Players (CHOPS) was formed in 2013.

After the bushfires, with some funding from the bushfire appeal, the Christmas Hills Mechanics' Institute Hall was resurrected from its derelict state. It is now a beautiful hall. Some of us got together and decided to form CHOPS with musicians from Christmas Hills and surrounding areas. The number of talented musos in our area is truly remarkable. We are a small ensemble of 13 players, and we rehearse in the hall on Monday night and give two or three concerts a year. Depending on the music chosen for CHOPS, I am now playing either viola or second violin, which I prefer. It's a great thing to do, to play music with others. We play a lot of baroque music which suits the ensemble. And no one takes themself too seriously. We have a good laugh during rehearsals and our egos are parked at the front door.

The other orchestra in which I have been playing violin since 2016, is the Footscray Gypsy Orchestra. It's a ragbag collection of about 30 mainly older musicians who play a variety of instruments. The vibe of the band is great. We do a lot of gigs. Our leader encourages people to get up and dance. It's an absolute buzz to feel the energy of an audience when it responds enthusiastically to our playing and cheers for an encore! It's intoxicating. I really enjoy playing the wide range of world music. It has also helped me get more used to playing in front of people, though performance anxiety still affects me.

I never thought in a million years that I would have to live through a pandemic. As the 2020-21 COVID-19 pandemic interrupted our lives, it meant that rehearsals of CHOPS and the Gypsy Orchestra had to stop. There were no gigs. Everything came to a crashing halt. While the orchestras couldn't get together, at certain times, depending on the COVID restrictions, small groups of people could meet, or you could have a single, constant visitor – a 'bubble-buddy'. In Christmas Hills, three of us formed a trio – Pip on cello, Linda and me on violin. We met at every opportunity when public health restrictions allowed. Playing with them was such a blessing during this horrendously fraught time, as the state of Victoria had the strictest and longest public health restrictions in the country. Playing music with friends was a lifeline. Linda and I also started playing duets.

Robbie and Dido had found a window in between lockdowns to go on a caravanning trip. While they were still away, a snap lockdown was called, so Linda became my bubble-buddy and we could get together to play violin duets. We played a stack of music, both classical and folk. Playing together has improved our musicianship markedly. Immersing ourselves in our violins and all the wonderful music took us away from the despondency of the pandemic that hung over all of us like a huge, black cloak. Music is now more important to me than ever and I imagine I will play in more ensembles when I can no longer play hockey.

I have said earlier that my voices are less troubling now but there is one facet of my waking life they still attempt to disrupt. While music is a gift and a joy, it is an opportunity for my mischievous voices to play their tricks. When I am reading music and an F sharp appears, my voices tell me to play an F natural and vice versa. The same with B flat and B natural. And bizarrely, it is just those four notes that they try to sabotage. Even as I am surrounded by a wall of music, the voices can cut through the noise to bark their commands. Because I anticipate my voices interfering, it can make playing music less pleasurable. Playing in tune on a violin is hard enough at the best of times, so having to second-guess my voices in order to play the right note is an added pressure. Surprisingly though, I think I mostly manage to defy them and play in tune. I don't get too many cross looks from my fellow players. I can see the comical side of this and ask myself what the hell do they know about music? But it also shows the darker side of how doing ordinary things can become victim of a psychotic mind.

I run a bi-monthly poetry reading at the Christmas Hills Hall called Poetry@Chrissy Hills where I invite a poet to be the featured reader and offer an Open Mic for the audience. It's a fun night with poetry, laughter, wisdom, and seriousness when needed. I have a regular audience that has been loyal to the reading for over ten years, with people often coming out on wintry nights to make the trek to Christmas Hills. We sometimes have musical performances to end the evening. Words and music are a good combination. Everyone says it is a welcoming and friendly reading which is why they keep coming.

During the pandemic, people's lives were disrupted in unimaginable ways. For the first time, many people were isolated and lonely and became depressed and anxious; their mental health was challenged. They finally had a glimpse of what me and my mad comrades had been living with for years. Our inclination was to say, 'Welcome to our world'. Here in Christmas Hills, even though we are 50 kms from the CBD and in a rural setting, our area was still considered part of Greater Melbourne and so we were subject to all the lockdown restrictions imposed on Melbourne. Our lives shrank, our days dawdled with little activity. The world beyond was mad. Trump was running amok in the USA, Boris was running a shambolic government in the UK, while all across the world conspiracy theories and the QAnon phenomenon were gaining traction. Anti-vaxxers were protesting and disrupters were taking to the streets and finding voice. The world was so mad during the pandemic that it made me, and my mad comrades, look like the sanest people on earth!

Christmas Hills was a haven away from this insanity. I felt lucky to be in a place where we were shielded from all this chaos, where we could walk in the bush and still feel human and be nourished by the space and the plants and animals. It gave us a sense that there could still be some order in our world. The survival of our household through the pandemic was largely due to Robbie and Dido's planning abilities and their practicality in problem solving. Our strategy to propel us through the empty days was to institute our 'COVID cuisine' regime, which was to have a whiteboard with the week's menu for a special evening meal mapped out. We could look at it through the day and look forward to a scrumptious meal to end the day. We also walked with our dog every morning after breakfast and again in the afternoon. Dr H was impressed with my COVID strategies to keep me sane.

During the lockdowns I started keeping a daily diary in haiku poems to document political and social events. I wrote thousands of haikus. I couldn't help but see the world through the prism of counting syllables. When I would see a sentence or hear a phrase, my fingers would immediately start tapping to count syllables to see if I could put them into the 5, 7, 5 syllabic pattern of a haiku. It was an obsessive exercise, but they were my sanity tool. These haikus found their way into a book, *The Poetics of a Plague: A Haiku Diary*, published by Spinifex Press in 2021.

I was thrilled to have another poetry book published in 2021, as there had been a time when I thought I would never write poetry again. Back at a gig in the 2009 Melbourne Writers Festival, I was interviewed by the poet Alicia Sometimes about this book, *Flying with Paper Wings*, who asked what was next for me. I answered that there would be no more books. I felt I had exhausted my creative engine and had nothing more to say. But then, in 2012, a poetry fever possessed me. Poems tumbled onto the page in a flood of words I couldn't stop. The world was one big unfinished poem. My Muse had returned. It was an inspired time where I felt productive and creatively alive. The poems eventually became two books, both published in 2015 – *Chiaroscuro* published by Black Pepper and *The Mad Poet's Tea Party* published by Spinifex Press.

The commissioned show with Meryl Tankard and Elena Kats-Chernin, finally happened. The show was called *Mad* in which Elena had set my poems to her wonderful music. Directed by Meryl, it was a mixture of song, dance, acted scenes and filmic images devised by Regis Lansac. There were two performances at the Brisbane Festival in 2012 at a theatre in Fortitude Valley. Elena was there in person to play the piano. Mara Kiek was the singer, Celia Ireland the actor and Hannah Scanlon the dancer. I had to pinch myself that this show was really happening; that my words could inspire such creatively abundant artists to conceive this thoroughly stimulating and entertaining theatre piece. It remains a highlight for me.

The opera I mentioned earlier in this book didn't happen nor did the book collaboration with Heidi Everett. We did get a book of poems and drawings together but couldn't find a publisher. But Heidi did get me to do a stand-up comedy gig. It was five years ago, and I was 65. What was I thinking? It's one thing to make your friends laugh in your own loungeroom, but to be paid to make an audience of strangers laugh, is another thing altogether. It was terrifying. It was one of the maddest things I have ever done. Madder than being in Larundel! But I must say, my carcass is not lying on that stage. I didn't die on stage. In fact, people thought I was very funny and laughed at the appropriate times. The power you feel when you move an audience to laughter, or tears, is irresistible and seductive. One might want more of it. But I won't be doing stand-up comedy again. Once is enough.

I have given up midweek ladies' tennis. Those days are behind me courtesy of a damaged Achilles tendon. But I am still playing hockey though I no longer run on the field. I am now the goalkeeper for Essendon Hockey Club in both Open Age and Masters competitions. I even fulfilled a bucket-list wish to play representative hockey when I played for the women's ACT 65s team at the Hockey Australia Women's Masters Championships in Cairns in 2022. It was two weeks of full-on hockey played in sweltering heat and stifling humidity. It was like entering a cult with idiosyncratic traditions and rituals. I wasn't sure about how to fit in with this cult, always feeling a little like a fish out of water. But the players were very welcoming of me, and I did enjoy the hockey experience.

As a goalkeeper, I stand in front of the goals and have ballistic missiles hit at me. It's a tough gig and whenever a goal is scored against me, I take it personally. When I do make a good save, my goalie ego just about bursts out of my chest, and I feel ten feet tall. When I was a forward trying to score goals, that goal mouth seemed so small. Now that I am a goalie defending it, it is so big. I am now 70 which scares me. When I lament getting old and my body declining, I need to remind myself and celebrate that I am still vertical and mobile and healthy enough to play hockey! What a privilege.

All things must come to pass and so it was that the Healesville discussion group, which had been meeting weekly since 1988, finally came to an end in 2021. It was a COVID casualty. Having talked up a storm for 33 years, its time had come. We ran out of members and out of puff. I am grateful for having had the opportunity to sit with interesting people and discuss poetry and ideas in a friendly, thoughtful and safe environment. Over the years many of the members have died and I remained as the last one standing of the original group. Through its many incarnations, and right up to the end, I was always the youngest member!

Over the years I have learnt that schizophrenia humbles the ego. It can pull the rug out from under your feet in an instant. You cannot take your sanity for granted. As for my advocacy work, my public loony life is not as active as it used to be. I don't give as many talks or go to as many conferences. It's a young and emerging world, not old and submerging like me. I feel a bit irrelevant to the 'Lived Experience' advocacy world, which is populated by younger, more optimistic, advocates. My only relevance now is that I am a historic figure because I remember the old days of Larundel and the era of institutions.

That is why I decided to write a book about Larundel, which closed in 1999. Many people don't know what Larundel was. Even scarier is the fact that people now working in mental health don't know about Larundel. Around 2011, I decided to interview people about their experiences of Larundel. Over the course of six or seven years I interviewed 80 people – former inmates and staff. It was a broad range of people bringing with them a variety of experiences of Larundel. It took ten years from the first interviews to the publication of the book in 2020. I co-opted my dear friend and carer advocate, Margaret Leggatt, into co-authoring it with me. *Out of the Madhouse: From Asylums to Caring Community?* ended up winning the oral history prize at the 2020 Victorian Community History Awards.

In reflections while writing about the 'Madhouse', Larundel, I realised that in my own memoir – this book – I had used 'medical model' language and theories to unpack and make sense of my experiences of schizophrenia. I used deficit language such as *sufferer* and *suffer from* when describing living with schizophrenia, which feeds into the pessimistic medical model, condemning myself and others to negative self-perceptions and outcomes. It's not language I would use these days. But there is other language I do use now which is in response to the power of language and with Mad Pride in mind. As you have already seen, I have coined the term 'mad comrades' with which I acknowledge our lived experience solidarity.

I had also praised the advent of the atypical antipsychotic medications – though with some reservations. I don't feel as positive about them now. Not after seeing how my mad comrades are suffering the effects of taking them. We were promised then that these new atypical antipsychotic medications brought onto the market in the mid-1990s – Olanzapine, Seroquel, Risperidone – would erase our voices and tame our delusions and not burden us with unpleasant side-effects. It turned out these drugs unleashed on us debilitating side-effects, and their efficacy was questionable. Our Sophie's Choice, as people living with schizophrenia, is supposed good mental health at the cost of appalling physical health, which includes obesity, diabetes and cardiovascular disease. I struggle with my weight, though thankfully I am quite healthy, unlike many of my mad comrades. For reasons often associated with the medications, the life expectancy of patients with schizophrenia is reduced by between 15 and 25 years. This is truly shocking. When I reflect on my mad journey, I see, alarmingly, that my adult brain has never known life without antipsychotic drugs! It is a wonder I can still operate, let alone have the wherewithal to write these words.

A lot has happened in the mental health world since writing this book. What are my thoughts today, in 2024, on the issue of the medical model as applied to mental health? I am prepared to say there is such a thing as schizophrenia/mental illness, which is a medical condition that causes a person to have problems relating to the world. But in saying that, I see myself as a constellation of many forces that culminated in my diagnosis at 23 – medical, social, genetic and childhood trauma. I have stressed however, that healing is more than taking a pill or seeing a clinician. The whole of me needed to heal and that came with the support of my Team, away from the psychiatric system. My mad comrade Julie says, *A life of total psychiatry will take away your soul.* And that is so true. For many years my life was defined by being just 'a psych patient', trapped in the pessimistic emptiness of hospital admissions, psychiatrist appointments, and Modecate injections, which at that time were my only measure of time passing. This, coupled with dealing with my wayward mind, was suffocating. It was a road to nowhere.

Psychiatry has always sat on very shaky ground with its main diagnostic tool being a clinician simply interpreting someone's words and behaviour in order to establish a mental illness. This hasn't changed in spite of all the neuroscientific research done over many decades. Any wonder it continues to attract heavy criticism. The perennial question remains: at what point do you pathologize behaviour? In response to this, the social model of mental distress is finding a stronger voice in the mental health world. It proposes that it is important to shift the discussion away from the medicalisation of the psyches of the mad and to look at the socioeconomic and environmental factors in the causes and treatment of mental distress; to look at the systemic barriers that preclude mad people from participating in mainstream society as well as their oppression in a society that still has a lot of stigmatising attitudes towards the mad. Pathological and deficit models of disability are rejected as 'sanist' ways of othering the mad by the Consumer, Survivor, EXpatient, Mad (CSXM) community which seeks to challenge these medical ideologies.

Heidi writes that,

> *the medical symptoms of people with schizophrenia and other lifelong mental health realities, are not the issue. It's the negative and burdensome outdated attitudes of medical model-based organisations that categorically paint a miserable picture of people who are actually doing a brilliant and functioning job at managing post-traumatic stress.*

Trauma is increasingly recognised as a key component as a cause of mental distress in the lives of so many people. The uncomfortable question is, who is perpetrating the trauma? Families unfortunately are in the firing-line which takes us back to the tensions of the simplistic family-blaming era of the 1960s, 70s and 80s. Trauma is complex, as is understanding its legacies.

An interesting development has been that we have never talked more publicly about mental health or had more fund-raisers for it, than we do now. When I was first diagnosed in 1976, people certainly didn't openly discuss their mental health challenges in the media. Now it's on the lips of everyone: sports-people who take mental health leave, politicians and celebrities who talk about their mental health struggles, kids who say they are suffering from anxiety. Mental health is even on school curricula. Every second person, usually someone personally touched by a family member or friend with a mental health condition, is running, walking, riding or climbing mountains to raise awareness and money for mental health charities and organisations.

I marvel at how PR juggernaut Beyond Blue has managed to normalise depression and anxiety, using celebrities as their ambassadors who market hope and recovery. Their PR has been so effective that everyone can relate to their message. In the wake of endless media coverage, people are pathologizing and self-diagnosing their sadness and anxiety as depression and seeking psychiatric treatment. The number of people taking antidepressants is astronomical. I have lived with the blackest of moods to see the world through a glass darkly and know how debilitating and distressing it can be. I understand depression. While depression and anxiety are relatable, who, without experience, can fully grasp being bombarded by the assault of unwanted voices or being captive to bizarre delusions? Sadly, it's not schizophrenia that people are open about, it's depression and anxiety because as they have become more acceptable, schizophrenia has slipped further into the murky shadows. It continues to be demonised by the media and Hollywood. I can't help but feel that a diagnoses war has been ignited, with schizophrenia and other complex mental illnesses being pitted against depression and anxiety to win the PR race and public acceptance. Where is the celebrity living with schizophrenia?

The mental health world is always in a state of flux with new theories entering the discussion around how best to understand and treat mental illness/distress. As I have spent so long thinking, talking, writing about madness, my own thinking has had to develop about the many complex issues around caring for people suffering mental distress. There is much debate in other nations working to reform their mental health systems – and more so since the COVID pandemic – but what system can ever be effective across the range and varying needs of those who need its support? Why can't we get mental health right? My feeling is that because mental illness/madness/emotional distress is an inherently messy experience, that everything around it will be messy too, including accepting, understanding and treating it. In *Out of the Madhouse: From Asylums to Caring Community?*

Margie and I interrogate the history of psychiatric treatments and Victoria's mental health system. We looked at what was lost and gained by closing the big madhouses like Larundel – seen through the eyes of people who experienced the system as survivors or carers.

What has changed in mental health since writing this book in 2009? What progress has been made? The 'Care in the Community' model of treatment, brought into being in the early 2000s after the closure of the big psychiatric hospitals in Victoria, became even more compromised. The system, which relied, I think, on the supposed efficacy of the new medications which were going to keep people out of hospital, has failed miserably. The medications weren't the wonder drugs Big Pharma would have had us believe. The much-vaunted Crisis Assessment Treatment Teams (CAT Teams) and Mobile Support and Treatment Teams designed to support and treat people in their place of choice or their homes, if they had a home, never really hit the mark as they were quickly swamped with an unmeetable demand and were under-resourced, under-funded and, to people's frustration, only available during business hours.

The number of people needing a hospital bed didn't diminish, and as the pressure on the small public psych wards became overwhelming, only people who were extremely unwell or a serious danger to themselves or others, were admitted. It became a case of if you are too unwell to be at home but not unwell enough to be in a public psych ward, there is nowhere for you to go apart from the various PARCs (Prevention and Recovery Centres) where there is a limit on how long you can stay. If you do happen to be admitted to a public psych ward, you will almost certainly find these places to be of the utmost, unspeakable torment.

Public psych wards are usually placed at the back of a general hospital where, it's said, the carpet ends, and the linoleum starts. Placing these wards in hospitals alongside renal, cardiac or spinal wards further medicalises mental distress/madness, cementing the medical model of treatment and taking away any notion of holistic healing.

If you are a woman, chances are you could be sexually or physically assaulted by a male patient in one of these wards. I have a friend who in 2022 was having a mental health crisis. She went to the Emergency Department of a big hospital seeking help. After waiting seven hours she was assessed by a clinician who her told her she wasn't suicidal enough for an admission. He then told her that she was too vulnerable to be in a public psych ward! That says it all. In the end, she went to a private psychiatric hospital where she spent four weeks and came out with a huge debt.

Almost everyone who goes into a public psych ward finds it so traumatising they never want to go back. Adding to the distress of these wards is the inappropriate presence of people on ice benders further complicating an already high-octane atmosphere. They are trauma factories. My mad comrades talk of their public psych wards experiences like soldiers coming home from the front. These wards do not even pretend to offer the mad a place of asylum in which to recover. There are no curative gardens in which to find respite. Patients are often discharged mad because someone madder needs their bed, leaving carers to bear the brunt of looking after loved ones with complex needs mostly unsupported and with no resources.

If you can afford 'top cover' health insurance, you can access care in expensive private psychiatric hospitals. But good luck trying to find a private psychiatrist as many have closed their books. And as most of them charge exorbitant rates, it's more likely only the worried wealthy can afford them. Some psychiatrists bulk bill patients on low incomes but it's at their discretion.

Disturbingly, many mentally ill are homeless or end up in jails which have become the new institutions. Across the mental health system, crisis is endemic. I am not surprised that many of my mad comrades have a deep and profound resentment and distrust of psychiatry and the mental health system. With such failings, it has made some people question whether closing Larundel really was a progressive policy.

It was recognised that after 20 years of 'Care in the Community', this model was so broken a Royal Commission into Victoria's Mental Health system was held in 2020. It reported to the government in February 2021. The Victorian Government has committed to carrying out all the recommendations. Realistic or pie in the sky?

I was interviewed by one of the Commissioners and offered my opinions, stressing the need for safe, affordable, supported accommodation – a place to call home – for people struggling with mental distress. Among the Commission's recommendations is the proposal to expand the Lived and Living Experience Workforce (LLEW) in the Department of Health and across the mental health sector. People will bring their experience of mental distress into non-government mental health organisations, workplaces and government departments to advise on and co-design policy and mental health practice. Their expertise is to be valued and remunerated. I look at the job descriptions and skills expected of applicants for these positions and think there is no way I would qualify. Anyone who has had a long-term debilitating mental illness that has prevented them from working and upskilling would be excluded from these jobs by the skill set required. These LLEW advocates generally don't have schizophrenia and may have some or no experience of involuntary admissions to public psych wards.

I can't help but wonder if these appointments are being seen as the panacea for the broken system? It puts a lot of pressure on them to be the rescuers and influence the systemic changes so desperately needed. More importantly, will they really be listened to and consulted in good faith by the bureaucrats when making policy decisions? I am told a lot of good things are happening in the Department with the LLEW but there is some disquiet. LLEW people on various advisory and research bodies have reported perceived toxic and tokenistic working environments that have caused them great distress. This is not the outcome wanted when trying to reimagine and recreate a kinder mental health system.

The rollout of the new and supposedly enhanced mental health system will be overseen by the Mental Health and Wellbeing Commission. Will softer language make a real difference to the treatment of people's mental distress? Will it make psych wards kinder, more humane, healing places from which people leave better off, not worse off? How can the dignity and human rights of people be upheld when they are forced to have treatment? Will women be safer? Will the focus be shifted away from medical-only solutions to looking after the whole person and their complex needs? How will it help carers be better supported in their challenging roles? Will the findings and recommendations see the advent of a better, more accessible and efficacious mental health system where people don't see themselves as psychiatric survivors? But I worry because the Royal Commission's recommendations were very medical model-based and didn't offer much for other modalities of healing. Will this be offset by the Department of Health's inclusion of LLEW expertise and the co-design approach when implementing the Royal Commission recommendations? Is it possible the mental health system will be truly transformed, and the purely medical approach currently being taken will be defused? We watch with interest.

* * *

When I re-read this memoir, I was struck by how sad it is. So much has happened to me over a long period of time. I have been thinking a lot lately about my parents and realise I never really understood or appreciated how miserable they must have been in their awful relationship. How my mother's drinking was perhaps a result of her being trapped in a situation over which she had no control and couldn't easily leave – she had no education or financial independence. Her drinking may have been a form of self-medication to ease her unhappiness. Maybe she was depressed and never received the care she needed. My mother and father were so tragic, two people caught in a web of hate and self-destruction. I wonder, did they ever ask themselves what their bad behaviour was doing to their children? What I witnessed never goes away. So, how do I feel about them now? After years of unresolved conflicting emotions, I see them through sorrowful eyes from a safe distance. Even though I am still affected by their legacy, and I can dissolve into a deep melancholy when horrific memories flood my senses, I am less distresed and able to see that that was then, and I am in the now, a better now.

If only my younger, troubled self, who carried the weighty baggage of childhood trauma, who was condemned all those years ago to irretrievable madness, had had a crystal ball in which to see the future; to know that it would be alright. If only she could have seen the miracle that I am still here; that my brain is still functioning after all the meltdowns and medications I have taken; that I have a balanced life which pleasingly straddles a few different worlds – music, sport, writing and advocacy. I am so grateful that I have managed to keep Robbie and Dido, and all my friends and my Team intact. The other thing that struck me was the absence of anger in the story. I am just not an angry person, and I am not sure why.

Wellbeing is something we all aspire to. My mad comrades Heidi and Julie are examples of living beyond the confines of a diagnosis and finding wellbeing. They continue to go from strength to strength. Heidi, a proponent of the social model of mental distress, founded Schizy Inc., of which I am the Chairperson. Schizy Inc. is an organisation that encourages people with schizophrenia and other mental health realities to be creative artists and writers outside the mental health system.

Heidi found that being a practising artist has given her hope and purpose and the will to find and maintain her wellbeing. She reflects that, *I tell my story in the psychiatric system and I get medicated. Tell the same story in the arts and it gets celebrated. Heidi is testament that for her, the pen is mightier than medication.*

Julie, on the other hand, is taking on the bureaucracy. Her official title is 'Senior Lived Experience Adviser – Lived Experience Branch, Department of Health', and she is one of the people advising bureaucrats on crucial decisions around mental health policy and ensuring the Lived Experience/consumer voice is central to systemic change. Julie is one of the few in the department with a schizophrenia diagnosis and decades of experience of multiple involuntary admissions to a public psych ward. Julie is thriving in spite of her up-and-down struggle to stay sane. Both Heidi and Julie are beacons of what is possible with purposeful and meaningful living.

I recognise that not everyone will overcome their emotional distress in the way Heidi, Julie and I have. We have been fortunate to find a formula that works for us; something we do not take for granted. Not all can dig their way out of madness. Sometimes it's luck, sometimes it's a concerted struggle to reach the surface and breathe sane air. And mostly it is something you need to be supported in doing. I have had my own asylum and a supported healing environment in my home in Christmas Hills. Even though I have managed to muddle my way through my madness, I would never say I am paragon of recovery. For some, recovery is a much more difficult path. And often a menacing shadow lurks behind you – I can't fully trust my mind, which has taken me to such dark places.

The last 15 years have been kind to me. I have landed in a good place. I am much more at ease with myself now and don't find being alone as scary as it once was. I am settled even as things beyond my control are starting to happen. Friends are starting to die which is devastating, while other friends have moved on to new locations away from the area and away from me. I suppose this happens as we age. I miss not having them close by and now have to negotiate a new way of honouring these friendships. I am also finding that as I am ageing, apart from my body starting to give way, I feel short-changed that I am not benefiting from the getting of wisdom! Somehow, I expected to come up with more certain answers about the causes and cures of madness – my own included. Yet, uncertainty about everything rules more than ever.

Another interesting change is that my poetry is different now. Even though I now see myself as an old and submerging poet, I still have the urge to create. I want my poetry to move angels to tears and make a stern God laugh. I no longer write obsessively about my madness. My 'Christmas Hills Rhapsody' is an epic poem but gentle in its mood and voice. It's about being connected and centred and safe. I couldn't have written it even a while ago but now I am in a mind space where I can appreciate and celebrate and write about the good things with which I am blessed. I write more widely and with more humour, with a mind that sees the absurdity of this nonsensical world. As the distance between me and my madness grows, my poems are less fraught and less about my demons. And just as our hills came back to life after the fires and rang with a bush chorus, I, too, came alive and found my song with a *grateful gladness*.

> It is where we find ourselves when,
> everywhere and everything and everyone
> is lost in the temporal temple,
> with its prowling bitumen serpents and concrete canker,
> and the barren glass and steel,
> and bricks and mortar dwellings.
> My Arcadian hills, *our* Christmas Hills,
> are for me dear and true,
> where we live in our cherished pastoral dream.

ACKNOWLEDGEMENTS

This book began several years ago as a written conversation with Coral Hull, who was the first person to encourage me to write my story in prose. I thank Anna Lanyon who encouraged me all the way. Anna's own writing and editing skills helped me to create something worth reading. I am indebted to Jackie Yowell who worked as an editor during the writing of this book. Jackie encouraged me to believe I could turn my hand from poetry to prose; that I could write this book; that I might even begin to think of myself as 'a writer'. Not only did Jackie guide me with a wise, intelligent and critical eye, but her compassionate and intuitive understanding of the painful issues I faced in writing this book helped me to crystallise, and see more clearly, the events that have shaped my life. Jackie nurtured me, encouraged me and gave generously of herself, spurring me on when my own failings were set to overwhelm me. I also wish to thank Hardy Brosow for casting his critical eye over an early manuscript and giving me honest and forthright feedback. Thank you to Werner Pelz for the many intriguing discussions on memory and much, much more. Sadly, Werner died during the time I was writing this book. To Sarah and Leigh, thank you for your encouragement and unwavering belief in this telling of my story and for making its publication possible. Leigh also kindly read many drafts of the book and offered her astute editorial advice. And

I wish to thank the following friends and colleagues for their encouragement and editorial suggestions: Anne Vines, Fran Whitty, Jillian Hiscock, Debbie Golvan, Michelle Wade, Mirella Di Benedetto, Veronica Holland, Margaret Leggatt, Barbara Hocking, Christine Fletcher, Margie Nunn, Kay Donnelly, Kay vanden Driesen, Virginia Westwood, Anne Deveson, Liz Olle, Jill Duncan, Julie Malmborg, Vassi Bouzalas, Jo Buchanan and Kylie Moppert. All took the time to read versions of the book and were always positive and optimistic when I felt less so. I wish to acknowledge Heather Kaufmann and Elke Brosow for their passionate support; both have sadly passed away. I thank Emily Rolfe for proofreadinging and Ian Syson of The Vulgar Press for publishing this book and giving it the opportunity to reach a wider audience. To my dearest friends Lynne and Felicity: thank you for always being there. To my furry friends: Ruby our dog, and Neville and Robert our cats, thank you for the peaceful moments when I can cuddle and pat you. And to my heavenly angels, Robbie and Dido, without whom . . .

The poems and fragments of poems I have used in this memoir, and the books from which they have been taken, are as follows: 'Every Friday Night', 'Vespers', 'Feline Love', 'Baggage', 'No Tears'; 'Liberation' comes from the suite of poems called Mein Führer, all from *Blood Relations* (Spinifex Press, Melbourne, 2000); 'Here I sit', 'Julian', 'As She Gently Brushed My Long Hair', 'Death Rising', 'Sitting on the Balcony of B Ward', 'Whisper My Friend' from *Poems from the Madhouse* (Spinifex Press, Melbourne, 2002); 'The Far Side of Madness' and 'Homecoming' from *Loose Kangaroos* (Domain Press, Melbourne, 1998). The poem 'The Social Worker' is unpublished. Chapters of this book have appeared in *Meanjin*, *Overland* and *Anastomoo*.

REFERENCES

Anthony, W.A. (1993). 'Recovery from mental illness: The guiding vision of the mental health service system in the 1990s.' *Psychosocial Rehabilitation Journal*, 16(4), 11–23.

Cawte, John. (1998). *The Last of the Lunatics*. Melbourne University Press: Melbourne.

Deveson, Anne. (2003). *Resilience.* Allen & Unwin: Sydney.

Hodder, T., M. Teeson and N. Buhrich. (1998). *Down and Out in Sydney: Prevalence of Mental Disorders, Disability and Health Services Use among Homeless People in Inner Sydney*. Sydney City Mission: Sydney.

Jablensky, A., J. McGrath, H. Herrman, D. Castle, G. Oye, V. Morgan and A. Korten. (1999). 'People Living with Psychotic Illness: An Australian Study 1997–98.' An Overview. *National Survey of Mental Health and Wellbeing, Bulletin One.*

Kapur, S. (2003). 'Psychosis as a State of Aberrant Salience: A Framework Linking Biology, Phenomenology, and Pharmacology in Schizophrenia.' *American Journal of Psychiatry*, 160, 13–23.

Laing, R.D. (1967). *The Politics of Experience and the Bird of Paradise*. Penguin Books: Harmondsworth.

Lambert, T., D. Velakoulis and C. Pantelis. (2003). 'Medical Comorbidity in Schizophrenia.' *Medical Journal of Australia*, 178(9) Supp 5 May: S67–S70.

McLean, Richard. (2003). *Recovered, Not Cured: A Journey through Schizophrenia*. Allen & Unwin: Sydney.

Read, J., J. van Os, A. Morrison and C. Ross. (2005). 'Childhood Trauma, Psychosis and Schizophrenia: A Literature Review with Theoretical and Clinical Implications.' *Acta Psychiatrica Scandinavica*, 112, 330–50.

Other books by Sandy Jeffs available from Spinifex Press

The Poetics of a Plague: A Haiku Diary

The 2020–2021 COVID-19 Pandemic

What was it like to live in Melbourne during the 2020–2021 lockdowns? Capturing the day-to-day struggles of lockdown, the daily news, Dan Andrews' 11 a.m. morning press conferences, the tensions between Victorians and the rest of Australia, Trump's chaotic America, the conspiracy theories that circulated and battling her own mental health, Sandy Jeffs takes us through the whirlwind of events in imaginative haiku poems. These became her sanity while the world spiralled into madness.

First wave fear is back.
Before an end was in sight
now there is no end.

Trying to make sense
of an unravelling world
that is downright mad.

This is not only a book about the pandemic but also about political wins and political failures. From Dan Andrews to Donald Trump. Each day brings news that creates despair or joy: the pandemic numbers and the voting numbers side by side. And as the world is in the grip of COVID madness, sanity is found in poetry.

Light in a dark time
Best start to a better day
Aptly delightful

—Peter Doherty, medical scientist and Nobel Prize winner

ISBN 9781925950366

The Mad Poet's Tea Party

In this moving collection of poems, award-winning writer Sandy Jeffs shares her journey through madness over four decades, drawing inspiration from Lewis Carroll's *Alice in Wonderland* and the motley gathering of characters at the Mad Hatter's tea party. Both delightful and insightful, playful and serious, witty and whimsical, *The Mad Poet's Tea Party* provides a devastating commentary on how our society treats those with mental illness from the perspective of someone who has experienced all its interventions. It captures in poetic form the enigmas and contradiction in madness.

but I am madness
and madness is me
it holds you captive
like a hapless bunny
caught in the headlights.

Sandy Jeffs lives her art and opens up her unique soul to us. Her writing makes us laugh, enlightens and moves us with her bewitching words. This book is a treasure and testament to her wonderful gift.

—Elena Kats-Chernin, award-winning composer

I never imagined describing madness could be so rich, so vivid and so full of humour – Sandy's words make me want to dance.

—Meryl Tankard, choreographer and director for stage and film

ISBN 9781742199498

The Wings of Angels: A Memoir of Madness

Not since Sylvia Plath and Anne Sexton has anyone written so candidly about madness. Sandy Jeffs' poetry has a stark dignity, capable of conveying 'shudders of intense fear'. Yet in the midst of her rigours, she can access a voice both wild and funny. Sandy Jeffs' leavening sense of humour peoples her darkness with the sirens of the supermarket, a tinsel paradise and high-tech technicolour Armageddon. After all, God is only a word and angels, although mad, sing the wanderer into paradise.

We hum the songs
remember the tuneful phrases
of the angels, the artists in residence.

The Wings of Angels: A Memoir of Madness continues Sandy Jeffs' articulation of the spirit and reality of the underworld of the mind that pushes itself into existence through her own schizophrenia ... never romanticising madness, she writes with grit and candour of the dark confusion, the well of suffering inside mental illness.

—*Blue Dog*

This poetry is clear and concise with no smokescreens of pretence. It is directly from the unconscious yet nowhere is there babble. Always there is the driving force of intelligence, questioning the reality of delusion and the reality of the concrete. Always there is the powerful, simple, at times Biblical rhythm; a certainty of purpose; and a precision of craft.

—Robyn Rowland

ISBN 9781876756512

Blood Relations

The poems in this collection are an evocative documentation of the harrowing experiences of a child living in a hostile and unhappy home. The reader is shown the pain, the bitterness and the mixed emotions that accompany the experiences of growing up in a family torn apart by domestic violence and alcoholism.

Bearing witness was unbearable.

... only a language 'scoured' of artifice and sentimentality can encompass the experiences of *Blood Relations*.

—Jennifer Strauss

Sandy Jeffs' poems inhabit the darkness at the heart of the dysfunctional family. The ravaged emotionality of these poems will speak to anyone who has felt its pain.

—Doris Brett

Sandy Jeffs depicts the terrible, violent relationship between her parents and its effect on her ... her spacing, timing and self editing are superb, creating disciplined intensity which many readers will find impressive and cathartic, reinforced by the work's wider social dimensions.

—Jennifer Maiden, *Australian Book Review*

ISBN 9781875559985

Poems from the Madhouse

1994 FAW Anne Elder Award
1994 Commended, Human Rights Award

Poems from the Madhouse invites readers into the paradoxical world of insanity: the confusion and clarity, the courage and fear, the bleak despair and the black comedy. Only a poet could make us hear the thundering whisper of insanity, the endless circling of the revolving door, the sheer practicality of whatever gets you through the night. Here are portraits of other people in wards filled with restless wanderers. In the end, it is humour, a thesaurus of monickers that enable the reader to emerge sadder, wiser, but not hopeless.

Brutal Madness, come no more to my home.
Do not cast your shadow over my door,
Lest you steal me away
Taking me into your arms
To transport me to your far-off prison.

Their direct appeal lies in [the poems'] combination of comedy and despair, of terror and courage.

—Jennifer Cooke, *Australian Bookseller and Publisher*

Sandy Jeffs powerfully creates madness as cultural institution and social inscape. Her vivid, cogent poetry fully conveys the harsh peremptoriness of insanity and is at the same time empoweringly sane.

—Kerry Leves, *Overland*

This is disturbing but quite wonderful poetry because of its clarity, its humour, its imagery, and the insights it gives us into being human, being mad, being sane. I read and read – and was profoundly moved. I delighted in it as poetry, I was touched by its honesty, courage and vulnerability.

—Anne Deveson

ISBN 9781876756345

If you would like to know more about Spinifex Press, write to us for a free catalogue, visit our website or email us for further information on how to subscribe to our monthly newsletter.

Spinifex Press
PO Box 105
Mission Beach QLD 4852
Australia

www.spinifexpress.com.au
women@spinifexpress.com.au